Austerity and Working-Class Resistance

Austerity and Working-Class Resistance

*Survival, Disruption and Creation
in Hard Times*

Edited by Adam Fishwick and
Heather Connolly

ROWMAN & LITTLEFIELD
INTERNATIONAL

London • New York

Published by Rowman & Littlefield International, Ltd.
Unit A, Whitacre Mews, 26-34 Stannary Street, London SE11 4AB
www.rowmaninternational.com

Rowman & Littlefield International, Ltd. is an affiliate of
Rowman & Littlefield
4501 Forbes Boulevard, Suite 200, Lanham, Maryland 20706, USA
With additional offices in Boulder, New York, Toronto (Canada), and London (UK)
www.rowman.com

British Library Cataloguing in Publication Information
A catalogue record for this book is available from the British Library

ISBN: HB 978-1-78660-352-4
ISBN: PB 978-1-78660-353-1

Library of Congress Cataloging-in-Publication Data

Names: Fishwick, Adam, editor. | Connolly, Heather, 1978– editor.
Title: Austerity and working-class resistance : survival, disruption and creation in hard times / edited
     by Adam Fishwick and Heather Connolly.
Description: London ; New York : Rowman & Littlefield International, [2018] | Includes index.
Identifiers: LCCN 2018015290 (print) | LCCN 2018017706 (ebook) | ISBN 9781786603548 (elec-
     tronic) | ISBN 9781786603524 (cloth : alk. paper) | ISBN 9781786603531 (pbk. : alk. paper)
Subjects: LCSH: Working class—Social conditions—21st century. | Working class—Political activ-
     ity. | Protest movements. | Economic policy—Citizen participation. | Social policy—Citizen
     participation.
Classification: LCC HD4855 (ebook) | LCC HD4855 .A97 2018 (print) | DDC 306.3/6—dc23
LC record available at https://lccn.loc.gov/2018015290

Contents

Introduction

Working-Class Resistance in Hard Times

Adam Fishwick and Heather Connolly

This volume arose from of a series of interactions and two workshops hosted by the Centre for Urban Research on Austerity (CURA) at De Montfort University. The contributors were brought together through their commitment to the working-class struggles that their chapters seek to represent as either an activist or an engaged observer. The project developed through an organic engagement across contributors' shared interest in emerging sites and practices of resistance and from how these are understood via distinct disciplinary lenses. Consequently, the volume speaks from across a range of sites and spaces of resistance, explicitly foregrounding the different levels at which we observe them, with insights from sociology, politics, international relations, labour relations and media studies on migrant labour, workplace occupation, social movements and digitalised resistance.

The collection that has emerged from this collaboration marks an attempt to shed new light on the possibilities of working-class resistance in the current moment, offering an alternative view but still speaking to recent contributions – for example, from social movement studies (Cox and Flesher Fominaya 2013; della Porta 2015) or from labour relations (Doellgast et al. 2018; Gall 2013). It does this through a collaborative, interdisciplinary approach to several core questions that inform the contributions to this volume: (1) How are different working classes surviving in the context of increasing hardship, and does this produce resistance? (2) In what ways are they disrupting the institutions and structures that reproduce the political economic order? (3) To what extent can we observe resistance(s) that are creating something new within and against this? A broader question underpinning these core questions is: How far can we engage with and learn from across the range of sites and spaces identified in this volume to facilitate a broader challenge across the globe? The collection seeks to develop an ongoing dialogue around these questions by assessing the impact and continuing development of working-class resistance in and against what we term *hard times*.[1]

To do this, the volume is less an assessment of the vibrant range of 'anti-austerity' social movements that have emerged (although several chapters do make significant contributions to these debates – see Shibata and Bailey; Kiersey in this volume). There have been detailed and influential accounts of these movements elsewhere (see della Porta 2015; Flesher Fominaya and Hayes 2016). The volume is, instead, about understanding the sites, spaces and practices of *working-class resistance* that have begun to emerge over the last decade, assessing them through the theoretical lens of survival, disruption and creation that we outline in this introduction. In doing this, our contributors offer a critical understanding of the concept of working-class resistance that advances beyond a static notion of class, situating this, as elaborated below, in contexts of 'hard times' that combine austerity with a broad-based transformation of political economy, work, everyday life and subjectivity that is at once responsive to and generative of new protests and new modalities of resistance.

The contributions to this volume are unashamedly radical in their content, engaging unapologetically in solidarity with their objects of analysis. The authors aim to place the agency of the marginalised and actions of the op-pressed in a range of sites and space at the fore of understanding the (re)construction of the world around us. Each focuses on the coalescence of local, micro, oft-concealed resistance(s) on vibrant, explosive moments of social protest, and on the mutually constitutive relationship between the two (Douzinas 2013; see Moore; Price in this volume). What ties these contribu-tions together is an attempt to understand concretely how the actors, sites and struggles of resistance we have identified are central to constructing new ways of organising and of mobilising, as well as surviving and creating new ways of living in the face of these hard times.

It is a volume rooted in a radical critique of an era characterised by what Ana Dinerstein (2014) describes as the deepening 'hopelessness' of neoliber-alism. In part, we follow her critique as we set out to explore the way various actors are already 'organising hope' today, linking different various Marxist-inspired theoretical perspectives that each foreground the importance of a dynamic working-class agency. This is not to fetishise the significance of what remain sporadic acts of protest, still-marginal practices of resistance and the uneven growth of collective action. In fact, as noted in several of the contributions (see Moore; Mckenzie; Fishwick in this volume), the direct opposition to and suppression of these new practices of resistance is power-ful and leads, more often than not, to the defeat, dissipation or placation of resistance. But, drawing on social movement and mobilisation theory, what our volume shows is that where individuals feel aggrieved and grievance is felt as an injustice, there is always the possibility for individual and collective resistance to develop (Kelly 1998; Tilly 1978). One of the main aims of this volume is to foreground this ever-present potential, countering the marginalisation of working-class agency in everyday life and academic literature, by bringing to the fore those that are confronting the seemingly inexorable rise of hard times.

The chapters focus primarily on a series of Western European cases, with comparative cases drawn from Argentina and Japan. Most important, the volume covers different spaces from workplaces, trade unions, social movements and digital labour. Each chapter recognises the grounding of these emergent challenges and significance of specific spatial and temporal contexts in giving rise to the diverse, but, as we show, related modalities of working-class resistance (Cox and Flesher Fominaya 2013, 4). What we observe, therefore, as 'new' phenomena cannot be detached from that which preceded it, hence taking that context seriously in the constitution of the various sites and forms of struggle:

> At any period in the development of capitalism, it is in essence the *same* social actors, production processes, means of communication and transport, and cultural orientations necessary to the construction and maintenance of the system which are also used to undermine it. 'Capitalism creates its own gravediggers', or at least its own resistance, in very literal ways . . . *the creativity of capitalism and that of its opponents are not separate, but a cycle of commodification and creative resistance.* (ibid., 257; authors' emphasis)

In this sense, the volume connects and contrasts the creativity of struggles mobilised from diverse contexts and their interconnection with the material and affective dimensions of the latest phase of capitalism's own creativity in disarming resistance and heightening exploitation, exclusion and immiseration. But before turning to the creativity and potential of this resistance, we must first ask: What are these 'hard times' that we confront today?

RESISTANCE AGAINST WHAT?
HARD TIMES AS CONTEXT AND CONFRONTATION

Over the last decade, the discourse and practice of austerity have come to dominate political economy across the Global North, echoing the harsh structural adjustments enforced across the Global South in the 1980s and 1990s. In principle, it entails the reduction of government spending in sectors from welfare to healthcare, a shift in the burden of indebtedness from the state to the private individual, and protections for the financial system and threats to it by debtors. However, in practice, the processes involved encompass a wider range of practices than this overarching logic and differ across specific national and regional contexts. Moreover, as Graham Hayes (2016) has shown, austerity represents something more than worsening material conditions. In defining austerity through the lens of the social movements and the range of resistances to it, he argues that austerity is exercised along multiple axes, as fiscal, ideological, political, and civic 'regimes of austerity' that represent a 'continuation and . . . intensification of established neoliberal dynamics' aimed at closing down 'democratic space'.

Such an argument is convincing. As a mode of economic governance, austerity has comprised the slashing of national and local government budgets. As the Organisation for Economic Co-operation and Development (OECD) reports in its 2016 *Social Expenditure Update*, although average public expenditure has remained relatively stable – or even marginally increased – since the 2008 financial crisis, real rates of growth in social expenditure have declined dramatically across all areas. Tellingly, and of significance to all of the cases in this volume, labour market spending has been most strongly affected, with growth in real terms falling from just under 12 per cent between 2005 and 2009 to around minus 2 per cent between 2010 and 2014 (OECD 2016, 2–3). In fact, it is only public spending on pensions – illustrating most starkly the significance of aging populations across the OECD – that continued to grow at a real rate above 1 per cent between 2010 and 2014 (ibid., 3).

The rhetoric of public indebtedness and real spending cuts has, therefore, been central to a broader restructuring of governance and the state. Hugo Radice (2014), for example, argues that the Structural Deficit (SD) targets imposed as part of the European Council Fiscal Pact in 2012–2013 have been crucial in placing structural limits on social spending. Evidence for this structural change in economic policymaking can be seen across Europe and is also reflected in countries across the OECD and, increasingly, elsewhere.[2] In Greece, a series of euphemistically named 'Memoranda of Understanding' imposed by the European Union, European Central Bank, and IMF (the now infamous 'Troika') in the wake of the financial crisis devastated public spending and led to deepening recession. The results were dramatic. Unemployment increased from around 10 per cent in 2009 to 23.6 per cent in 2012, and wage shares of GDP declined significantly from a little more than 60 per cent to 53.2 per cent over the same period (Milios 2013, 185–87). The short-lived, and ultimately futile, battle by the radical-left coalition Syriza ended in the further slashing of public spending on pensions and other public provision, with cuts of more than four billion euros and a shifting tax burden from the rich to poor (Amaral 2016, 49). In the UK, moreover, deep public-sector cuts – hitting local government budgets and unprotected ministries in particular – have been justified by the profligacy of earlier public spending. As Liam Stanley (2016) has described, this 'anticipatory governing logic' was not simply about enforcing budget cuts, but rather aimed at securing the discipline of private indebtedness, in what Hayes (2016, 26) defines as the fiscal 'regime of austerity' that underpins broader 'political, cultural, and institutional' crises.

Building upon these critical readings, hard times, as we understand them in this volume, represent more than just a transformation of economic governance through austerity. Maurizio Lazzarato (2012) explicates these core features of this contemporary conjuncture as being characterised by a new system of governance (or 'command') that

> constitute[s] specific relations of power that entail specific forms of production and control of subjectivity . . . 'the indebted man' . . . You are free insofar as you assume *the way of life* (consumption, work, public spending, taxes, etc.) compatible with reimbursement. The techniques used to condition individuals to live with debt begin very early on, even before entry on the job market. (Lazzarato 2012, 30–31)

Consequently, and as is noted in many of the contributions to this volume, the transformations that characterise this conjuncture seek to 'manage out' emerging modalities of resistance, through the harsh repressive apparatus of the state, at work through the transformation of the labour process, in the political settlements that are reached to placate and disarm more radical mobilisations, and via the logic of indebtedness manifested at the structural-political level of the state by the prevalent discourse and practice of 'austerity'.

Our understanding of this conjuncture is also informed by the work of critical scholars who have shown how the last decade has been characterised by a transformation of political economy, work, everyday life and of subjectivity itself. Literature on 'authoritarian neoliberalism' highlights how austerity is just one facet, albeit an important one, of the combination of legal, political, economic and repressive practices of states that suppress the exercise of dissent (Bruff 2014; Tansel 2017). Research into changing conditions of work – which include increased precarity, as popularised in Guy Standing's notion of 'the precariat' (Standing 2011) and heightened material and affective monitoring and surveillance via digital technologies (Moore and Robinson 2016) – illustrates the intersection between austerity as a mode of economic governance and the deepening intensification of exploitation in work. Or, as Standing (2014) has noted more recently, the working class – or his precariat – has not only been stripped of its security at work but also increasingly, as 'denizens', denied rights as citizens. Feminist thinking on social reproduction, the household and everyday life, moreover, demonstrates the fundamentally gendered character of this shift at work and beyond. As Silvia Federici (2014) shows, women act as the 'shock absorbers' for the brutal effects of increased unemployment and of the growing 'depletion' brought about by the sudden reduction of public provision in housing and social care (Rai et al. 2014). This notion of 'shock absorbers', moreover, is perhaps useful when thinking about the role played by migrant workers and the workings of racialized systems of exploitation (see Connolly and Contrepois in this volume). Finally, research into the subjective transformations wrought by heightened individualism, precarity and fragmentation highlights how new ideational logics derive and intersect with these material impacts of austerity in reshaping our understanding of politics, society and even ourselves (Lorey 2015; Chandler and Reid 2016; Hayes 2016).

Yet emerging from these multifaceted hard times in which we all now live has been the generation of new sites for working-class struggle, bringing new actors into these struggles, and, at the same time, diminishing the potential of struggles themselves, particularly in the conflict-ridden urban settings of several of our contributions (Andretta et al. 2015; Mckenzie; Fishwick; Shibata and Bailey in this volume). In response, the remainder of our volume turns to what Lazzarato terms 'the most urgent task . . . imagining and experimenting with forms of struggle which are as effective at bringing things to a halt as strikes were in industrial society' (Lazzarato 2012, 163). So, in the spirit of Simon Springer's (2016) call – 'fuck neoliberalism' – it is to this task that we dedicate the remainder of this introduction and volume.

RESISTANCE AS SURVIVAL, DISRUPTION AND CREATION

In the following section, we focus on understanding the new sites, spaces, practices and modalities of working-class resistance that have emerged in these hard times. We focus on three key themes that underpin each of the contributions in this volume: resistance as survival, resistance as disruption, and resistance as creation. Here we draw on a range of literatures and examples. We highlight some of the interconnections between those visible moments of radical social protest and mobilisation typically the domain of traditional social movement studies, of their integration in or instigation by more organised actors or institutions that is central to the work of labour relations and trade union scholars, and to the unseen or unrecognised practices of resistance that ferment and emerge 'outside of or underneath' these two domains, examined increasingly by the field of resistance studies (Courpasson and Vallas 2016; Vinthagen 2016; see Price in this volume).

Resistance as survival

As hard times have impacted the lives of the great mass of the world's population, ordinary people have been forced to organise and mobilise not through a sense or desire to overthrow and confront, but simply to survive.

The relationship between resistance and surviving under difficult conditions of work and everyday life has been a central theme in thinking on resistance since the influential work of James Scott (1990) on so-called infrapolitics and the hidden practices of resistance. Despite wide-ranging critiques of his approach in this early work, of his inadvertent demobilising of resistance as a radical act and his overstating of discrete everyday acts as constituting 'resistance' (Gutmann 1993), the notion of resistance as a mode of survival is important for each of our contributions.

In considering some of the experiences explored by our contributors – by the working classes of increasingly impoverished postindustrial communities, recent migrants in insecure, precarious work, workers facing imminent unemployment and poverty, or individuals facing intensifying work monitored by new digital technologies – the need to focus on survival becomes increasingly pressing. Trade unions continue to play an important defensive role in ameliorating the worst effects of declining wages, heightened surveillance and increasing insecurity (see Cillo and Pradella; Connolly and Contrepois; Moore in this volume). The need to survive in hard times can also be shown as the basis for many of the most active, radical mobilisations we have seen emerge over this last decade. Migrant workers in poorly paid, unprotected cleaning jobs employed on university campuses in London, for example, have been the backbone of the resurgence of a radical trade union tradition in the UK led by the Independent Workers of Great Britain (IWGB) and United Voices of Workers (UVW) (Alberti 2016; Woodcock 2014). Neighbourhood and workplace assemblies have proliferated, not only in Argentina (see Fishwick in this volume) but also in Greece and Spain. Struggles against unemployment and eviction – losing your livelihood or your home – have produced new sites of struggle (Arampatzi 2016a; Arampatzi 2016b; García-Lamarca 2017; Romanos 2013). The dramatic decline in employment, lack of social provision and dearth of decent housing here and elsewhere have generated resistance required simply to survive.

Directly connected to this question of survival, moreover, is an understanding of the means by which simply surviving the damaging impact of the current conjuncture is a fundamentally disruptive and simultaneously creative process. Consequently, and as do many of the authors highlighted in the preceding section, we move to thinking about how working-class resistance in its diversity of forms can directly, if sometimes inadvertently, generate disruption and create new ways of living within and beyond these hard times. This can derive, for example, from the occupation and repurposing of space intended for capital accumulation, the formation of new subjectivities and solidarities in conflict, and the affective, embodied foundations of collective action in new sites and spaces.

Resistance as disruption

Resistance disrupts in different ways. It can be a short-lived temporary moment, as an explosion of popular dissent, or an organised mobilisation aimed
at halting the normal functioning of capital or the state. Rosa Luxemburg
famously addressed this distinction in *The Mass Strike* around the question of
spontaneity and the disruptive nature of protest and resistance. She argued
that the explosive, organised, more visible practices of disruption are underpinned by a long historical development of multiple axes of struggle: 'It is
absurd to think of the mass strike as one act, one isolated action. The mass
strike is rather the indication, the rallying idea, of a whole period of the class
struggle lasting for years, perhaps for decades' (Luxemburg 2005/1906).
Understanding the foundations and the generative impact of resistance as
disruption necessitates that we foreground these practices – as our contributors do in this volume – and make them central to understanding the reshaping of the world around us.

Refocusing on the significance of disruption leads us, then, to think about
how the governing logic of these hard times emerges – at what it is aiming
and how it is seeking to restrict any forms and sites of agency that may
challenge the class interests that underpin it. Huke, Clua-Losada and Bailey
(2015) address this in their notion of a 'disruption-centred political economy'
that seeks to understand the modes of governance that have arisen in Europe
after the 2008 crisis and that underpin the current conjuncture. The disruption-centred political economy approach demands that we subvert our typical
thinking on governance. The authors show that it is only through a focus on
disruptive practice that we can understand the logic of domination, as well as
the possibilities to transcend it. The logic of hard times, from this view, is
then borne of a continuing need to constrain the potential impact of disruptive resistance, which, although at times imperceptible, remains fundamental
to the outcomes of the institutional forms of domination that are most visible
(Huke et al. 2015, 7). Modes of governance that seek to establish the conditions for heightened exploitation and immiseration, therefore, are secondary
to the resistance that they seek to necessarily constrain.

The multiple axes of hard times – political economy, work, everyday life
and subjectivity – can hence be understood as combining to ameliorate,
dissipate and fragment the disruptive energies of resistance. Yet, as we have
noted, in each area that we see these being brought to bear – oftentimes with
great effect – we see the generation of new modalities of resistance. Thus, we
argue that resistance can be seen as always already present. Such a view has
been central to the development of the autonomist tradition, which several of
our chapters draw upon directly (see Shibata and Bailey; Kiersey; Fishwick
in this volume). Harry Cleaver (2000/1979) and Antonio Negri (2005/1977),
for example, highlighted the continuing efforts at what Negri termed the

'self-valorization' of the working class to break away from the totality of capitalist social relations that constitute us only as 'labour' to be exploited. In this view, to understand the centrality of disruptive resistance, we must acknowledge the necessary 'separateness' of our resisting agency, the 'continuity of destruction, of abolition, of overcoming' in the making of our world around us, and the 'no possible immediate translatability' of these practices to the categories mobilised to organise and mobilise us within the 'totality of capitalist social relations' (Negri 2005/1977, 236–39). From here, resistance then becomes central to comprehending the mobilisation of modes of governance that seek to suppress, pacify and destroy it.

Thinking concretely about how this is organised in response to the multiple points at which these modalities of resistance become significant, we can reflect briefly on questions of work and migration – two key sites assessed by our contributors in the chapters that follow. In the workplace, we can consider Chris Smith's (2006) 'two indeterminacies of labour power'. In his argument, Smith points out that workers can disrupt the labour process – and hence the accumulation of capital – along the axes of effort and mobility. To put it simply, workers can choose to withhold their labour power if they want to resist their exploitation, or they can leave their employment and relocate. Such practices speak to the micro, hidden modalities of resistance referred to in the previous section, but enable us, crucially, to comprehend the strategies of capital and the state mobilised to restrict the free exercise of agency under these so-called indeterminacies. Considering our conjuncture of hard times, for example, the reduction of the welfare state and the increased monitoring of us in the workplace combine to limit our capacity to withhold our labour power or to easily relocate within an increasingly precarious labour market. On migration, Maribel Casas-Cortés, Sebastian Corrubias and John Pickles (2015) argue that we can see this mobility as an autonomous act of disruptive resistance. Repression and the 'ordering' of migrant movements through border controls and restrictions on citizenship and working rights can then be linked to limiting this possibility.

Disruption, therefore, is central to understanding the significance of resistance – the dual questions of how opposition, contestation and struggle can confront domination and how domination is in turn reshaped by these emerging practices are at the core of our volume. Anti-austerity social movements have exemplified this disruptive turn, with Occupy and its various guises in the 'movement of the squares' confronting the lived hard times that were being consolidated across the globe during and after 2011. What also emerged in these spaces, however, was a deliberate attempt not just to disrupt but also to create. Through a range of horizontalist political practices, actors mobilised in protest and resistance have continued to embody the notion that there remains an alternative to these hard times.

Resistance as creation

Understanding resistance and mobilising it in the context of the contributions in our volume also requires a move from seeing how protest and resistance confronts – in the vigorous and disruptive modalities outlined above – to how these practices also mark a creative moment. In this vein, we observe an alternate phase in the relationship between protest and resistance. Practices of resistance generate new social relations, ways of being and subjectivities:

> We see resistance as an enactment of alternative power relations, a creative mode of *potential* or 'power-to' that constructs alternative forms of subjectivity and sociality even as it challenges dominant expressions of *potestas* or 'power over'. (Juris and Sitrin 2016, 32)

Consequently, we also see resistance as a continuous process of activity information, drawing together diverse moments of social conflict and reshaping the surrounding environment, as well as being reshaped by engagement with that environment itself (Kurkik 2016, 60–61). This can be observed in a range of practices, notably in horizontal politics that confront, intersect with and seek to overcome the multiple axes of these hard times.

Thinking about the importance of place and space in the generation of these practices of creative resistance is also key. New spaces that are taken and brought under the control of resisting actors are central to understanding the modalities of change that can emerge:

> The place/resistance nexus is therefore fundamental to account for practices that are elaborated to escape usual controls and expectations; but it is also a way to understand the role of space in shaping specific meaningful initiatives in direct relationship with the very place where they are taken. (Courpasson and Vallas 2016, 10)

Hence our contributors focus on a range of spaces – the institutional spaces of the trade union, the organisational spaces of the workplace, the virtual spaces of digital labour and the public spaces of the city – for making sense of the emergent alternatives across these sites. In drawing together lessons from the successes of and constraints upon these forms of resistance in the spaces shaped and shaping this conjuncture, our volume looks to understand how these intersect in surviving, disrupting and creating against and beyond these hard times.

The role of self-organisation and prefigurative practice is crucial to understanding the importance of resistance. Returning to the occupations of workplaces, housing and other public spaces, we see how these enable the construction of new bases of solidarity in new forms. Maurizio Atzeni (2010) talks of the 'living encounter' with solidarity that occurs in the workplace, which is at the root of the contradiction of capitalism whereby the socialisation of the working class is required for production, but where efforts also must be continually mobilised to constrain and restrict this lived solidarity in work. However, in spaces beyond the capitalist workplace, new solidarities are able to form unhindered by direct efforts to restrict them. In cooperatives or in housing that is taken over and repurposed within and against capitalism, there is ample evidence of new bases for social relations that extend through and beyond these spaces, providing new ways of being that enable survival but also seek to create something wholly new. In capturing these dynamics in Latin America, for example, Raúl Zibechi (2012) talks not just of social movements but also of 'societies in movement' in which a range of new emergent practices proliferate across societies – mobilised explicitly from below – in looking to remake the world around them.

It is around these three axes – resistance to survive, to disrupt and to create – that our chapter contributions focus. To what extent can the different spaces in which we observe these modalities help us to understand the possibilities (and limitations) of those we observe at other sites? How far are they capable of transforming their immediate environments, and what has been the effect of these efforts? And what are the prospects of generalising a broader basis for comprehending the chances of resisting – and winning – in these hard times? It is to a consideration of these questions in the following chapters that we now turn.

CHAPTER SUMMARIES

Each of our contributions engage, in different ways, with this framework of working-class resistance as survival, disruption and creation. In Mckenzie (chapter 1), the focus is on surviving in hard times and against the power of organised politics. In Shibata and Bailey (chapter 2), survival, disruption and creation run through each of the different cases they draw on from the UK and Japan. In Cillo and Pradella (chapter 3), the actions of migrant workers are those of survival, but they also offer the hope of renewed disruption through creative acts of resistance. In Price (chapter 4), historical and contemporary forms of oppression in Spain have generated newly disruptive modes of resistance that can offer hope for revolutionary practice. In Connolly and Contrepois (chapter 5), the continuing efforts to organise undocumented immigrant labour in France are assessed through this lens of survival, disruption and creation. In Kiersey (chapter 6) the issue of 'time' for disruptive practices to generate new 'counter-power' is linked to the challenges of horizontal, working-class resistance in Ireland. In Fishwick (chapter 7) the acts of survival by workers in Argentina have been transformed into a creative model of resistance that can – potentially – offer a site for confronting a renewal of hard times in the country. In Moore (chapter 8), everyday acts of survival in the new workplaces of digitalised labour in the UK and Europe offer important possibilities for disrupting this increasingly exploitative and degenerative form of production.

In chapter 1, Lisa Mckenzie draws on extensive ethnographic fieldwork to examine the various resisting practices and lived experiences of members of the New Era and Focus E15 housing protests. Although garnering substantial celebratory national attention when confronting attempts to evict long-term residents from this housing in East London, this chapter shows how the ultimate defeat and relocation of participants around the country has important implications for how we understand the possibilities and limits of resistance today. This chapter highlights how the combination of the housing crisis and intransigent local authorities pose a unique and substantial challenge to those looking to survive and fight back in these hard times.

In chapter 2, Saori Shibata and David Bailey draw on an autonomist Marxist approach through a 'disruption-centred' critical political economy, arguing that to understand the implementation of austerity measures, we need also to incorporate modes of resistance into our analysis. Through detailed analyses of social struggles in the United Kingdom and Japan, they demonstrate the impact of different forms of resistance on the rolling out of austerity reforms in these two countries. They show how disruptive resistance reshapes these two 'low resistance models of capitalism', through either 'militant refusal' in the United Kingdom or more organised mobilisations in Japan.

In chapter 3, Rossana Cillo and Lucia Pradella explain how immigrant workers in the Italian logistics offer the most substantial challenge to the mode of political economic governance in the country. Situating their understanding of resistance firmly in the global transformation of production relations, they demonstrate the logics and practices of resistance that are being mobilised anew at the point of production. They highlight a critical dynamic in the emergence of new sites of working-class resistance as migrant workers confront deindustrialisation, structural reform and austerity that underpins the transformation of capital accumulation.

In chapter 4, Stuart Price presents a left libertarian perspective on resistance in Spain during the Civil War (1936–1939) and in relation to the Catalan crisis today. He shows how these earlier experiences can help us to understand the complexities of working-class struggles in and around Catalonia, illustrating how assaults on democracy and through neoliberalism generate new sites of potentially revolutionary social and political practice. His chapter engages a notion of 'proletarian intransigence' to critically engage both with the power of the state and with radical theoretical perspectives on resistance that turn to the state as a solution.

In chapter 5, Heather Connolly and Sylvie Contrepois examine the engagement between undocumented immigrant workers in France – the *sans papiers* – and traditional French trade unions. Utilising empirical findings drawn from extensive fieldwork, the chapter shows how workers operating under conditions of increasingly heightened precarity, not only of work but also of claims to residency and citizenship, have organised new strategies for survival that, in turn, have reshaped the institutional spaces of the trade unions. This offers an important rereading of the role of trade unions and how they build on new forms of solidarity.

In chapter 6, Nicholas Kiersey draws on the experience of relations between radical Greek and Spanish social movements and parliamentary politics to interrogate the emergence of anti-austerity politics in Ireland. The chapter argues for an incorporation of time for resistance to understand the often-conflicting relations between horizontal forms of organising and vertical engagements with the state and political institutions. This acknowledges the often insecure and difficult terrain upon which new 'local' working-class resistance emerges, highlighting the necessity of creating 'time' for this, and for associated new radical subjectivities, to develop.

In chapter 7, Adam Fishwick examines the possibilities that persist within the 'concrete utopias' (Dinerstein 2014) of the worker-recuperated enterprises in Argentina. Reflecting on the impact of renewed austerity measures under the government of Mauricio Macri, he argues that the innovations that have taken place in these spaces prefigure possible modes of resisting the heightened precarity and growing impoverishment that have characterised the country since late 2015. He shows that, although these have often been premised on strategies of surviving against earlier crises, the ways of organising work and life, particularly in engagement with wider communities, can offer a way to challenge the worsening hard times of Macrismo.

In chapter 8, Phoebe Moore addresses new sites of resistance in digitalised labour. The chapter develops an innovative theoretical understanding of the affective relationship between new forms of digital work, the transformation of subjects, and the potential to refuse and resist in the digital workplace. Drawing on interviews across a range of fieldwork sites, the chapter documents how increasingly monitored and precarious workers in the digital workplace – including workers in the 'gig economy' – are developing new micro-level resistances. It argues that practices of survival can act to disrupt this new form of work, but also that techniques to control 'affect' are pervasive and difficult to overcome.

The volume concludes, finally, with a short reflection that returns to our core questions of how resisting actors survive, disrupt and create. Building on responses in the preceding chapters, we highlight crucial conceptual and empirical themes that have emerged from the contributions and in the dialogues generated around them. We discuss the distinction between effective and meaningful resistance and the importance of 'being unreasonable' today. Finally, we conclude by reflecting on what can be learnt across these sites and spaces – asking, 'Where to next?' in the face of a multifaceted crisis that shows little sign of abating.

NOTES

1. This volume opens an alternative perspective on the 'politics of hard times' addressed in the seminal work of Peter Gourevitch (1986), and which has been recently revisited on the politics of the 'new' hard times (see Kahler and Lake 2013). Yet, rather than address the remaking of policy and politics in the multifaceted crises of hard times, the contributions to this volume examine how those impacted most directly by the increasing hardships and precariousness of work and everyday life in this conjuncture survive, disrupt and creatively (re)build.

2. Recent turns to fiscal austerity in Argentina and Brazil, enforced under various conditions of political crisis, highlight the furtherance of this trend in austerity policymaking across the globe (Casullo 2016; Fortes 2016).

BIBLIOGRAPHY

Alberti, Gabriella. 2016. 'Mobilizing and Bargaining at the Edge of Informality: The "3 Cosas Campaign" by Outsourced Migrant Workers at the University of London'. *WorkingUSA: The Journal of Labor & Society* 19(1): 81–103.

Amaral, Aaron. 2016. 'The Struggle Against Syriza's Austerity Program'. *New Politics* 16(1): 49–56.

Andretta, Massimiliano, Gianni Piazza and Anna Subirats. 2015. 'Urban Dynamics and Social Movements'. In *The Oxford Handbook of Social Movement Studies*, edited by Donatella della Porta and Mario Diani, 200–215. Oxford: Oxford University Press.

Arampatzi, Athina. 2016a. 'The Spatiality of Counter-Austerity Politics in Athens, Greece: Emergent "Urban Solidarity Spaces"'. *Urban Studies* Online First. Accessed 25 March 2017. doi: 10.1177/0042098016629311.

Arampatzi, Athina. 2016b. 'Constructing Solidarity as Resistive and Creative Agency in Austerity Greece'. *Comparative European Politics* Online First. Accessed 25 March 2017. doi: 10.1057/s41295-016-0071-9.

Atzeni, Maurizio. 2010. *Workplace Conflict: Mobilization and Solidarity in Argentina*. Basingstoke: Palgrave Macmillan.

Bruff, Ian. 2014. 'The Rise of Authoritarian Neoliberalism'. *Rethinking Marxism* 26(1): 113–29.

Casas-Cortés, Maribel, Sebastian Corrubias and John Pickles. 2015. 'Riding Routes and Itinerant Borders: Autonomy of Migration and Border Externalization'. *Antipode* 47(4): 894–914.

Casullo, Maria Esperanza. 2016. 'Argentina Turns Right, Again'. *NACLA: Report on the Americas* 48(4): 361–66.

Chandler, David and Julian Reid. 2016. *The Neoliberal Subject: Resilience, Adaptation, Vulnerability*. London: Rowman & Littlefield International.

Cleaver, Harry. 2000/1979. *Reading Capital Politically*. Leeds: AK Press.

Courpasson, David and Steven Vallas. 2016. 'Resistance Studies: A Critical Introduction'. In *The Sage Handbook of Resistance*, edited by David Courpasson and Steven Vallas, 1–28. London: Sage.

Cox, Laurence and Cristina Flesher Fominaya. 2013. *Understanding European Movements*. London: Routledge.

della Porta, Donatella. 2015. *Social Movements in Times of Austerity: Bringing Capitalism Back into Protest Analysis*. Cambridge: Polity Press.

Dinerstein, Ana. 2014. *The Politics of Autonomy in Latin America: The Art of Organising Hope*. Basingstoke: Palgrave Macmillan.

Doellgast, Virginia, Nathan Lillie and Valeria Pulignano. 2018. *Reconstructing Solidarity: Labour Unions, Precarious Work, and the Politics of Institutional Change in Europe*. Oxford: Oxford University Press.

Douzinas, Costas. 2013. *Philosophy and Resistance in the Crisis*. Cambridge: Polity Press.

Federici, Silvia. 2014. 'The Reproduction of Labour-Power in the Global Economy and the Unfinished Feminist Revolution'. In *Workers and Labour in a Globalised Capitalism: Contemporary Themes and Theoretical Issues*, edited by Maurizio Atzeni, 85–107. Basingstoke: Palgrave Macmillan.

Flesher Fominaya, Cristina and Graeme Hayes. 2016. 'Special Issue: Resisting Austerity: Collective Action in Europe in the Wake of the Global Financial Crisis'. *Social Movement Studies* 16(1).

Fortes, Alexandre. 2016. 'Brazil's Neoconservative Offensive'. *NACLA: Report on the Americas* 48(3): 217–20.

Gall, Gregor. 2013. *New Forms and Expressions of Conflict at Work*. Basingstoke: Palgrave Macmillan.

García-Lamarca, Melissa. 2017. 'From Occupying Plazas to Recuperating Housing: Insurgent Practices in Spain'. *International Journal of Urban and Regional Research* Early View. doi: 10.1111/1468-2427.12386.

Gourevitch, Peter. 1986. *Politics in Hard Times: Comparative Responses to International Economic Crises*. London: Cornell University Press.

Gutmann, Matthew. 1993. 'Rituals of Resistance: A Critique of the Theory of Everyday Forms of Resistance'. *Latin American Perspectives* 20(2): 74–92.

Hayes, Graham. 2016. 'Regimes of Austerity'. *Social Movement Studies* 16(1): 21–35.

Huke, Nikolai, Monica Clua-Losada and David Bailey. 2015. 'Disrupting the European Crisis: A Critical Political Economy of Contestation, Subversion and Escape'. *New Political Economy* 20(5): 1–27.

Juris, Jeffrey and Marina Sitrin. 2016. 'Globalization, Resistance, and Social Transformation'. In *The Sage Handbook of Resistance*, edited by David Courpasson and Steven Vallas, 31–50. London: Sage.

Kahler, Miles and David Lake. 2013. *Politics in the New Hard Times: The Great Recession in Comparative Perspective*. London: Cornell University Press.

Kelly, John. 1998. *Rethinking Industrial Relations: Mobilisation, Collectivism and Long Waves*. London/New York: Routledge.

Kurkik, Bob. 2016. 'Emerging Subjectivity in Protest'. In *The Sage Handbook of Resistance*, edited by David Courpasson and Steven Vallas, 51–77. London: Sage.

Lazzarato, Maurizio. 2012. *The Making of the Indebted Man: An Essay on the Neoliberal Condition*. Los Angeles: Semiotext(e).

Lorey, Isabelle. 2015. *State of Insecurity: Government of the Precarious*. London: Verso.

Luxemburg, Rosa. 2005/1906. *The Mass Strike*. London: Bookmarks.

Milios, John. 2013. 'Neoliberal Europe in Crisis: Syriza's Alternative'. *Studies in Political Economy* 91(1): 185–202.

Moore, Phoebe and Andrew Robinson. 2016. 'The Quantified Self: What Counts in the Neoliberal Workplace'. *New Media & Society* 18(11): 2774–92.

Negri, Antonio. 2005/1977. 'Domination and Sabotage: On the Marxist Method of Social Transformation'. In *Books for Burning: Between Civil War and Democracy in 1970s Italy*, Antonio Negri, trans. Arianna Bove, Ed Emery, Timothy S. Murphy and Francesca Novello, 231–90. London: Verso.

OECD. 2016. 'Social Expenditure Update 2016'. Accessed 5 April 2017. http://www.oecd.org/els/soc/OECD2016-Social-Expenditure-Update.pdf.

Radice, Hugo. 2014. 'Enforcing Austerity in Europe: The Structural Deficit as a Policy Target'. *Journal of Contemporary European Studies* 22(3): 318–28.

Rai, Shirin, Catherine Hoskyns and Dania Thomas. 2014. 'Depletion: The Cost of Social Reproduction'. *International Journal of Feminist Economics* 16(1): 86–105.

Romanos, Eduardo. 2013. 'Evictions, Petitions and Escraches: Contentious Housing in Austerity Spain'. *Social Movement Studies* 13(2): 296–302.

Scott, James. 1990. *Domination and the Arts of Resistance: Hidden Transcripts*. Michigan: Yale University Press.

Smith, Chris. 2006. 'The Double Indeterminacy of Labour Power: Labour Effort and Labour Mobility'. *Work, Employment and Society* 20(2): 389–402.

Springer, Simon. 2016. 'Fuck Neoliberalism'. *ACME: An International Journal for Critical Geographies* 15(2): 285–92.

Standing, Guy. 2011. *The Precariat: The New Dangerous Class*. London: Bloomsbury Academic.

Standing, Guy. 2014. *A Precariat Charter: From Denizens to Citizens*. London: Bloomsbury Academic.

Stanley, Liam. 2016. 'Governing Austerity in the United Kingdom: Anticipatory Fiscal Consolidation as a Variety of Austerity Governance'. *Economy & Society* 45(3–4): 303–24.

Tansel, Cemal Burak. 2017. *States of Discipline: Authoritarian Neoliberalism and the Contested Reproduction of Capitalist Order*. London: Rowman & Littlefield International.

Tilly, Charles. 1978. *From Mobilization to Revolution*. Reading, MA: Addison-Wesley Publishing Company.

Vinthagen, Stellan. 2016. 'We Continue to Develop Resistance Studies'. *Journal of Resistance Studies* 2(1): 5–11.

Woodcock, Jamie. 2014. 'Precarious Workers in London: New Forms of Organisation and the City'. *City* 18(6): 776–88.

Zibechi, Raúl. 2012. *Territories in Resistance: A Cartography of Latin American Social Movements*. Leeds: AK Press.

Chapter One

Resisting and Surviving Organised Politics

The Case of the London Housing Movement

Lisa Mckenzie

It seems that the holy grail of any organised political activist group or professional political campaign is to have a connection and reach into what we might call the 'grass roots'. 'The grass roots' in terms of political campaigning means 'local people', those situated closest to a particular issue. These types of bottom-up campaigns often start out as last-resort attempts to save or change or end local or national government policy and/or practice. Grassroots campaigns can also grow in opposition out of unwanted private industry interference that may be having a negative effect on a community or group. Communities, groups and individuals in society that have little legitimate institutional or political power often start campaigns out of desperation, and through feelings of embattlement when other forms of complaint have come to a dead end. Grassroots campaigners are mostly made up of people who have little to no personal power as individuals and are not practised or confident in fighting against institutional power. Consequently, they come together as a collective, even if it is for only a short period of time in an attempt to make their voices heard together.

This chapter focuses on recent grassroots housing campaigns in London that have been predominantly led by working-class women forced into struggle. These small campaigns took on the daunting position of resisting government and for-profit organisations, global and local institutional power. The chapter uses ethnographic data collected over three years by myself during two campaigns in East London; both campaigns were set up by women attempting to save the communities where they lived. These types of

campaigns are not rare, despite 'official' and organised campaigning structures that often complain and report that they cannot engage with local communities, or that local people, particularly those in working-class communities, are difficult to engage in politics. Yet social media is filled with small,
local campaigns using Twitter and Facebook, creating their own websites, in
addition to the more traditional organising. These small-scale grassroots
groups usually start up by engaging their communities and bringing attention
to local issues, such as the closing of a community centre, school or hospital;
however, not all local grassroots campaigning is seen as 'legitimate'. This
follows Stephanie Lawler's research (2002) in relation to working-class
women campaigning and protesting in Portsmouth against what they believed was a local government initiative in rehousing convicted sex offenders
into their neighbourhood. There had been a widespread national media response to the protests, which Lawler (2002) argued used the narrative of 'the
mob' to delegitimise the campaign. Although the protests caused wider debate throughout the general public and media relating to British criminal law
and the rehabilitation of sex offenders, Lawler (2002) was not critiquing the
protest or aims of the protest. Rather, these are the ways that the women's
campaign had been delegitimised:

> What I am concerned with here is, first, the way in which the concept of 'the
> crowd' or 'the mob' is strategically used to legitimate some forms of protest
> and to pathologize others, and, second, the ways in which class and gender are
> built into the heart of notions of 'the mob'. (Lawler 2002, 103)

What Lawler (2008) later highlights through her book *Identity* is the
marked class difference between women protesters. Middle-class women are
seen as 'concerned', and their concerns are therefore legitimised through
their class positions, while working-class women's protests are conversely
read as 'not knowing the right things', 'not doing the right things' and not
'looking right' (Lawler 2008, 139–41). Consequently, working-class concerns that are on the outside of a political party or an organised trade union
are delegitimised (Mckenzie 2015; Skeggs 1997).

Consequently, very few of the many small-scale local campaigns are
picked up by the national media or supported by organised political parties,
as their 'local social capital' (Mckenzie 2015) is seldom recognised by professional and party political activists as legitimate. Yet grassroots groups find
their 'fight back' has emerged organically out of anger and frustration toward
organised and institutional power. This chapter argues that party politics,
charities, and NGOs in addition to local and national government are part of
the Marxist concept of a cultural and political superstructure that works with
the capitalist economic base that creates and maintains unequal and oppressive social structures.

THE GLOBAL CITY: THE NEOLIBERAL LANDSCAPE

At the heart of the campaigns discussed within this chapter is gentrification and displacement, which are vital issues in relation to providing a critical account of whether local campaigns can either win or lose. The concepts of victory and defeat can often be a complicated outcome to decide upon when grassroots movements take on powerful institutions. The centre of contention, and consequently the flashpoints around these conflicts of housing in London, have arisen between local and national government policy and those being displaced by these policies. This chapter argues that the very act of resistance should not be underestimated.

Urban working-class resistance movements have been set up in all global and large cities in opposition to the gentrification process as a form of class cleansing, displacement and dispossession (Watt 2010; Watt and Minton 2016). The debates around gentrification have been around for more than fifty years since Ruth Glass (1964) linked housing and class struggle together in London during the early 1960s where she lived in Islington, North London. Glass's research focused on her concerns over the rehabilitation of Victorian lodging houses, but also how the community was moving away from renting and towards owning of property, leading to property price increases and the displacement of working-class occupiers by middle-class incomers. Hence, she created the term *gentrification* with the intention of capturing the class inequalities and injustices created by capitalist urban land markets and policies that lead to the rising house expense burden for low-income and working-class households. At the same time, this captures the devastating experiences of displacement, eviction and homelessness that she argues are the outcomes when capital accumulation is priority over family and community.

Tom Slater (2014) has argued for the importance in retaining this level of critical commitment in studying gentrification and also in retaining its focus on class inequality, which over time has begun to disappear from the debate. Slater (2014) responded to an article in the *Guardian* newspaper (Ball 2014) that suggested gentrification was a 'natural process' in an urban environment. Slater was indignant in his response that 'there is nothing natural about gentrification', arguing vociferously why we need to ensure that the language of gentrification stays true to Glass's original concept centred upon class struggle.

However, Tim Butler and Chris Hamnett (2009) have put forward the notion that processes of deindustrialisation and professionalisation have had an intense impact upon working-class Londoners, as London's 'old' traditional, industrial, manual working class is being replaced, not displaced, by professional and managerial groups with the concomitant effect that 'the middle class is the biggest (but not the only) class in town' (Butler and Hamnett 2009, 226).

Others, including Slater (2006, 2009), Davidson (2008) and Watt (2008), have challenged this 'evolutionary narrative' by 'attacking the way "professionalisation" downplays ongoing social and political struggles over space in contemporary London' (Davidson and Wyly 2012, 404). London remains a city with extensive multiethnic, working-class areas and populations, while class struggles over the uses and appropriation of space in London continue, even if the notion of an ethnically homogenous, manual working class is anachronistic: 'We should not mistake the changing appearance of class structure with the disappearance of class antagonism' (Davidson and Wyly 2012, 396). Gentrification is, however, increasingly noticeable in East London, partly caused via the 'collective social action' of clusters of middle-class gentrifiers in areas such as London Fields in Hackney (Butler and Robson 2003), but also via large-scale capitalist processes of new-build developments connected to rounds of regeneration, as in London Docklands (Foster 1999; Butler and Robson 2003; Bernstock 2009; Minton 2012). This logic has had severe consequences for working-class people in contemporary Britain through the current crisis of underfunding in social housing, deals between local councils and property development companies and social cleansing – the process that removes poorer residents from a community in favour of higher-earning people.

Recent research undertaken by the estate agent Savills (Emmett 2016) has calculated that London is now the most expensive city to live and work in the world. This research by a leading estate agent has measured the cost of space an individual needs for accommodation, together with the space needed to work in office rental costs, totalling a figure of £80,700 a year per person. This reduces people to a market-value figure of their wealth; as Skeggs says, only seeing value from within the blinkers of capital's logic and removing all recognition of the values that live beyond value (Skeggs 2014).

This connection between an individual's market value and their moral and social value have been central in producing new ways of exploitation through the fields of culture and media, strengthening established forms of class differentiation but also inventing new forms of class prejudice. Consequently, even the ways working-class people try to organise themselves against power are judged as legitimate or illegitimate, depending upon who, or what, they have on their side.

The poorest people and the neighbourhoods where they live within the UK have already been established and been conceptualised and known through many forms, and the definitions constantly shift. Those definitions have led to specific and often negative understandings of those communities, and it is through this negative baptism that there has been a growing stigmatisation of the poorest people in the UK. Levels of symbolic violence towards working-class people, and in particular those that live in council housing, are unprecedented.

QUESTIONS OF VALUE

Defining working-class people as valueless has taken on new forms in recent years, in often very negative ways. Since the 2008 banking crash and especially since 2010 there has been a development in working-class women's representation. This has manifested itself into a growing genre of popular television programmes that 'watch the poor' in pseudo-documentary formats, a phenomenon known as 'Poverty Porn'. This trend of 'watching the poor' has produced programmes like Channel 4's *Benefit Street*; my favourite, *Dogs on the Dole*; and even the BBC has cashed in with *We Pay Your Benefits*. There is also a whole host of the genre on Channel 5 that is shown nightly at prime time. This genre of television has become an outlet for those 'hard-working families' that Westminster politicians have helpfully differentiated for us against 'Benefits Britain' to vent their anger, and it has given them someone to blame for the rising inequalities in Britain and the continued precarity that millions of families are experiencing. These are based on simple but well-used narratives – the benefit-claiming, young, single mother taking too much from the state, or the lazy benefit family with no intention of ever working. These are myths and stories rather than coherent narratives, but they are still extremely damaging and hurtful to these communities and individuals – a type of violence that is not physical but symbolic. Symbolic violence hurts families and has severe consequences for communities because the removal of social goods either through 'brownfield' regeneration or through austerity measures can be justified because the poor can be blamed for their poverty.

However, recent and rigorous research by Shildrick et al. (2012) shows clearly that poverty in the UK is caused by an insecure employment market where people move from no pay to low pay, to zero-hours contracts and to welfare benefits. In addition, the crisis for homes that has been purposefully orchestrated by successive government policy on housing has meant that there has been an inflated property market and a lack of genuine affordable rented accommodation and a rise in 'buy to let' private landlords (Dorling 2014). Consequently, social goods that the poorest in society have needed and relied upon are being removed and justified through the narrative of value: who is of value and who is not.

However, for the local working-class communities that live within these spaces that are highly valued as investment interests to global capital, what they see are multimillion-pound housing developments rising from familiar places that seem to be inexhaustible in their grab for space and creating a place that is foreign to them. This process of gentrification that is dispossessing local and established communities in London works on two levels: by forcibly removing existing communities, and also by making them feel unwelcome in a community they have lived in for generations. Many residents who are suffering this form of dispossession describe themselves as living on 'reservations' or on 'islands', as one elderly woman told me, in 'a sea of hipsters'.

It seems that social cleansing, social apartheid and social inequality have been accepted as 'common sense' by the political elites of London. There is the notion that London is a special place where the special people live, and if you cannot afford to live in London, you need to leave. However, the unintended consequences of this hard-line neoliberal thinking are that political movements are growing in working-class communities around a class consciousness of struggling in London. This grassroots activism is thriving amongst those groups that are being treated harshly and have very little or no power; they are fighting for their lives and the futures of their children, as we did in 1984 against pit closures. This fight has become especially apparent amongst working-class mothers, who were not politically active until faced with eviction, like the Focus E15 women. There are now campaigns all over London – from Hendon to Lewisham – fighting forced evictions and the unfair inequality and struggles that Londoners are now experiencing in their everyday lives.

2013: THE YEAR OF HOUSING ACTIVISM

During 2013, I wrote a blog for the London School of Economics that was full of hope. I had recently moved to London and become engaged in the London housing movement. I wrote, 'A spectre is haunting London and that spectre is the rumble of grass roots civil disobedience, activism and dare I say a people's anarchism'. I believed this at the time – London on one level was and still is an oppressive, aggressive and hard-to-survive-in place. The global elite had set up camp in London. London had become their playground. Rents are sky high, wages are being pushed down by austerity measures and global competition, and the actual incomes amongst working-class people were falling because of new welfare benefit changes. Yet there was a sense of hope and a real resistance coming from the grass roots, and they were led by young, working-class women. I believed the sense of solidarity and hope during 2013 was connected to being two years away from a general election, and different communities and organisations were forming out of a sense of social justice rather than being divided on party and political lines.

I came across and got involved in the housing campaigns that were springing up all over London. Local people, usually women, were at the forefront all over London from the campaign in Hoxton that fought a tremendous battle against an American vulture capital company that had joined up with an extremely wealthy Conservative member of parliament and property tycoon to buy a social housing estate.

NEW ERA

The New Era estate in Hoxton has a long history of providing affordable housing and has been home to working-class Londoners for seventy years. Several generations of the same families have lived on this estate, and it has been a safe and stable community that has thrived. One of the mothers leading the campaign described the estate as 'in her blood'; it was much more than bricks and mortar – it was her home. However, once the American property firm Westbrook Partners bought the estate from its previous owners, a philanthropic trust, Westbrook planned to treble the community's rents and 'uplift' them from a social rent to a market rent. This would mean that the existing tenants would have been forced out. At the time, property prices in the capital had risen by 25 per cent and were selling at an average of £450,000, whilst wages had drastically failed to keep pace.

Hackney in general (and the areas surrounding Hoxton in particular) has been at the sharp end of this dramatic change. This part of London has been at the forefront of a gentrification process that has without mercy displaced communities that could not keep up with the rising cost of living in the trendy Shoreditch area of London.

After a very public campaign that was supported by a wide spectrum of political views, even the Conservative mayor of London, Boris Johnson, spoke in support of the campaign. The *Guardian* newspaper on the Liberal left, and even the *Daily Mail* on the Conservative right, ran stories in support of the campaign that had hit a nerve with the general public that this was unfair. This was an easier case to make because the residents of New Era were the working-working class, employed in service work and care assistants for the National Health Service, and in the building trade for men.

The actor and comedian Russell Brand took a starring role alongside the mothers who were at the forefront of this campaign after meeting them as they collected signatures for a petition in their local neighbourhood, where Russell Brand also lived at the time. The campaign, which had been quite small, consisting only of the residents and a few local housing activists, grew very quickly once the media attention started to shine upon it. The organising committee consisted of local trade unions, members of the Socialist Worker Party, and residents and activists that met in the local pub and organised a march to the Member of Parliament's office. I was part of this committee for a short time, and I soon realized there was a two- or even three-tier campaign happening between the actual residents, the experienced campaigners and Russell Brand. I have been part of many grassroots campaigns and attended hundreds of protests and marches; however, the march organised by the New Era campaign to the Member of Parliament and property developer's local office was unusual. It took place at 10 a.m. on a Saturday morning and ended at 11 a.m. promptly to fit around Russell Brand's book signings at Waterstones Book shop in central London. It was an odd protest that ended in Russell Brand climbing on the scaffolding around the MP's office and nailing a sign to it while the crowd clapped and cheered. This was followed by a Hare Krishna food cart turning up to distribute free food organised by Brand, as he was whisked away in a black limousine and the protest dissipated into nothing.

I have no doubt that the celebrity status and media attention Mr Brand brought to the campaign was positive and brought about a much quicker-than-usual end, which also attracted other more experienced activists from trade unions and political parties. Consequently, the campaign was efficient but short, and lacked building the class-consciousness and solidarity that often comes out of grassroots campaigning.

The last march of the campaign was at the beginning of December in 2014 to Downing Street, where a petition of 350,000 signatures would be delivered to the door of the prime minister by three of the mothers who were leading the campaign and Mr Brand. The whole estate and Russell Brand arrived at the Westbrook Partners office in Mayfair on two coaches. I was at the protest outside the office with about two hundred other housing protesters from all over London. Most of them were part of their own local campaigns to save their housing estates; the social cleansing since around 2012 in London has been endemic, and there are approximately two hundred small and local campaigns. There was a scrum of media reporters wanting an interview with Mr Brand. He struggled to keep the campaign and the women at the forefront and centre of the media interest. Although to his credit he told the reporters that it was not about him but the campaign, the media was still more interested in him and his thoughts. Despite Russell Brand not wanting to be the story, to some extent, it was. An A-list comedian turned political activist was the story the media picked up on, and the campaign to save people's homes was secondary. The petition was delivered, and the New Era community was on a high because they had enjoyed the day. As one of the women said to me, 'I want to do this for the rest of my life'. The community had undoubtedly been empowered and politicised during this campaign.

The campaign came to end at the end of December 2015, after a hard year in which the New Era community had no idea from day to day whether they would be evicted and what would happen to them. The unprecedented media attention had forced both the Conservative MP and the Westbrook Partners to relent, and they decided to sell the housing estate to another social housing scheme, Dolphin Living. The deal was brokered by the local Labour mayor of Hackney, Labour councillors, and members of Parliament that had been reluctant at best, and obstructive at worst, to support this campaign in its early days. The *Independent* newspaper ran the story with the headline 'New Era housing estate saved by Russell Brand becomes first to introduce "means-tested rent"'.

Although this was a victory, it was not an all-glorious victory. The deal was brokered that 'Dolphin Living' would design a scheme to ensure that less-well-off tenants were not priced out of their homes while generating funds to refurbish the estate by renting vacant flats on the estate at market rate. Under this scheme, residents would need to provide information on their income and factors such as the number of children in a household. Dolphin Living in March 2016 released a statement on its website relating to the means-tested rent scheme.

> This news demonstrates Dolphin Living's ongoing commitment to providing truly affordable homes for working Londoners. The rent policy launched today offers tenants a choice in how much rent they are likely to pay in the future by giving them the option of either signing up to a new personalised rent scheme, primarily based around household income, or remaining on a standard rent (a fixed annual increase of CPI inflation plus 4.5%). (Dolphin Living 2015)

The result for the New Era residents was that the community kept their homes, although they did proceed onto a means-tested rent system that had no assurances that as properties became vacant they would continue to be rented as 'social housing' with a genuinely affordable social rent.

Despite the solidarity and the success of the campaign led by the women on the estate and the unprecedented amount of media attention the campaign received, it ended abruptly as the new means-tested scheme was agreed on.

FOCUS E15

I first met the Focus E15 campaign in 2013 when a group of very young mothers living in a local homeless hostel had set up a street stall in order to garner support from their local community in Stratford in East London. At this point they were fighting eviction from 'Focus E15', which was the name of a rundown temporary hostel for homeless young people (and their babies, in the case of the young mums) that they were living in. In 2013, the coalition government in the UK was taking harsh and draconian measures to cut the national deficit by cutting spending that ultimately affected public services. Local governments as part of these austerity measures were told to cut their own budgets and make 'efficiency savings'. Newham council in East London decided to cut the £41,000 that it paid towards support for the young people in the Focus E15 hostel. When the funding cut was announced, the East Thames Housing Association, which manages Focus E15, said that it could not continue to house the women and their small children. Consequently, the women were served notices to leave. Living in this temporary accommodation was not what the women really wanted; as one mother told me, 'It's not ideal but it's not on the street either'. The young mothers hoped and believed that by sticking it out in the hostel it would mean at some point they would be offered a permanent home in the borough.

Undoubtedly this was not a good situation for families, and the women had mixed feelings about the Focus E15 hostel. The mothers had to live under very strict rules; as one woman told me at the time, 'You're only allowed to have someone stay for three nights a week, even if it is your mum coming around to help'. The women said that the rooms were tiny, with fold-out beds; in truth, the accommodation was supposed to be temporary, equipped for a few months at the most – a bed and basic facilities for a short space of time for young homeless people – but some of the women and their children had been there several years. Jasmin Stone, who was at the time only nineteen years old (her daughter was eighteen months), had lived in the hostel for just over a year, and she told me, 'It's not fit for a mother and a baby, there's damp and the repairs don't get done'. The mothers complained about mold and broken garbage chutes, and they also noted that they had problems with rodents. However, the hostel had become a home of sorts for the women, and they had certainly built and created a close-knit community out of their struggle. As they constantly said, 'It's better than being on the streets with your baby in care'. This was the mothers' worst fear.

All of the mothers while they were living in the hostel hoped and prayed for an offer of social housing, at an affordable rent and near their friends and family. They were desperate to start their lives in stable homes. These offers never came. The women were terrified of being pushed into the highly unstable, unaffordable private rental sector, and they knew even this was unlikely because they were on benefits. The added worry for these mothers was to beat the benefit cap, now and in the future. Newham council would send them to live miles away in some distant town like Hastings, Sheffield, Birmingham, and Liverpool where private rents were cheaper and tenants on benefits could still be placed. That would remove young mothers from their families and friends in Stratford, whom they relied on and who could provide all-important free childcare when the women went into training and work – which they all wanted to do. They also knew that other towns didn't want them; they would be added pressure to any council. Consequently, out of frustration, anger, and pure desperation, the Focus E15 campaign began. Initially the young mothers held a street stall that asked passersby to sign their petition for decent, reasonably priced social housing for people with low incomes and benefits in the borough. The women wanted social housing in particular. They wanted social housing for everyone. They readily walked up to Broadway shoppers, explained their housing problems and asked people to sign.

Thousands signed, and many spoke of their own housing troubles – steep and fast-rising rents, bullying landlords, scandalous overcrowding, slow repairs when things broke, mould, damp and maggots, and short-term tenancies that left people vulnerable to sudden homelessness. There was a general understanding as well that people on low incomes were as entitled as anyone else to basics like housing. By February 2014, several thousand people had signed the Focus E15 petition, which the women planned to take to Boris Johnson, the then mayor of London. Jasmin Stone became a key spokesperson in this campaign, a very shy young mother who was only nineteen years old and found her voice by speaking directly to local people and their shared fears when she said from the start that 'we just want to know where we're going to live. It's been really horrible, because they [the local council] say they don't know where any properties [for us are]'. Newham council had recently changed its housing allocation policy to prioritise people who were in work ahead of people who were not. The Focus E15 mothers were a 'difficult' demographic – young, poor, working class, mostly single mothers and homeless. They did not have the 'respectable' working-class narrative that the New Era residents had been awarded by the wider media and the wider political sphere.

Jasmin told me at the time, 'We've been to see the mayor, Robin Wales . . . and he was really negative about everything. He said to us that he was "cross with our campaign"'. Jasmin explained to me that the local MPs and councilors and mayor their campaign had lobbied had all told them the same: 'There's no housing'.

However, the campaign continued with a hopefulness and resilience that is very rare amongst those who are most marginalized. This group of young women were defiantly drawing strength and support from each other, but also with the help and support of other grassroots organisations and individuals. Artists, campaigners and the Revolutionary Communist Group offered support and mentorship. One of the women's most inspired actions came in mid-January when the group occupied a showroom flat in the East Thames building and then Newham council's housing offices. The local council, politicians and the media started to take them seriously, as they were becoming a nuisance. The Labour mayor and councilors ran a campaign against the mothers, accusing them of being 'troublemakers' going about this 'the wrong way' and being 'unreasonable', and of course always within the subtext of the old, underclass tropes of them being '"rough", lazy, and promiscuous' (Mckenzie 2015; Shildrick and MacDonald 2013).

The campaign is still going, and the mothers still meet weekly at their street stall outside the Wilkinsons store on Stratford High Street. They are supported by local families and other housing campaigns; however, none of the original Focus E15 mothers still live in this part of Newham; they have been moved further and out of the Borough, and in some cases out of the city.

MANAGING OUT RESISTANCE

Both New Era and Focus E15 campaigns were undoubtedly grassroots campaigns; neither one was connected or affiliated with any official political group or party, although many supporters of both campaigns had affiliations. None of the campaigns were being directly or indirectly 'managed'; they were community led and organised. Both campaigns were led by women who had clear and connected stakes in the fight they had been forced into; none of the campaigners before their campaigns had been involved in any type of mainstream political or social movement previously. Some of the Focus E15 mothers are still active in the housing campaigns in Newham and across London and can be seen at the street stall in Stratford and at the various rallies and demonstrations that continue in the city despite being 'cleansed' out of the neighbourhood. However, the New Era campaign and campaigners are not involved in the wider housing movement in London, and the campaign is closed.

In January 2018 I was contacted by some of the New Era residents. They had been given notice that Dolphin Living planned to demolish the New Era estate. The landlord wrote to residents in August 2017 to say it was considering a number of options for the estate, including refurbishing existing homes and rebuilding the entire estate. The landlord said the best option would be to demolish and rebuild the estate, adding into the development a substantial amount of 'for sale' market-rate apartments as the 'only way' to deliver all the improvements it wants to carry out without residents having to pay more in rent. Meetings were held in January 2018 with residents, and Dolphin Living said 84 per cent of residents supported the demolition and rebuild plan. One of the residents told me, 'We are exhausted, we can't go through all that again'.

None of this is surprising as the emotional and physical effort, time and resources that are needed in taking on institutional power are immense, and most grassroots campaigns have little (if any) of those resources by their very nature. Most local grassroots campaigns are thrown reluctantly into positions of constant negotiating with institutional power, initially with the agency/ organisation they have issue with, and then later with local government officials. Eventually, as in both cases here, the negotiation of power continued through elected government officials. Both campaigns faced similar problems. Initially elected officials ignored them, and then they patronised them. The Labour MP for the constituency where the New Era estate was had been invited to a meeting held by the campaign. The residents were clearly upset that their estate was under threat and that the Labour Party was not support-ing them – the MP told them she didn't have time 'for this' and left, while the mayor of Newham tried to physically attack the campaign and had to be held back by Labour councillors at a 'Family Fun Day' (Prynn 2014). However, he later made a public apology of sorts in a national newspaper, where he excused his behaviour as about 'London's housing crisis', yet still insisted that the initial decision to close the hostel and offer the mothers 'alternative' housing in places hundreds of miles away 'was the right one'. As the election was called in 2015, the housing campaigns right across London were finding it increasingly difficult to garner support wider than their community. The Labour Party and the trade unions were in election mode, and the housing campaigns in London that had direct battles with Labour councils became inconvenient and politically difficult.

The campaigns found that they had to fight their local councils, MPs, and mayors, which amounted to overwhelming pressure for those communities. With a general election looming in May 2015, organised party political acti-vists and party machines focused on electioneering. Local grassroots cam-paigns were being asked to 'wait' and were encouraged to put their own campaigning on hold and join the party election campaigning. This had a devastating effect on the London Housing Movement in particular because most of the grassroots housing campaigns were fighting against local govern-ment decisions that were predominantly being made by Labour Party coun-cillors and mayors. In the 2015 election, the Conservative Party won and formed its first government in twenty years. Divisions within the Labour Party opened with the left-wing candidate Jeremy Corbyn overwhelmingly winning and becoming leader of the party. Following this left-wing victory, the grassroots housing campaigns were asked again to 'wait' and support a Jeremy Corbyn–led Labour Party. Two further years of turmoil ensued with-in the Labour Party as they fought amongst themselves, and again the hous-ing campaigns were asked to wait. The negative attention about Labour councils' social cleansing their working-class tenants out of London was unwelcome by a party as it struggled within itself.

Political time moves slowly – it moves in parliaments and elections – but community time moves very differently. The people who are fighting for their communities become very easily exhausted over a few months of cam-paigning, and they have little to no resources. They do not have two years or five years of resources in them. The campaigns fold, or the residents are moved out or make concessions that are not beneficial to them because they simply cannot fight on.

MISSED AND MANAGED NARRATIVES

The poorest people often have no choice but to resist. The structure of a neoliberal society pushes towards resistance, success or annihilation; it is the capitalist model. The restructuring of urban space that Harvey (2008) identifies as accumulation by dispossession is producing increasingly antagonistic class relations that are in turn making such relations and their accompanying social injustices more apparent to those whose right to the city is being threatened. In turn this is leading to greater class resentment and in some cases anger against 'them' – corporate wealth and power – a resentment and anger whose political consequences are as yet unforeseen but are no doubt being played out on the streets and estates of London. Class struggle in itself is resistance, and campaigns that start from local communities that build up a sense of collectivist ideas and actions are successes within themselves despite the outcome of the campaign. However, these small-scale resistances find it difficult (if not impossible) to fight institutionalised power independently of institutionalised power. The grassroots London housing campaigns that are in direct struggle with their local council officials that are part of local government and wider national party politics are easily suffocated, and the fire in their anger can be put out by organised politicians and their supporters if the campaigns' aims are in direct opposition to those of their elected officials, especially when the political cycle has moved into election time.

CONCLUSION

As we also learned from the New Era campaign, well-intentioned and well-meaning celebrities, or even philanthropists, can suffocate the genuine anger that arises from injustice and inequality. Consequently, the important process of building class solidarity through struggle is not recognised as a legitimate successful outcome. Instead, the only measure that is used in political campaigning is the ultimate outcome of the campaign rather than the process of consciousness-raising and creating class solidarity.

   To conclude, it is important to ask what we can gain from these stories from housing campaigns in London and about the process of resistance. Resistance does not necessarily mean winning, and we need to understand victory in many ways when we are considering the constant uphill fight that grassroots campaigns have. Their campaigns start through hurt and anger and desperation. They have little to no resources, but their very act of resistance is a victory in itself. What happens too often is their campaigns are coopted by well-meaning outsiders who sometimes have their own agendas; sometimes they don't, and often they are well meaning but naïve regarding the struggle that working-class people face that is structural and systematic.

BIBLIOGRAPHY

Ball, Philip. 2014. 'Gentrification Is a Natural Evolution'. *The Guardian*. 19 November 2014. https://www.theguardian.com/commentisfree/2014/nov/19/gentrification-evolution-cities-brixton-battersea.

Bernstock, Penny. 2009. 'London 2012 and the Regeneration Game'. In *Olympic Cities: 2012 and the Remaking of London*, edited by Gavin Poynter and Ian MacRury, 201–18. Farnham: Ashgate.

Butler, Tim, and Chris Hamnett. 2009. 'Walking Backwards to the Future – Waking Up to Class and Gentrification in London'. *Urban Policy and Research* 27(3): 217–28.

Butler, Tim, and Garry Robson. 2003. 'Negotiating Their Way In: The Middle Classes, Gentrification and the Deployment of Capital in a Globalising Metropolis'. *Urban Studies* 40(9): 1791–1809.

Davidson, Mark. 2008. 'Spoiled Mixture: Where Does State-Led "Positive" Gentrification End?' *Urban Studies* 45(12): 2385–2405.

Davidson, Mark, and Elvin Wyly. 2012. 'Class-Ifying London: Questioning Social Division and Space Claims in the Post-Industrial Metropolis'. *City* 16(4): 395–421.

Dolphin Living. 2015. 'New Rent Policy at the New Era Estate'. 18 March 2015. http://dolphinliving.com/new-rent-policy-at-the-new-era-estate/.

Dorling, Danny. 2014. *All That Is Solid: How the Great Housing Disaster Defines Our Times, and What We Can Do About It*. London: Allen Lane.

Emmett, Susan. 2016. 'Making Better Use of Land'. *Savilles*. 4 May 2016. http://www.savills.co.uk/research_articles/187788/202104-0.

Foster, Janet. 1999. *Docklands: Cultures in Conflict, Worlds in Collision*. London: UCL Press.

Glass, Ruth. 1964. *London: Aspects of Change*. London: MacGibbon & Kee.

Harvey, David. 2008. 'The Right to the City'. *New Left Review* 53: 23–40.

Harvey, David. 2010. *A Companion to Marx's Capital*. London: Verso.

Hodkinson, Stuart, Paul Watt and Gerry Mooney. 2013a. 'Social Housing, Privatisation and Neoliberalism'. *Critical Social Policy* 33(1): 3–77.

Hodkinson, Stuart, Paul Watt and Gerry Mooney. 2013b. 'Introduction: Neoliberal Housing Policy: Time for a Critical Re-Appraisal'. *Critical Social Policy* 33(1): 3–16.

Lawler, Stephanie. 2002. 'Mobs and Monsters: Independent Man Meets Paulsgrove Woman'. *Feminist Theory* 3(1): 103–13.

Lawler, Stephanie. 2005. 'Disgusted Subjects: The Making of Middle-Class Identities'. *Sociological Review* 53(3): 429–46.

Lawler, Stephanie. 2008. *Identity; Sociological Perspectives*. Cambridge: Polity.

Mckenzie, Lisa. 2015. *Getting By: Estates, Class and Culture*. Bristol: Policy Press.

Minton, Anna. 2012. *Ground Control: Fear and Happiness in the Twenty-First Century City*. London: Penguin UK.

Prynn, Jonathan. 2014. 'Newham Mayor Sees Red at Woman Campaigning for Homeless Single Mothers'. *Evening Standard*. 3 February 2015. http://www.standard.co.uk/news/politics/newham-mayor-sees-red-at-woman-campaigning-for-homeless-single-mothers-100 20164.html.

Shildrick, Tracy, and Robert MacDonald. 2013. 'Poverty Talk: How People Experiencing Poverty Deny Their Poverty and Why They Blame "the Poor"'. *Sociological Review* 61(2): 285–303.

Shildrick, Tracy, Robert MacDonald, Colin Webster and Kayleigh Garthwaite. 2012. *Poverty and Insecurity: Life in Low-Pay, No-Pay Britain*. Bristol: Policy Press.

Skeggs, Beverley. 1997. *Formations of Class and Gender: Becoming Respectable*. London: Sage.

Skeggs, Beverley. 2004. *Class, Self and Culture*. London: Routledge.

Skeggs, Beverley. 2014. 'Values beyond Value? Is Anything Beyond the Logic of Capital?' *British Journal of Sociology* 65(1): 1–20.

Slater, Tom. 2006. 'The Eviction of Critical Research from Gentrification Studies'. *International Journal of Urban and Regional Research* 30(4): 737–57.

Slater, Tom. 2009. 'Missing Marcuse: On Gentrification and Displacement'. *City* 13(2-3): 292–311.

Slater, Tom. 2014. 'There Is Nothing Natural about Gentrification'. *New Left Project*, 24 November. www.newleftproject.org/index.php/site/article_comments/there_is_nothing_ natural_about_gentrification.

Wales, Robin. 2014. 'I Apologise to the Focus E15 Families, but This Is a London Housing Crisis'. *The Guardian*. 6 October 2014. https://www.theguardian.com/commentisfree/2014/ oct/06/apologise-focus-e15-london-housing-crisis-newham.

Watt, Paul. 2008. 'The Only Class in Town? Gentrification and the Middle-Class Colonization of the City and Urban Imagination'. *International Journal of Urban and Regional Research* 32(1): 206–11.

Watt, Paul. 2010. 'Unravelling the Narratives and Politics of Belonging to Place'. *Housing, Theory and Society* 27(2): 153–59.

Watt, Paul, and Anna Minton. 2016. 'London's Housing Crisis and Its Activisms'. *City* 20(2): 204–21.

Wintour, Patrick. 2011. 'George Osborne to Cut £4bn More from Benefits'. *The Guardian*. 11 September 2011. https://www.theguardian.com/politics/2010/sep/09/george-osborne-cut-4bn-benefits-welfare.

Chapter Two

Contesting Austerity in Low-Resistance Capitalist Contexts

Saori Shibata and David Bailey

The age of austerity that followed the 2008 global economic crisis represents a significant period of study for those with an interest in political economy, particularly with regard to attempts to restructure relations of production, distribution and exchange that have been witnessed during this period. It also represents a key period of investigation for those seeking to understand the role of resistance within political economy. The present chapter explores these themes, with a particular focus on the interaction between austerity and different forms of anti-austerity resistance: to identify patterns of austerity and the impact that they have had upon the national and global political economies of contemporary neoliberalism, and to understand the ways in which these have themselves been responses to, accompanied by, and in turn witnessed subsequent attempts to contain and control different types of resistance.

As we have argued elsewhere (Huke et al. 2015; Bailey and Shibata 2014), existing models of political economy have shown a tendency to overstate the smooth reproduction of the social relations that comprise capitalism and neoliberalism. This has included a focus on the way that austerity measures have been imposed upon advanced industrial democracies. Instead, we seek to conceptualise the reproduction of the social relations of capitalism as a process that is unavoidably marked by tension, conflict and antagonism (for a similar argument, see Lebowitz 2003). As such, in seeking to develop a critical political economy account of the so-called age of austerity, we argue, we need also to draw attention to the patterns of contestation associated with efforts to impose austerity. In seeking to understand the 'age of austerity', therefore, we need a model of political economy that takes seriously capitalism and neoliberalism, *and* their contestation. The present chapter seeks to develop such a model, paying particular attention to the different patterns of contestation associated with different national models of capitalism.

Drawing on research into capitalist contexts with comparatively low levels of resistance, we seek to highlight the way in which different models of capitalism have a tendency to be associated with different patterns of opposition to austerity, with different associated outcomes. In particular, as we argued in a recent paper, within the more coordinated market economy (CME) of Japan we see proposals for austerity to be routinely obstructed by relatively moderate and institutionalised expression of public opposition. In contrast, in liberal market economy (LME) contexts such as that of the UK, where there is an absence of mechanisms of coordination and negotiation, more widespread and innovative forms of opposition are required in order for proposals for austerity to be successfully obstructed (Bailey and Shibata 2017). In addition, the more 'standard' forms of opposition – non-disruptive public opposition, such as demonstrations and marches – tended to be more common in Japan's CME context, whereas more innovative and militant forms of opposition were more likely in the UK case (Bailey and Shibata 2017). As such, we argue, whereas CMEs have a tendency to experience the gradual erosion of welfare rights and solidaristic institutions in a relatively institutionalised and iterative relationship between austerity and organised opposition to austerity, LMEs in contrast experience more severe attempts to impose austerity measures, although these also tend sometimes to face sporadic eruptions of significant, unpredictable and unconventional forms of more militant types of resistance which, once mobilised, prove difficult to re-contain. It is these two different models of contested capitalism and how they have played out in the so-called age of anti-austerity that we aim to introduce and explore in the present chapter.

In developing such an approach to contestation and resistance and its centrality to political economy, we draw upon an approach that Holland (2011) terms 'minor Marxism'. By this, we mean the attempt to understand and conceptualise capitalism from the disruptive perspective of labour (see also Bailey et al. 2018, 18–33). Broadly set out, such a perspective seeks to develop the claim, associated with the Italian *Operaismo* and post-*Operaismo* traditions of the 1960s and 1970s, and especially the work of Mario Tronti, that we should seek to reverse the assumptions of more conventional Marxist approaches (which aim to conceptualise the relations of domination that constitute capitalism), and in doing so to highlight the way in which labour represents the primary form of (disruptive) agency in capitalist relations. From this perspective, it is not so much that labour is exploited by capital, but rather that capital seeks (but unavoidably fails) to capture and contain the vibrancy of workers' agency. Indeed, it is the necessity of this agency – upon which capital (and therefore capitalists) depend – that pre-

vents capital from securing the relations of domination that capitalist authorities strive to stabilise (in order to perpetuate). Thus, workers unavoidably
exist beyond and outside of the capture and domination that capital and
capitalists seek to impose (for a good summary, see Burgmann 2013). For
those adopting such a perspective, what is of particular interest is the ongoing
expression of working-class agency and practice of escape, which manifests
itself in different ways in different capitalist contexts, and which thereby set
the terms upon which capitalists must seek (but necessarily fail) to secure the
relations of domination that constitute capitalism. As Tronti puts it, 'Capitalist development becomes subordinated to working class struggles; it follows
behind them, and they set the pace to which the political mechanisms of
capital's own reproduction must be tuned' (Tronti 1964).

From the perspective of 'minor Marxism', therefore, we understand capital and capitalists to be struggling to achieve the unattainable goal of a
controlled and contained working class. Such a problem, however, need not
manifest itself empirically in the same way in different contexts; indeed, it
would be surprising if it did. Whilst different attempts to resolve this central
dilemma of capitalism will result in similar outcomes – in the sense that
efforts to achieve control can be expected to result in the production of new
problems and tensions due to the impossibility of that goal – the specific
form that those problems and tensions take are likely to be different in
different contexts, as a result of the form of working-class agency expressed
as well as the particular efforts adopted in an attempt to contain it. As such,
'minor Marxism' might be considered *both* a theory of disruptive subjectivities (Pasquinelli 2014) *and* an attempt to understand the impact of the disruptive actions and potentialities that these subjectivities produce (Huke et al.
2015).

As we set out in more detail below, we expect both the forms of disruptive working-class agency and the practices of containment pursued by capitalist and state authorities to co-vary across national contexts. In this sense,
we build on the assumptions inherent in the 'varieties of capitalism' or 'comparative capitalisms' literatures – which consider different forms of capitalist
relations to be comparable across different national contexts – but we do so
in a way that is more focused on patterns of disruption than on relations of
domination (for one of the more useful discussions of the comparative capitalisms approach, see Ebenau et al. 2015). In particular, we anticipate that
what are typically considered coordinated market economies (CMEs) within
the varieties of capitalism approach are also likely to be characterised by
patterns of working-class agency that are associated with more institutionalised forms of resistance, as well as a greater likelihood that both capitalist
firms and political authorities will seek some kind of formal incorporation of
the expressions of agency that these generate, all as part of the process of
seeking to achieve a more coordinated response to the intractable problems

facing capitalist societies. In contrast, in what are typically considered to be liberal market economies (LMEs), we expect that expressions of agency and dissent are likely to be un-institutionalised, and as a result also more likely to be relatively spontaneous and 'subterranean', and that likewise the response of economic and political authorities to such instances of dissent is likely to be exclusionary, repressive, non-institutionalised and reactive, itself reflecting the typically less coordinated responses to the intractable problems facing capitalist societies witnessed within LMEs.

In exploring the different types of resistance, contestation and agency within different socio-economic models of capitalism, we also seek to develop our understanding of resistance. Drawing on the framework developed in the introduction to this volume (Fishwick and Connolly, this volume), we consider the way in which the different models of contested capitalism discussed below will evince each of the aspects of resistance that have been conceptualised – survival, disruption and creation. In terms of survival, we consider especially the degree to which acts of resistance are driven by the experience of (or fear of increasing) material hardship. In the sense that resistance acts to disrupt attempts to impose austerity measures, we consider the degree to which this disruption (if it happens) occurs in the form of a disruption of legitimating narratives and/or the more direct disruption of policy implementation. Finally, with regard to the potential for resistance to result in the creation of new and alternative sources of hope, we focus especially on the degree to which resistance stems from established institutions, or whether it prompts the creation of new organisations, movements and other forms of association through which dissent can be mobilised and articulated. Each of these questions we turn now to consider in more detail.

THE CRITICAL POLITICAL ECONOMY OF AUSTERITY

Most accounts of the onset of an austerity agenda across the advanced industrial democracies, from around 2010 onwards, highlight the way in which this resulted from the prior experience of the 2008 crisis. In particular, contributions to the critical political economy literature tend to highlight the way in which the neoliberal phase of globalised capitalism had by 2007–2008 become exhausted. The growth model pursued prior to 2007 was one of deregulation, market liberalisation, downward pressure on the wage share, an expansion of the world market in order to take advantage of low-paid labour in the third world, and an erosion of welfare entitlements (Kotz 2008). This was combined with the promotion of debt-led growth in order to offset problems associated with declining consumption and legitimacy and produced an inflation of certain finance-dependent assets, most obviously housing (Tridico 2012). As this growth model began to experience problems, including declining opportunities for further growth, a declining rate of profit, limits to the levels of debt that could be accrued, and faltering consumption levels, the symptoms of this slowdown were felt first in the housing sector (Resnick and Wolff 2010). The so-called subprime crisis of 2007 sparked a collapse in confidence and a subsequent crisis in the financial industry, eventually leading to the fall of Lehman Brothers in 2008 and an ensuing global economic crisis. In order to rescue the global economy, advanced industrial democracies almost universally moved in 2008–2009 to adopt a policy of fiscal expansion to provide immediate relief to (especially) the financial industry, and a sharp reduction in interest rates combined with quantitative easing as a means by which to inject support into the economy through unconventionally loose monetary policy.

Whilst these measures acted to stabilise global capitalism, one of their effects was a sharp rise in government deficits and debt. In some cases, such as in Southern Europe, this produced a collapse in confidence within the debt market, sparking a new Eurozone crisis (Bellofiore 2013; Varoufakis 2013). In other cases, the fear that high levels of public debt might produce a similar crisis were deployed as grounds for reducing public spending. In each case, the perceived, imposed or proclaimed pressure for austerity measures was such that in almost all of the advanced industrial democracies attempts were made to reduce the generosity of the welfare state, thereby consolidating and accelerating an agenda of welfare retrenchment that had already been in place for much of the neoliberal period (Stanley 2014; Konzelmann 2014). One final consequence of this series of events has been the move in several states to adopt an increasingly authoritarian governing strategy as a means of control. This is in part the result of a decline in welfare provisions as an alternative means through which to incorporate labour and neutralise dissent (Bruff 2014).

Clearly this process has occurred in different ways in different contexts, mediated by conventional mechanisms typically identified within the political economy literature (such as union density, partisan politics and policy traditions), as well as more unconventional ones (such as social movements and everyday forms of workplace dissent) (Clift and Ryner 2014; Thomas and Tufts 2016; Bailey 2015). As is routinely observed, these mechanisms have a tendency to cluster together within particular varieties of capitalism (Hall and Soskice 2001; Heyes et al. 2012). As we have argued elsewhere, and introduced above, our knowledge and understanding of these different models of capitalism might improve if we are better able to consider the particular forms of contestation that mark them (Bailey and Shibata 2014). In the same way that we expect capitalist social relations to be structured in a particular way within a particular variety of capitalism, so we should also expect the contestation of those capitalist social relations to take particular forms within particular models of capitalism. As such, moreover, we might expect the contestation of the 'age of austerity' to take particular forms in particular models of capitalism.

THE CRITICAL POLITICAL ECONOMY OF ANTI-AUSTERITY

Drawing upon, and adapting, the varieties of capitalism approach to comparative political economy, we identify herein two alternative models of capitalist contestation. The first, which coincides with what are more commonly referred to as coordinated market economies (CMEs), we term here the incorporated contestation model (ICM), or ICM/CME, to make clear that these tend to overlap. The second, which coincides with what is more commonly referred to as the liberal market economies (LMEs), we term the excluded contestation model (ECM), or ECM/LME. The key differences are summarised below.

The incorporated contestation model (ICM/CME)

The ICM/CME model of capitalism, in which attempts are made to regulate capitalist relations in order that they be rendered more inclusive, stable and negotiated, tends to experience economic growth in a form that is less volatile and therefore might be expected to have a more compressed business cycle. This therefore includes lower levels of growth in upturns in the business cycle, alongside more moderate experiences of recession during downturns. These lower levels of growth are therefore likely to be associated with concerted attempts to restructure capitalist social relations in order to identify new opportunities for innovation, profitability and improved prospects of growth. The inclusive nature of capitalist relations in the ICM/CME model of capitalism is also associated with distinct patterns of contestation. In particular, we might expect both that acts of contestation are somewhat standardised and institutionalised and that there is a greater willingness to listen to and seek to incorporate those views expressed through acts of contestation, due to the tendency within CMEs to seek to incorporate key actors within a negotiated pattern of decision making. Finally, this pattern of behaviour might also be expected to be associated with a particular pattern of austerity politics. Due to the less volatile nature of economic growth, the moderate level of institutionalised contestation and a greater willingness to incorporate the views expressed through that contestation, we are also likely to witness only limited attempts to propose austerity reforms, but these attempts to introduce austerity measures are introduced consistently and in a prolonged manner over time (due to the inability, but perceived need, to introduce more substantial austerity measures in an attempt to inject growth in a context of sluggish economic performance). In terms of austerity politics, therefore, we are likely to witness ongoing attempts to introduce moderate austerity measures, which are themselves routinely contested, and that that contestation is partly successful in staving off more substantial forms of austerity, thereby contributing to an ongoing iteration between moderate proposals for austerity and institutionalised patterns of contestation and opposition.

The excluded contestation model (ECM/LME)

The ECM/LME model of capitalism, in contrast, is characterised by an absence of attempts to regulate capitalist relations, and indeed a more concerted attempt to produce more direct and unmediated relations of exploitation, through the construction of an institutional apparatus in which market exchange and a dependence upon either profit realisation or the pursuit of wage labour are the key means by which to sustain oneself. This less regulated model of capitalism is, as a result, susceptible to more volatile swings in the business cycle, experiencing striking boom periods but also being prone to sharp downturns once markets have become overinflated. As a result of both the models of growth that are adopted during upturns in the economy, which are largely dependent upon heightened opportunities for exploitation, and the more severe downturns, there tends to exist a corresponding pressure at certain times for more dramatic forms of austerity-focused restructuring. Further, due to the absence of negotiated forms of deliberation and contention within the ECM/LME model of capitalism, these tend to be marked by a lack of organised opposition, which ensures that in many instances the austerity measures that are proposed are also adopted relatively unopposed (or, at least, without successful opposition). This is not without, however, a greater tendency for underlying forms of hostility and 'everyday' or 'imperceptible' forms of opposition and resistance to become more prevalent, including what we might refer to as 'foot dragging', 'infrapolitics' or the 'weapons of the weak' (Scott 1990; Papadopoulos et al. 2008; Huke et al. 2015). This underlying resentment is only occasionally made more visible when we see what sometimes appear to be relatively spontaneous 'flashpoints' or un-institutionalised outbursts of opposition, which, when they do occur, oftentimes prove more difficult to contain. In terms of patterns of austerity-related policymaking, therefore, we see relatively severe attempts to impose austerity initiatives. Many of these initiatives are successful due to the lack of organised opposition and a tendency to seek to exclude and silence (rather than incorporate) those instances of opposition that do arise, albeit matched by a growth in 'subterranean' forms of resentment and everyday opposition that sometimes transforms into more visible forms of relatively spontaneous outbursts of resistance, and which when it does so is likely to require concessions and backtracking by the government in an attempt to contain such forms of opposition.

These two alternative critical political economy models of anti-austerity are summarised in table 2.1.

ANTI-AUSTERITY IN LOW-RESISTANCE MODELS OF CAPITALISM

We discuss in this section the different patterns of anti-austerity politics witnessed in the two different models of contestated capitalism conceptualised above. Both countries selected – the UK and Japan – have typically experienced low levels of overt resistance. This is due either to the long-standing construction of a relatively obedient and passive workforce, in the case of Japan, or to a more recent process whereby subordinate groups (especially organized labour) have been quieted through a process of disorganisation, disarticulation and repression, in the case of the UK (Bailey and Shibata 2017). By comparing two countries with similar levels of opposition to austerity we are able to explore the degree to which the particular model of contested capitalism – ICM/CME or ECM/LME – is associated with the particular form that resistance takes in each country. As such, we control for the level of resistance in order to explore the relationship between the particular model of contested capitalism and the types of resistance observed. As table 2.2 shows, the experiences of Japan and the UK during the neoliberal period up until 2010 broadly confirm the claims outlined above regarding growth and austerity patterns. That is, during the two periods compared (1979–1992, during which Japan experienced consistently higher levels of

Table 2.1. Critical political economy models of anti-austerity

Model of capitalism	Growth patterns	Contestation patterns	Austerity patterns
ICM/CME (e.g., Japan)	Less volatility, lower levels of secular growth	Standardised/ institutionalised contestation, willingness to compromise	Ongoing, gradual reforms during times of slow growth, met with consistent opposition and moderate austerity processes
ECM/LME (e.g., UK)	Greater market volatility, bubble-led growth, sharper or more frequent recessions	Absence of organised opposition, rising 'imperceptible' opposition, anger and resentment, sporadic outbursts of 'spontaneous' resistance and refusal	Relatively unopposed but severe austerity measures during periods of low growth, sometimes followed by concessions and backtracking when met with spontaneous outbursts

growth than the UK, and 1993–2007, during which the UK experienced consistently higher levels of growth than Japan), we see clear differences in both levels of volatility and the tendency to respond to sluggish growth through recourse to austerity policymaking. Thus, during the UK's low growth period (1979–1992) we see multiple recessions (1980–1981 and 1991) and relatively severe levels of austerity (nine austerity years and an 18.21 per cent decrease in welfare generosity). In contrast, during Japan's low growth period we see only a gradual move towards austerity policymaking, including five austerity years but a 3.24 per cent increase in overall welfare generosity. This suggests, therefore, that the proposal and execution of austerity measures tends to be more muted in Japan's ICM/CME model of capitalism. Given that Japan's period of low economic growth throughout the 1990s and 2000s coincided with growth in visible instances of worker-led acts of public opposition and dissent, this is perhaps unsurprising (Shibata 2016). This contrast, marking a greater tendency for austerity measures to be adopted in the UK's ECM/LME model of contested capitalism, is also confirmed by the data available for 2010 in the Scruggs et al. (2014) dataset. This is the final year of data available in that dataset, but also the year during which most advanced industrial democracies turned towards a pro-austerity agenda. It also witnessed austerity measures at double the size in the UK compared with that of the Japan case.

In order to compare the different contestation patterns in each national context we can also turn to a recent comparative survey of attempts to promote austerity that we have compiled and reported on in our *Anti-Austerity in*

Table 2.2. Comparing anti-austerity

	1979–1992	1993–2007	2010
Japan (ICM/CME)	High growth (4.21% p.a.) No recession Low austerity (5 austerity years, 4.26% increase in generosity)	Lower growth (1.15% p.a.) Recession (1998–1999) Gradual austerity (5 austerity years, 3.24% increase in generosity)	Low austerity (−1.15% generosity)
UK (ECM/LME)	Low growth (2.19% p.a.) Multiple recession years (1980, 1981, 1991) High austerity (9 austerity years, 18.21% decrease in generosity)	Higher growth (2.93% p.a.) No recession No austerity (5 austerity years, but 6.08% increase in generosity)	High austerity (−2.48% generosity)

Low Resistance Capitalism blog.[1] In doing so we seek to consider the different types of contestation experienced in the UK and Japan during the 2010–2015 age of austerity. The results of this comparison, in terms of the degree to which austerity proposals were successfully obstructed, have been reported elsewhere, highlighting the different routes towards successfully obstructing proposals for austerity policymaking (Bailey and Shibata 2017). In each case we present a brief overview of the austerity proposal initially made, the different types of opposition witnessed, and the eventual outcome, including details of any concessions made or consequences experienced by those who proposed the austerity measure. As such, the aim is to provide a collection of brief vignettes, the sum of which enables us to identify different patterns of contestation and austerity in different models of capitalist contestation. As we see, and as suggested in our discussion above, in the ICM/CME case of Japan, contestation takes on a standardised and institutionalised form and an apparent willingness of austerity advocates to compromise when met by this type of resistance. In the ECM/LME case of the UK, in contrast, we see an absence of organised opposition, rising 'imperceptible' forms of opposition, anger and resentment, and sporadic outbursts of 'spontaneous' resistance and refusal, and on those occasions where anti-austerity opposition does become more visible we see a tendency by austerity advocates to offer concessions and to backtrack in an attempt to regain control of opposition movements.

JAPAN: GRADUAL AUSTERITY, ORGANISED DISSENT, MODERATE CONCESSIONS

Japan experienced four major austerity proposals during the 2010–2015 period. These were reform to the Dispatch Workers Law, to introduce further flexibilisation into the Japanese labour market; a proposal to unilaterally reduce the generosity of existing public pensions in Japan; a proposal to increase the value-added tax (VAT) from 5 per cent to 10 per cent, in two stages; and a proposal to introduce legislation that would remove the need for employers to pay staff for overtime work (Zero Overtime Payment). Since we discuss Zero Overtime Payment elsewhere (see Bailey and Shibata 2017), this chapter focuses on the first three austerity proposals. Each proposal experienced different forms of opposition, although in each case this was largely coordinated by organised interests (especially trade unions) producing some kind of obstacle to austerity, as we detail below.

Dispatch Workers Law

In the aftermath of the global financial crisis, a makeshift camp for temporary agency workers (known in Japan as 'dispatch workers') was established by various groups – including unions, citizens' groups, volunteering groups and NPOs in one of Tokyo's parks – and which provided housing for many of Japan's precarious workers who had become homeless as a result of the 2008 crisis. This came to be known as *Hakenmura* and would come to represent a key symbol of anti-austerity resistance in Japan. The camp provided support for precarious workers, as well as unemployed and homeless people affected by the economic turmoil of late 2008. It also led to the creation of a loosely connected network of activists, named the 'Committee for the Amendment of the Dispatch Workers Law'. As the name suggests, this focused on attempts to seek changes to the Dispatch Workers Law (DWL) that regulates the conditions under which dispatch workers can be employed in Japan. The committee attracted participants from a number of institutions, each of whom were linked by their involvement in the temporary camp event and the general awareness that this had raised regarding precarious workers and the unemployed. In an attempt to improve the conditions faced by dispatch workers, the Committee staged demonstrations and public events that sought to engage trade unionists, members of the public, citizens' groups, and antipoverty civil society groups. In addition, this witnessed the participation of newer community unions, including the *Syutoken Seinen* Union and *Haken* Union, both of which played a key role in the Committee and which had been created to provide support for precarious and temporary workers who were unable to gain satisfactory representation within existing established unions.

In late 2013 Japan's Abe administration proposed that the existing Dispatch Workers Law (which regulates temporary agency employment, or 'dispatch workers') be amended, removing an existing requirement that jobs could only be filled by dispatch workers for a maximum of three years, and thereby regulating to increase the use of temporary agency workers (dispatch workers) within the Japanese labour market. This prompted a wave of public opposition throughout 2014 and 2015, which built upon the agenda-setting work that had already been done through the earlier efforts of the Committee for the Amendment of the Dispatch Workers Law. This new round of mobilisation in support of dispatch workers was largely coordinated by the major established trade union confederation *Rengo*, which staged a number of protest events, including public demonstrations in Yamanashi, Kumamoto and Kanagawa. Following the refusal of the Abe administration to back down on the proposal, further sit-in protests were staged by eight hundred trade union activists outside the national parliament in October 2014, again supported by *Rengo* but also this time by the established public sector trade union confederation, *Zenroren*. Similar protests were also witnessed during 2015, especially in Tokyo, and focused on the national parliament. Having successfully put opposition to the Dispatch Workers Law amendment on the national political agenda, Japan's trade union movement was able to push for concessions in the drafting of the legislation. As a result, and in an attempt to placate public opposition, Abe moved to introduce reforms to the legislation, whereby the government would take a larger role in the regulation of temporary agencies, promising that training would be provided for dispatch workers alongside a later increase in the minimum wage. These measures were widely interpreted as an attempt to offset the claims of the trade union movement that the Abe administration was acting to the detriment of low-paid and temporary workers. As such, ongoing organised opposition towards a further flexibilisation of Japan's labour market, therefore, was sufficient to produce a number of concessions designed to mitigate the impact upon precarious workers.

Pension reforms

In November 2012, under Prime Minister Yoshiko Noda's Democratic Party of Japan administration, the Japanese parliament passed an amendment to the National Pension Act that would reduce what it was claimed was Japan's 'overpayment' of its public pensions. The terms of this reduction were further clarified following the election to office of the Liberal Democratic Party, under Prime Minister Shinzō Abe, according to which a reduction of 2.3 per cent was set to phase in over three stages between October 2013 and April 2015. This reform was accompanied by a commitment, known as the 'macroeconomic slide', to ensure that public pensions would not rise at the same rate as wages and prices and would decline in times of wage or price deflation. In response to this pension-related austerity measure, Japan witnessed a number of acts of resistance, conducted by the elderly (and their unions and lawyers). Opposition to the reforms was quickly mounted and included lawsuits brought by the Japan Pensioners' Union against twenty-seven local prefectures, with more than 116,000 complaints filing for, or requesting, official investigations. In addition, public demonstrations were frequent, including the occurrence of so-called pensioners' riots in Nagasaki, Aomori and Kumamoto. This round of opposition also added to the problems already experienced in Japan's public pension system, which in 2007 had been forced to admit that it had lost the pension data of fifty-one million Japanese citizens. As a result, non-payment into the public pension scheme had risen to 37 per cent by 2013 (compared with a level under 20 per cent during the 1990s) amidst popular distrust towards the scheme. In response to these objections, both the Noda and the Abe administrations moved to adopt a number of relatively substantial concessions. The scale of the pension reduction was reduced from 2.3 per cent to 2 per cent, and Abe was eventually moved to announce an increase of 30,000 yen in temporary support for low-income pensioners, with the most draconian parts of the 'macroeconomic slide' being abandoned altogether. As had been the case with the attempt to reform the Dispatch Workers Law, therefore, significant and sustained organised opposition, conducted especially by the Japan Pensioners' Union, was sufficient to ensure that Abe was moved to offer significant concessions, including the abandonment of one of the major elements of the reforms.

Sales tax hike

In May 2010 the Hatoyama administration (Democratic Party of Japan, DPJ) announced that it would increase the national sales tax, despite promising not to do so in the election manifesto upon which it was elected. The proposal was so unpopular, however, that it contributed to the resignation of Hatoyama's successor, Prime Minister Naoto Kan, when he tried to implement it, and eventually led to a proposal to introduce a two-stage increase (from 5 per cent to 8 per cent, and then to 10 per cent), in part in order to soften its impact. Opposition to the tax hikes was frequent and often took the form of public demonstrations staged by the trade unions, especially oil industry unions, the *Zenroren*, and in July 2012 a street protest organised by twenty-three citizens' groups and trade unions in which fifty cars paraded through Kouchi. The scale of opposition to the proposal was such that it caused significant division within the DPJ, resulting in roughly equal proportions of the party membership being both for and against the proposal. Attempts to appease the dissent that followed witnessed promises to suspend the tax hike if economic growth was weak at the time of its planned implementation, in part as a result of a steep decline in the cabinet approval ratings of the DPJ government, and eventually seeing the government dramatically voted out of office in the December 2012 general election before it had a chance to actually implement the tax hike (Park and Ide 2014).

Upon his election to office, therefore, the new LDP prime minister, Shinzo Abe, was faced with the task of implementing the sales tax hike, which had already been agreed to under the previous administration. In particular, the question that the Abe government faced was that of when to introduce the tax increase. In seeking to mollify opposition, Abe promised both that the increase would be conditional upon there being strong economic growth in place and that the revenue would be used to increase social welfare spending (although the degree to which this latter commitment was upheld was later disputed). Abe also introduced a small 10,000 yen increase in social benefits for low-income people in order to offset the effect of the tax hike.

Following the first increase in sales tax, in April 2014, the incidence of non-payment of the tax rose and the economy experienced a drop in consumption that was sharper than anticipated. The Abe administration was also met by public demonstrations opposing the tax increase, again often organised by the national trade union confederations (*Kenroren, Zenroren* and *Rengo*) – for instance, in Tokyo, Fukushima, Osaka, Shiga, Nagano and

Tokushima – each of which sought to highlight the impact that the sales tax increase would have, especially upon the low paid. Opposition to the second tax hike, especially after the sharp drop in consumption following the first hike, was such that Abe proposed a number of substantial concessions, including temporary welfare payments for the low paid and those with children, a sales tax relief plan, and eventually a postponement of the hike altogether (first to April 2017 and then, later still, to October 2019). As such, at the time of writing (December 2017) the second tax hike has still not been introduced, in large part due to the different forms of public opposition that it experienced. With this third austerity initiative, therefore, we also see sustained and organised public protests galvanizing public opposition, eventually resulting in the government offering significant concessions.

In sum, therefore, we see in the case of Japan's ICM/CME model of capitalist contestation an ongoing succession of relatively moderate proposals for austerity, which have prompted organised and sustained protest actions, demonstrations and displays of public opposition, typically facilitated by established trade unions and other civil society organisations. We might consider these acts to represent an attempt to perform resistance in pursuit of the goal of survival (especially in the sense that resistance has been mobilised in an attempt to avoid a lowering of living standards for already precarious workers, pensioners and citizens). These events have also sought to disrupt the notion that austerity measures are in some way equitable or a positive development for Japan's model of capitalism. Whilst these protest events have been largely conducted by established trade unions and civil society groups, we have also witnessed, in some instances, the creation of newer forms of association, especially in the case of precarious workers, where we have seen the creation of both new independent trade unions and new protest movements that seek to advance the cause of temporary workers. In most instances, we have also seen that anti-austerity actions have been met by some form of concession from the Japanese government. As such, this broadly coheres with our expectations, as set out above and in table 2.1, whereby moderate austerity proposals are introduced gradually and consistently over time, largely in response to lower levels of growth, and which are in turn met with consistent opposition that is largely of an institutionalised kind, eventually resulting in the implementation of moderate austerity measures that are accompanied by concessions in an attempt to offset opposition.

UK: BETWEEN DEPOLITICISED AUSTERITY AND HEATED CONTESTATION

The UK's experience of both austerity and anti-austerity was more mixed than that of Japan. The period of full-blown austerity was launched in the UK with the new coalition government led by David Cameron, elected in 2010, and especially with its Emergency Budget of June 2010. This announced that the incoming government would adopt a round of public spending cuts that would seek to eliminate the government deficit by a target date of 2015. Many of the austerity measures adopted took a relatively technocratic form in an attempt to depoliticise the process of austerity policymaking. This was most obviously the case with the move to change the government's measure of inflation from RPI to CPI, which we have discussed in detail elsewhere (and which we therefore omit from the contested austerity measures we discuss below; for details of the RPI/CPI switch, see Bailey and Shibata 2017). This switch from RPI to CPI resulted in a substantial reduction in public sector pay and pensions, and (partly as a result of its technical nature) was relatively uncontested. A similar trend can also be witnessed with the Coalition's Bedroom Tax, the reduction in public sector pay, and the VAT increase, all of which are discussed in more detail below. In contrast, some of the more high-profile austerity measures did spark more widespread opposition, leading to either considerable efforts to reform the proposed austerity measure or significant consequences for the coalition in its attempt to implement it. This, as we shall see, is perhaps most evident regarding the opposition to the rise in university tuition fees. As a result of these diverging experiences of contested austerity measures, we divide our discussion below into two types: depoliticised austerity measures in which opposition was relatively muted (and, as a result, the measures were adopted relatively smoothly), and those austerity measures that experienced more heated opposition (and which tended to see either concessions offered or significant consequences for those who sought to impose the measure in question). These are each discussed in turn below.

Depoliticised austerity: Bedroom Tax

The under-occupancy penalty – or 'Bedroom Tax', as it became known – was proposed at the beginning of the Coalition Government as part of the 2010 emergency budget. In presenting the proposal the Coalition chancellor, George Osborne, claimed that spending on housing benefit had climbed above a reasonable or affordable level, and therefore it was necessary to reduce a proportion of a family's housing benefit for each 'spare room' that they had (14 per cent reduction for one 'spare room', and 25 per cent for two). Given that the penalty for so-called under-occupancy was a reduction in housing benefit, resulting in the possibility of eviction if rents could not subsequently be paid, the proposal was widely considered to be a punitive one. This was compounded by the fact that the definition of an unused room was difficult to pin down, in many cases resulting in penalties for disabled residents who required an additional room in order to be able to house equipment related to their disability, or in some cases to recently bereaved parents, or those with a very small 'spare room' that could not be used as a bedroom due to its size.

The punitive nature of the proposal was such that it received considerable public opposition, including a wave of protests that took place throughout early 2013 (i.e., on the eve of its implementation), including a protest of 2,500 people in Glasgow, 1,000 demonstrators outside Downing Street, and protests in many other cities across the country (including Leeds, Cardiff, Manchester and Birmingham), many of which were coordinated by newly created local anti–Bedroom Tax campaigns, eventually resulting in the creation of the Anti–Bedroom Tax and Benefit Justice Federation in May 2013. In some cases, moreover, the evictions that could arise from refusal or inability to pay the Bedroom Tax were also resisted. For instance, Coventry Against the Bedroom Tax successfully prevented the eviction of a resident of Coventry, through a combination of blockading the house in order to prevent the eviction and the adverse publicity that this created for the housing association seeking to carry out the eviction. Such cases of successful mobilisation, however, were relatively infrequent, and whilst the public opposition to the Bedroom Tax was widely recognised as having had a negative effect upon (especially) the Conservative Party's reputation, the government has nevertheless continued with the policy relatively unabated, seeking to legitimate the policy by shifting the language in a more depoliticised direction and thereby depicting it instead as the 'removal of the spare room subsidy'.

Depoliticised austerity: Benefit cap

As part of the 2010 Comprehensive Spending Review, the Coalition Government also announced a cap on benefits of £26,000. Whilst this threshold was depicted by the government as a relatively high level of income, it took no account of the cost of living for recipients, including the number of dependents of a household. It therefore had the potential to be especially harmful for vulnerable families with a large number of dependents and without an alternative source of income. Public opposition was relatively limited, with opposition largely coming from those in formal positions within organisations rather than from protests specifically focused on the cap, including criticism by church campaigners who sought the removal of child benefit from the calculation of capped benefits, and similar opposition from unexpected quarters, such as Emma Harrison, founder and chairwoman of A4e. However, no protest movement that was specifically focused on the benefit cap emerged. One of the main arguments put forward by the government in its attempt to build support for the initiative was a discourse of welfare dependency, according to which the benefit cap would help avoid people falling into some kind of 'welfare trap' and therefore also protect the interests of taxpayers. For instance, Chris Grayling, employment minister, said, 'We are making principled reforms that will finally tackle the trap of welfare dependency . . . The bill will also deliver fairness for claimants and for the taxpayers who fund the system'. Further, in defending the move, and later suggesting an additional lowering of the cap, David Cameron repeatedly highlighted the way in which it shielded taxpayers from unfairly subsidising those on benefits. For instance, in 2015, in announcing plans to lower the cap further to £23,000, Cameron said, 'People working 10, 11 hours a day, they don't pay their taxes to sustain people on welfare who are able to work'. Similarly, Osborne also defended the cap by stating, 'Those who campaign against a cap on benefits for families who aren't working are completely out of touch with how the millions of working families who pay the taxes to fund these benefits feel about this'. As such, in the absence of significant mobilisation against the benefit cap and given the government's depiction of the measures as a straightforward attempt to avoid profligacy on behalf of the taxpayer, the measure was adopted with minimal opposition, and indeed (as we have seen) in 2015 the Conservative Party moved to lower the cap further still, to £23,000.

Depoliticised austerity: Public sector pay

In its June 2010 'emergency' budget the Coalition Government also announced a two-year public sector pay freeze, applied to all public sector workers earning an annual salary of £21,000 or more, which it anticipated would save £3.3 billion by 2014–2015 (Bach and Stroleny 2013, 345). Low-paid public sector workers, in contrast, were exempt from the pay freeze, and instead received a £250 annual pay increase for both years. This pay freeze was done with no prior consultation with the public sector trade unions, thereby representing a decline in trade union influence within the pay bargaining process (Bach and Stroleny 2013, 350). Further still, the pay freeze was subsequently extended to a pay cap of 1 per cent per annum for 2013–2016 (and again, up until 2020, in the 2015 budget of the newly elected Conservative Government). The freeze therefore sought to impose considerable pay restraint across a large section of the UK workforce. However, in removing the lowest paid from the freeze, the government did at least attempt to mitigate the regressive effect of the proposal, presumably in an attempt to avoid more militant forms of opposition.

Following its announcement, the proposed pay freeze came under considerable vocal attack from public sector workers' trade unions – with trade union leaders portraying the move as an attack upon the public sector and seeking to mobilise opposition amongst their members. For instance, Dave Prentis, general secretary of Unison, talked of 'the government declaring war', describing public sector employees as 'innocent victims of job cuts and pay freezes' and noting, 'Freezing public sector pay when inflation is running at 5.1 percent and VAT is going up will mean a real cut in living standards for millions of ordinary workers and their families already struggling to pay rising bills'. There was, however, little in the way of an actual industrial dispute or more militant attempts to force the government to change course. This arguably reflected a lack of enthusiasm amongst the trade union membership to engage in industrial disputes that it was unclear could be won due to a relatively low level of union density and mobilisation and the acceptance within much of public opinion that a reduction in public spending was 'necessary' (Bach and Stroleny 2013, 352). In addition, we might note that the exemption of low-paid public sector workers from the pay freeze might have had the effect of mitigating opposition – especially as this had the effect of ensuring that the real pay of public sector workers fell less than for low-paid private sector employees. The government's plans to reduce the size of the public sector workforce (1.1 million job cuts planned for the period between 2010–2011 and 2018–2019 – on which, see Cribb et al. 2014) might also have contributed to a sense of limited bargaining strength.

It was not until March 2013 that we saw the first major pay-related strike amongst public sector workers in the UK, with the launching of a pay dispute by PCS members in the civil service on Budget Day 2013. As such, the government was relatively successful in using the language of necessity in seeking to legitimate its proposal, with Osborne claiming, 'The truth is that the country was living beyond its means when the recession came. And if we don't tackle pay and pensions, more jobs will be lost. That is why the government is asking the public sector to accept a two-year pay freeze'. In addition, the government focused on the positive implications of the pay policy, especially its ability to protect against job losses. For instance, in announcing a four-year extension of the pay cap in 2015, Osborne announced, 'There is a simple trade-off between pay and jobs in many public services'. In sum, there was no visible sign of the government moving to adopt concessions in response to the different forms of trade union opposition outlined above, in part, we argue, due to a lack of more consistent or militant forms of resistance.

Depoliticised austerity: VAT increase

In 2010 the coalition government also announced its plan to increase VAT from 17.5 per cent to 20 per cent, despite having earlier explicitly ruled out such a move. This was announced with the expectation that the rise would result in an increase in annual tax revenue of £12 billion. The proposed tax reform witnessed a wave of public criticism regarding the tax, focusing on the impact that it would have on inequality – due to VAT's regressive consequences, the impact on aggregate demand (which, it was feared, threatened growth), and the potentially inflationary effect due to its impact on prices. Criticism was, therefore, voiced by both social justice groups and business associations, witnessing the British Retail Consortium describe the tax rise as 'disappointing'. Public opposition to the rise, however, took a number of forms. The most visible opposition was only indirectly focused on the VAT increase, with UK Uncut using a range of innovative protest techniques to oppose tax evasion and avoidance, which it contrasted with (unnecessary) public spending cuts and the VAT increase. For instance, Murray Williams, a UK Uncut spokesman, declared, 'In a time when we're being told that we're all in this together and when we've all got to accept these harsh cuts to housing benefit and the NHS and take a hike in VAT . . . trying to claim that these companies then don't have to pay their fair share of that too – I just don't think that's on'. Partly in recognition of the unpopular nature of the tax rise, the government did move in its 2013 budget to introduce some conciliatory measures, including, for instance, the freezing of petrol duty, the freezing (and lowering) of duty on beer, and the reduction of National Insurance contributions; nevertheless, they did not substantially affect the direct implementation of the VAT increase. As such, there were few signs of direct consequences suffered by the government as a result of increasing the VAT.

Heated contestation: University tuition fees

In 2010 the new Coalition Government announced that it would increase tuition fees, with the maximum that universities were allowed to charge for undergraduate degrees raised from £3,375 per year to £9,000 per year, representing a near tripling of tuition fees and a major restructuring of the financial basis upon which higher education in the UK was to be funded (McGettigan 2013, 21–22). This prompted a rapid mobilisation of a student protest movement that was fiercely critical of the proposal. Opposition took two main forms – first, a round of public demonstrations timed to oppose the passing of the secondary legislation needed to implement the policies; second, militant direct action protests that largely consisted of occupations of university buildings in an attempt to highlight opposition to the impact that the fee rise would have on higher education. The anti-tuition-fee student movement emerged, somewhat unexpectedly, out of the official National Union of Students (NUS) demonstration that had been called for 10 November 2010 to oppose the tuition fee increase. The demonstration was expected to be a conventional march through central London, with the support of both the NUS and the academic staff union, UCU. However, disruption emerged on the route of the march as a group of more militant students entered the Millbank building that housed the headquarters of the Conservative Party. The scenes were striking – broadcast through traditional media as well as social media – including anarchist flags (amongst others) being waved from the roof of the building, students occupying the building, and a large group of protesters gathering outside the building. This event marked the beginning of the biggest wave of student mobilisation in more than three decades, forming a major part of the anti-austerity movement witnessed in the UK, including roughly one-third of all protest events for 2010 (Bailey 2014). This included sometimes violent protests, in which repeated clashes between student protesters and the police occurred, leading up to the vote in Parliament. The protests focused especially on the broken promise of the Liberal Democrats – the junior coalition partner – that they would oppose tuition fees once in office. Social media in particular was used to highlight the hypocrisy of the coalition partner.

Despite this opposition, the small amount of time between the announcement in October 2010 that tuition fees would be nearly tripled and the adoption of the necessary secondary legislation in parliament in December 2010 to implement the measure meant that there was little scope for concessions to be introduced. Nevertheless, the pressure upon the Coalition – and especially upon the junior coalition partner, the Liberal Democrats – was such that some kind of compromise needed to be struck. The main concession that the Liberal Democrats pushed for and achieved within the coalition was the agreement that the £21,000 repayment threshold (below which graduates would not begin repaying their loan) would raise annually in line with inflation (McGettigan 2013, 23).[2] A secondary concession was the requirement that universities charging more than £6,000 in annual fees were required to negotiate an 'access agreement' with OFFA (Office for Fair Access), which would show how some of the revenue from the tuition fees would be used to widen participation – for instance, by increasing support for students from lower income backgrounds. This is estimated to have a cost of between 20 and 30 per cent of the tuition fee revenue that comes from fees above £6,000 (c. £670 million, up from c. £400 million prior to the reforms) (McGettigan 2013, 31). In addition, any unpaid loans that remain after thirty years will be written off. In total, therefore, these amounted to significant concessions and reduced the degree to which the government was able to increase revenue through the austerity measure. Indeed, the calculation of the amount that could be expected to be repaid was significantly written down in 2014, by around £3 billion (compared with the 2010 estimate) (McGettigan 2015). Also as a result of the concessions introduced, the savings achieved by the increased tuition fees were estimated to be only 5 per cent of the total support spent by the government per student (Crawford et al. 2014). Despite these concessions, moreover, the Liberal Democrats suffered a massive loss of electoral support following the tuition fee rise, with most commentators explaining this directly as a result of the tuition fee issue – with the inconsistency of the tuition fee position of the Liberal Democrats ensuring that the party was tarnished with an image of duplicity and dishonesty, an image that the tuition fee protesters worked hard to establish and embed within popular consciousness. In the case of the tuition fee rise, therefore, we witness a wide range of major and vocal opposition, and although the measure went ahead, it nevertheless was accompanied by a number of concessions that ended up having a significant impact upon its effect, as well as witnessing major political consequences for the Liberal Democrats due to their complicity in implementing the measure.

Heated contestation: Workfare

After its election in 2010 the Coalition Government adopted a 'Workfare' scheme that consisted of three main initiatives – the Work Programme, the Work Experience Scheme and the Community Work Placement Scheme. This represented both a privatisation and an intensification of the previous Workfare (Welfare-to-Work) scheme introduced by the preceding New Labour Government. The Coalition's Workfare programme introduced a range of measures that would significantly increase the compulsion placed upon the unemployed to take up work placements, leading some critics to describe the scheme as a form of forced labour. Further, the use of sanctions ensured that some of the poorest members of society would be targeted for punitive measures. The Workfare programmes were highly controversial, sparking instances of a range of types of resistance, including: sometimes successful attempts to 'game' the incentive structure placed upon those firms implementing the scheme (Rees et al. 2014); a series of attempts to publicly disrupt the retail employers who were taking part in the scheme (for instance, witnessing occupations and protests directly outside the high street stores of participating firms, such as Tesco and Holland and Barrett); and a successful legal challenge brought against it by two benefit claimants who were forced to do unpaid work in order to continue to receive their benefits. As a result, the implementation of Workfare became increasingly problematic, with many firms pulling out of the scheme and the government eventually being forced to capitulate in 2012 over its commitment to sanctions for its work experience scheme as a result of pressure from employers that did not want to be associated with sanctions and the related compulsion to undertake unpaid labour. In sum, therefore, the Coalition Government's Workfare scheme represented a highly regressive austerity proposal, but one that was substantially obstructed as a result of ongoing and militant forms of disruptive opposition, much of which was orchestrated by the newly created group Boycott Workfare, set up with the direct intention of opposing the government's Workfare initiatives.

In sum, therefore, the UK experienced more dramatic proposals for austerity than those witnessed in the Japan case; yet, due in part to the liberal nature of its socioeconomic relations, on many occasions it witnessed little in the way of effective resistance. Nevertheless, when more 'spontaneous' forms of innovative and militant forms of refusal did emerge (in the case of anti-tuition fees and opposition to Workfare) we see more successful efforts to obstruct and impede the imposition of austerity, requiring concessions in an attempt to re-contain those outbursts of dissent. In terms of the three aspects of resistance guiding our discussion – survival, disruption and creation – we can see each of these present in the UK case, but they are obviously most apparent in the two cases of what we term *heated contestation* mentioned above (the anti-tuition fee protests and the anti-Workfare campaigns). Thus, both of these anti-austerity movements focused on survival efforts in the sense that they sought to avoid either the experience of lifelong debt (and associated hardship) in the case of the tuition fee campaigns or the more immediate forms of hardship resulting from a Workfare regime that sought to impose benefit sanctions as a threat placed upon those who refused to engage with the Workfare scheme. As we have seen, each of these campaigns also had a considerably disruptive impact, acting in part to disrupt the operation of the policies being advanced. Thus, in the case of the anti-tuition fee protests we see the concessions that were extracted by the movement eventually reducing considerably the degree to which the government was able to lower its costs in providing higher education. Likewise, in the case of the anti-Workfare movement, the scheme suffered a number of problems as a result of participating organisations dropping out of the scheme as they sought to avoid the negative publicity with which it had become associated. In terms of resistance as a form of creation, each of the more vibrant anti-austerity movements also witnessed the creation of new forms of association and new ways of organising. In the case of the anti-tuition fee campaign we saw the creation of a rival organisation – the National Campaign Against Fees and Cuts (NCAFC) – which sought to challenge the more established National Union of Students (NUS), in part due to dissatisfaction with the NUS and its muted opposition to tuition fee rises (for more detail, see Bailey et al. 2018, 179–85). In the case of the anti-Workfare movement we also see the creation of a new organisation, Boycott Workfare, which sought especially to utilise social media campaigning to target the Workfare regime (for more detail, see Bailey et al. 2018, 138–46).

CONCLUSION

This chapter has argued that we need a model of contested capitalism through which to understand the comparative political economy of anti-austerity. It suggests that we can see two different models of contested capitalism, and that these see different patterns of austerity policymaking and resistance to austerity. First, we posit what we term an incorporated contestation model (ICM/CME), in which proposals for austerity tend to be lesser in scope but more sustained over time, and in which governments proposing austerity interact with, are more receptive to and act to incorporate the views more meaningfully of organised expressions of opposition and dissent. Through our discussion of the case of Japan we have sought to show how we can see these trends, with much of the resistance to austerity measures that we have observed taking the form of public demonstrations, typically organised by established trade unions and civil society organisations, and with an apparent willingness on the part of the government to offer concessions to pacify this opposition. This we could see with the development of Abe's pension reforms, which were significantly downscaled in the face of public opposition, and with the implementation of a regressive sales tax, which has been postponed, also as a result of organised public opposition. We should perhaps note, however, that rather than considering this to be a successful attempt to deal with capitalism's intractable dilemmas, instead such an approach has subsequently prompted both new and ongoing problems for Japan's socio-economy (Shibata 2017).

In addition, we posit an alternative, excluded contestation model (ECM/ LME), in which austerity proposals tend often to go unchallenged, in large part due to the absence of significant organised social opposition movements, but which nevertheless at certain times apparently witness the eruption of more 'spontaneous' forms of innovative and militant opposition, which, when they do arise, have a tendency to see more successful efforts to obstruct and impede the imposition of austerity, requiring concessions in an attempt to re-contain those outbursts of dissent. We saw this in the case of both the anti-tuition fee movements in the UK and the anti-Workfare campaigns, alongside the more muted opposition to initiatives such as the cap on social security benefits or the reduction of public sector pay.

In terms of the three aspects of resistance that have been conceptualised in the present volume – resistance as survival, disruption and/or creation – we see instances of each of these in both of our models of contested capitalism, and indeed in each of our case studies, albeit manifesting themselves differently empirically in each case. With the more incorporated model of contestation that we discuss in the case of Japan, as well as the more exclusionary approach that we consider in the case of the UK, we see resistance occurring as a form of survival. In particular, we see instances of resistance emerging as a means by which to challenge and oppose the threats to living standards that are associated with the adoption of austerity measures and the removal (or heightened conditionality) of welfare provisions. Nevertheless, the means through which these survival-oriented forms of resistance are articulated tend to vary between cases, with a more institutionalised expression of these efforts in the more incorporated case of Japan and less institutionalised in the more exclusionary case of the UK. We also see resistance having a disruptive effect in both cases. In the case of Japan we see a disruption of the narratives that have been employed to justify austerity measures, targeting the notion that austerity measures are equitable, and focusing on the way in which they are harming the Japanese socioeconomic model, and as a result disrupting the attempt to legitimate austerity proposals. In the case of the UK, resistance (especially in its more explosive forms, as seen in the anti-tuition fee protests and the anti-Workfare campaigns) have acted more directly to disrupt the operation of austerity policies, either producing important unexpected consequences for those advocating austerity or producing significant obstacles in the way of those seeking to implement austerity measures. Finally, in both cases we see ways in which resistance has led to instances of creation, especially the creation of new organisations and other forms of association through which to mobilise and articulate dissent. In Japan's case, however, resistance was less likely to result in the creation of such new types of organisation, partly because of the continued presence of recognised and established institutions (although nevertheless we have seen the creation of new independent unions seeking to advance the interests of a growing group of precarious workers within the Japanese labour market). In the UK case, in contrast, the absence of institutions that provide a realistic opportunity through which to express dissent (or at least to have a meaningful chance of such dissent being heard) has on occasion prompted the creation of new organisations and alternative forms of association.

In sum, our chapter suggests that an account of resistance during the so-called age of austerity can benefit by drawing on both the comparative capitalisms' literature and an approach to political economy that we term *minor Marxism*. In doing so, we claim, we are better able to identify the problems, pitfalls and difficulties faced by those seeking to impose austerity measures in different socioeconomic contexts, as well as highlight the different ways in which resistance has been (and remains) able to facilitate survival, disruption and the creation of alternatives, despite the best efforts of those same austerity advocates. Whilst resistance happens differently in different socioeconomic contexts, therefore, capitalism nevertheless remains invariably contested, regardless of the different efforts to resolve the intractable tensions that unavoidably arise from the attempt to secure a system based on exploitation and domination.

NOTES

1. Each of the cases detailed are elaborated upon, with references to the original sources used, in our *Anti-Austerity in Low Resistance Capitalism* blog: https://antiausterity lowresistancecapitalism.wordpress.com/.

2. Although in 2015 it was announced that this commitment was to be abandoned and instead the threshold would be frozen until at least April 2021 (see Bolton 2016).

BIBLIOGRAPHY

Bach, Stephen, and Alexandra Stroleny. 2013. 'Public Service Employment Restructuring in the Crisis in the UK and Ireland: Social Partnership in Retreat'. *European Journal of Industrial Relations* 19(4): 341–57.

Bailey, David J. 2014. 'Contending the Crisis: What Role for Extra-Parliamentary British Politics?' *British Politics* 9(1): 68–92.

Bailey, David J. 2015. 'Resistance Is Futile? The Impact of Disruptive Protest in the "Silver Age of Permanent Austerity"'. *Socio-Economic Review* 13(1): 5–32.

Bailey, David J., Mònica Clua-Losada, Nikolai Huke and Olatz Ribera-Almandoz. 2018. *Beyond Defeat and Austerity: Disrupting (the Critical Political Economy of) Neoliberal Europe*. London: Routledge.

Bailey, David J., and Saori Shibata. 2014. 'Varieties of Contestation: The Comparative and Critical Political Economy of "Excessive" Demand'. *Capital and Class* 38(1): 239–51.

Bailey, David J., and Saori Shibata. 2017. 'Austerity and Anti-Austerity: The Political Economy of Refusal in "Low-Resistance" Models of Capitalism'. *British Journal of Political Science*.

Bellofiore, Riccardo. 2013. '"Two or Three Things I Know about Her": Europe in the Global Crisis and Heterodox Economics'. *Cambridge Journal of Economics* 37(3): 497–512.

Bolton, Paul. 2016. 'Student Loan Statistics'. House of Commons Library Briefing Paper. Available at http://www.parliament.uk/briefing-papers/sn01079.pdf.

Bruff, Ian. 2014. 'The Rise of Authoritarian Neoliberalism'. *Rethinking Marxism* 26(1): 113–29.

Burgmann, Verity. 2013. 'The Multitude and the Many-Headed Hydra: Autonomist Marxist Theory and Labor History'. *International Labor and Working-Class History* 3(1): 170–90.

Clift, Ben, and Magnus Ryner. 2014. 'Joined at the Hip, but Pulling Apart? Franco-German Relations, the Eurozone Crisis and the Politics of Austerity'. *French Politics* 12(2): 136–63.

Crawford, C., R. Crawford and W. Jin. 2014. 'Estimating the Public Cost of Student Loans', IFS Report R94 (London: Institute for Fiscal Studies). Available at https://www.ifs.org.uk/comms/r94.pdf.

Cribb, Jonathan, Carl Emmerson and Luke Sibieta. 2014. *Public Sector Pay in the UK*. London: IFS.

Ebenau, Mathias, Ian Bruff and Christian May. 2015. *New Directions in Comparative Capitalisms Research: Critical and Global Perspectives*. Basingstoke: Palgrave.

Hall, Peter, and David Soskice. 2001. 'An Introduction to Varieties of Capitalism'. In *Varieties of Capitalism: The Institutional Foundations of Comparative Advantage*, edited by Peter Hall and David Soskice, 1–68. Oxford: Oxford University Press.

Heyes, Jason, Paul Lewis and Ian Clark. 2012. 'Varieties of Capitalism, Neoliberalism and the Economic Crisis of 2008?' *Industrial Relations Journal* 43(3): 222–41.

Holland, Eugene W. 2011. *Nomad Citizenship: Free-Market Communism and the Slow-Motion General Strike*. Minneapolis: University of Minnesota Press.

Huke, Nikolai, Monica Clua-Losada and David J. Bailey. 2015. 'Disrupting the European Crisis: A Critical Political Economy of Contestation, Subversion and Escape'. *New Political Economy* 20(5): 725–51.

Konzelmann, Suzanne J. 2014. 'The Political Economics of Austerity'. *Cambridge Journal of Economics* 38(4): 701–41.

Kotz, David. 2008. 'Contradictions of Economic Growth in the Neoliberal Era: Accumulation and Crisis in the Contemporary U.S. Economy'. *Review of Radical Political Economics* 40(2): 174–88.

Lebowitz, Michael. 2003. *Beyond Capital: Marx's Political Economy of the Working Class*. Basingstoke: Palgrave Macmillan.

McGettigan, Andrew. 2013. *The Great University Gamble: Money, Markets and the Future of Higher Education*. London: Pluto Press.

McGettigan, Andrew. 2015. 'Cash Today: Who Profits from Student Loans?' *London Review of Books* 37(5).

Papadopoulos, Dimitris, Niamh Stephenson and Vassilis Tsianos. 2008. *Escape Routes: Control and Subversion in the 21st Century*. London: Pluto Press.

Park, Gene, and Eisaku Ide. 2014. 'The Tax-Welfare Mix: Explaining Japan's Weak Extractive Capacity'. *Pacific Review* 27(5): 675–702.

Pasquinelli, Matteo. 2014. 'To Anticipate and Accelerate: Italian Operaismo and Reading Marx's Notion of the Organic Composition of Capitalism'. *Rethinking Marxism* 26(2): 178–92.

Rees, James, Adam Whitworth and Elle Carter. 2014. 'Support for All in the UK Work Programme? Differential Payments, Same Old Problem'. *Social Policy and Administration* 48(2): 221–39.

Resnick, Stephen, and Richard Wolff. 2010. 'The Economic Crisis: A Marxian Interpretation'. *Rethinking Marxism* 22(2): 170–86.

Scott, James C. 1990. *Domination and the Arts of Resistance: Hidden Transcripts*. New Haven: Yale University Press.

Scruggs, Lyle, Detlef Jahn and Kati Kuitto. 2014. 'Comparative Welfare Entitlements Dataset 2. Version 2014-03'. University of Connecticut and University of Greifswald. Available at http://cwed2.org/.

Shibata, Saori. 2016. 'Resisting Japan's Neoliberal Model of Capitalism: Intensification and Change in Contemporary Patterns of Class Struggle'. *British Journal of Industrial Relations* 54: 496–521.

Shibata, Saori. 2017. 'Re-Packaging Old Policies? "Abenomics" and the Lack of an Alternative Growth Model for Japan's Political Economy'. *Japan Forum* 29: 399–422.

Stanley, Liam. 2014. '"We're Reaping What We Sowed": Everyday Crisis Narratives and Acquiescence to the Age of Austerity'. *New Political Economy* 19(6): 895–917.

Thomas, Mark P., and Steven Tufts. 2016. 'Austerity, Right Populism, and the Crisis of Labour in Canada'. *Antipode* 48(1): 212–30.

Tridico, Pasquale. 2012. 'Financial Crisis and Global Imbalances: Its Labour Market Origins and the Aftermath'. *Cambridge Journal of Economics* 36: 17–42.

Tronti, Mario. 1964. 'Lenin in England'. *Classe Operaia* 1. Accessed January 9, 2018. www.marxists.org/reference/subject/philosophy/works/it/tronti.htm.

Varoufakis, Yanis. 2013. 'From Contagion to Incoherence: Towards a Model of the Unfolding Eurozone Crisis'. *Contributions to Political Economy* 32: 51–71.

Chapter Three

Power of Labour and Logistics

Immigrant Struggles in Italy's Logistics Industry

Rossana Cillo and Lucia Pradella[1]

The global economic crisis erupted at a moment of decline for the 'alter-globalisation movement' but laid the foundations for the emergence of a potentially stronger movement and reopened a space for discussing substantive alternatives to neoliberalism. This chapter grounds the discussion of alternatives in an International Political Economy (IPE) analysis of the crisis and the struggles that emerged in response to it. Despite an increasing awareness among IPE scholars of the limits of finance-led narratives and the need to analyse the multiple societal aspects of the crisis, limited research has been done so far on contestation movements and alternative strategies. This lacuna depends on a still prevailing reified conceptualisation of social classes and on a view of labour as a passive factor of production.

Any reflection on alternatives, in our view, needs to start from the centrality of production and labour relations, and of workers as subjects. In this light, processes of international production restructuring and immigration appear to be relevant not only in diagnosing the roots of the crisis but also in reflecting on alternatives to it. If a rich literature exists on the negative consequences of these processes on the wage share, labour conditions and trade union structural and associational power, less research has so far been done on their potential for the renewal of the labour movement. Processes of international production restructuring, however, have led to the formidable growth of the class of wage labourers and increased their potential power at the point of production. In this context, international migration represents a link between processes of class recomposition in the global South and in the North.

The logistics sector exemplifies the contradictory dynamics of global production restructuring and working-class recomposition, highlighting the links
between resistance as survival, as disruption and as creation. In this chapter
we first discuss the link between global production restructuring, the growth
of logistics and workers' power. We then focus on Italy, where the global
economic crisis is determining an unprecedented process of deindustrialisation, and austerity and harshening immigration restrictions have reinforced
the deregulation, casualisation and racialisation of employment relations, further weakening organised labour. Deindustrialisation, however, is matched
by the growth of the logistics sector. This growth, which reflects Italy's
importance in international transport routes, is leading to the reorganisation
of logistics along the lines of just-in-time (JIT) production. After presenting
working conditions in the sector, we analyse the wave of strikes in logistics
since 2008, by far the most important struggles in Italy in the wake of the
crisis. Finally, we reflect on challenges for the renewal of the labour movement in Italy and beyond.

GROUNDING ALTERNATIVES IN PRODUCTION RELATIONS

Recent publications in IPE show an increasing awareness of the limits of
finance-led narratives of the crisis. For Alan Cafruny (2015) the crisis points
to the need to embrace political economy in the classical sense of the term: as
the study of production and power relations broadly conceived. Drawing on
literature on production transformations in Europe within a global context
(e.g., Simonazzi et al. 2013), Gambarotto and Solari (2014) seek to overcome
the invisibility of the real industrial and social damage provoked by the
crisis. An increasing number of scholars, moreover, pay attention to the
'everyday political economy' of the crisis and its consequences on marginalised social groups (Green and Hay 2015).

As Huke et al. (2015) recently argued, however, even critical IPE scholars
mainly focus on mechanisms of domination rather than on contestation
movements and alternative strategies. This lacuna, in our view, depends on
an 'ever-present temptation to suppose that class is a thing, and to portray
labour as a mere factor in global production, and workers as passive and
adaptive' (Amoore 2006, 23). These a-relational conceptions of social
classes and passive representations of workers cause serious shortcomings in
our understanding of 'the multiple societal inter-connections within the political economy of the crisis' (Green and Hay 2015, 334) and close down
strategic reflections on alternatives.

Exploring alternatives, in fact, requires understanding that production is
not a technical process but a terrain of struggle, where essentially political
questions of power, time and distribution are contested. Our chapter starts

from the centrality of production and labour relations, which necessarily implies adopting an international perspective. The crisis, in our view, highlights both a persisting crisis of profitability and the uneven effects of the neoliberal process of international production restructuring on the EU15 economies. Production relocation to low-wage countries has led to a worldwide but uneven development of a cheap labour economy, a trend that has become even more pronounced since 2007–2008. In the EU, this process is taking place unevenly among sectors and member states, reflecting the polarisation and international specialisation of the EU productive structure (Pradella 2015; Simonazzi et al. 2013).

Workers, however, are not mere factors of production that passively adapt to economic 'imperatives'; they are political subjects who can shape the global system itself. While these transformations certainly unleashed a downward spiral in workers' power and welfare in Western Europe, they also swelled the global class of wage labourers (which is now composed of 3.1 billion workers globally; see Foster et al. 2011) and led to the growth of labour militancy worldwide. This growth preceded the crisis and was reinforced by it: since 2010, widespread labour unrest in countries like China, Bangladesh, India and South Africa has been accompanied by anti-austerity movements in Europe and the United States, while revolutionary movements shook the Arab world, overthrowing military dictatorships in Egypt and Tunisia (Pradella and Marois 2015).

International migration, moreover, has led to the emergence of what Saskia Sassen calls a 'global class of disadvantaged workers', a class that is 'more global and hence indicative of the future, rather than of a backward past, than is usually assumed' (2007, 189). This 'global class' is composed of both immigrant and native-born workers facing increasing precarity as a consequence of international political economy dynamics (Basso 2015, 93). Immigrant workers thus represent a link between South and North, between the struggles of new working classes in the making and old working classes being unmade. Immigrant workers are not passive victims but central actors in the new kind of collective subjectivity that is needed to offer an alternative to the crisis.

The logistics sector is a good example of the contradictory dynamics of global production restructuring and working-class recomposition. This explains why, since the 2000s, a growing body of literature has looked at the logistics sector as a site of power and struggle.[2] While numerous studies have analysed the evolution of the sector in Italy and the relationship between intermodal transport, containerisation and work organisation (Appetecchia 2014; Bologna 2010; Mariotti 2015), the literature on logistics struggles in Italy is still underdeveloped. Mainly self-organised by immigrant workers from North Africa and Asia and organised by the independent union Si Cobas, the struggles that developed in Italy's logistics sector from 2008 onwards have been the most important struggles against the crisis so far and have attacked key neoliberal practices such as multinational corporations (MNCs) outsourcing work to cooperatives employing low-paid immigrant workers. After 2011, these struggles drew inspiration from the uprisings in the Arab world and North Africa.

These struggles well exemplify the links between resistance as survival, disruption and creation. Started as a reaction to workplace exploitation and racism, the wave of strikes in Italy's logistics has built on logistics workers' capability of disrupting tightly integrated supply chains. Mainly led by immigrant workers, over the years these struggles have become an example for the entire labour movement, showing how trade unions can resist austerity through rank-and-file organisation. The disruptive and creative aspects of logistics workers' resistance have been underestimated in the literature. While some scholars have denounced the extremely exploitative working conditions in Italy's logistics sector (Benvegnù 2015; Ghezzi 2010), in fact, little research has contextualised these conditions within political economy dynamics nationally and internationally. This lack of analysis, in our view, limits our understanding of the potential of these struggles in terms of both disruption and elaboration of alternative strategies. Anna Curcio (2014, 389), for example, envisages the potential for a common struggle between logistics, precarious workers and youth. A similar perspective is advanced by Cuppini et al.'s (2015) biopolitical analysis of processes of antagonistic subjectivation in the logistics sector. In this chapter we show that the logistics workers who have mobilised in recent years in Italy are organising as workers, not just as precarious workers, and are promoting a process of class recomposition at both national and international levels. In order to argue this, we draw on participatory observation and recent enquiries into logistics struggles in Italy published in academic journals, the Italian press and trade union websites.

GLOBALISATION, LOGISTICS, AND WORKERS' POWER

Since the end of the 1950s, and over the last twenty years in particular, a 'logistics revolution' has taken place (Allen 1997). With the international integration of the production, circulation and final consumption of commodities, the logistics sector has acquired an increasing centrality. As transport has gained importance in the overall production process, the speed of circulation has become vital to capital accumulation (Cowen 2014b, 101). The logistics revolution is closely linked to the rise of neoliberalism and JIT production. While trade deregulation and production relocation led to the emergence of global supply chains (Cowen 2014b; Mariotti 2015), with the spread of the Toyota Production System these chains have been reorganised along JIT and 'zero inventories' principles.

In order to respond to fluctuating markets, the Toyota Production System seeks to reduce waste (of time, space and materials) with the ultimate goal of maximising labour intensity (Basso 2003, 39; Ohno 1988, 58). Transport is part and parcel of JIT global supply chains; its organisation aims at guaranteeing 'the right delivery times, the integrity of loads, and prompt information on the shipment's condition' (Mariotti 2015, 3). JIT production changed qualitatively after the rise of Walmartism and the shift in dominance from manufacturers to retailers. Walmartism realised one of Toyotaism's main principles: the shift from producers seeking to shape their markets to retailers increasingly directing production (Ashton 2006). This had deep effects on production processes and the overall relationship between capital and labour. The acceleration of capital circulation, in fact, created new possibilities for labour exploitation.[3]

> Wal-Mart has forced its suppliers to cut costs, made it more difficult for companies to compete on any terms other than price, and made it close to impossible for manufacturers and service providers to pass on the cost of improvements in products and services to consumers in the form of price increases. (Bonacich and Wilson 2008, 7)

The logistics revolution is based on a series of technological innovations accelerating commodity flows and reducing transport costs. The use of satellite, communication and information technologies and shipping containers played a central role. As Deborah Cowen (2014a; 2014b) highlights, all these technologies were developed within the military and then adopted in the corporate world of management in the wake of World War II. Containers allowed for a significant reduction of 'the time required to load and unload ships, reducing port labour costs and enabling tremendous savings for manufacturers' (Cowen 2014b, 41; Mariotti 2015, 2). This explains why containerisation is generally considered the single most important technological innovation underpinning the globalisation of trade and production.

The increasing use of information technologies since the 1990s has been essential to coordinate accelerating global processes of production, circulation and the distribution of commodities. Walmart was the leading corporation in this field. By forcing its suppliers to use bar codes to collect data from retailers at the point of sale, Walmart was able to manage supplies from manufacturers more efficiently and reduce inventory costs along the supply chain. Since the early 1980s, moreover, Walmart has used its own satellite system to govern the flow of goods in its own fleet of trucks and pioneered the cross-docking system. In the 2000s it forced its suppliers to replace bar codes with radio-frequency identification technologies in order to track commodity flows still more accurately (Bonacich and Wilson 2008, 6–12). Crucially, these innovations allowed Walmart to monitor the movements and actions of more than a million employees. Walmart has thus

> achieved among the highest rates of productivity growth for the entire service economy, while keeping the wages of its 'associates' at or barely above the poverty level and while also relying on the taxpayer to keep the children of Walmart employees out of poverty. (Head 2014, 35)

The logistics revolution, however, has not just intensified labour exploitation and weakened organised labour but also created vulnerabilities both in individual workplaces and throughout the network that strengthen workers' mobilisations. Crucially, JIT production increases the potential for disruption. 'With the elimination of the buffer supply of parts, a strike that stops production in one key parts factory can bring assembly operations throughout the corporation to a halt within a matter of days or less' (Silver 2014, 53). The logistics industry exemplifies how the organisational and technological changes associated with globalisation actually strengthen workers at the point of production. Since tightly integrated supply chains depend on the smooth operation of their parts, they are highly vulnerable to disruption. The length of the chain, the role of transport and storage nodes within it, the seasonality of certain logistics-dependent sectors, the unbalanced but mutually dependent relationship between firms and subcontractors: all these factors increase the impact of workers' mobilisations far beyond individual workplaces, companies and the logistics sector itself (Bonacich and Wilson 2008).

Logistics workers have realised that they hold a strategic position in global supply chains (Neilson 2012). They have thus understood that the internationalisation of the working class resulting from neoliberal globalisation creates new vulnerabilities for the sector. Indeed, 'the system of global production and international distribution brings workers together in an unprecedented manner, by linking them to the same industry and supply chain . . . [and] joining them in a potential commonality that could be used to put intense pressure on that firm from multiple angles' (Bonacich and Wilson 2008, 47). While production restructuring and neoliberal labour market reforms have weakened workers' bargaining power at the labour market level, therefore, globalisation increases the workplace bargaining power of those who still have a job, forming the conditions for their common organisation. For Beverly Silver (2014, 54), 'understanding the combined impact of these two countervailing trends on workers' power is a key for understanding the future of the working-class in twenty-first century global capitalism'.

CRISIS, AUSTERITY AND PRODUCTION
RESTRUCTURING IN ITALY

These two countervailing trends are also visible in Italy. As is well known, the global economic crisis has decelerated the dynamism of the global economy but accelerated the global shift of production towards the Global South (Timmer et al. 2014, 109, 106; Eurofound 2014). Between 2007 and 2012, the share of world manufacturing output value of the EU declined from 27 to 19 per cent, while China's manufacturing share increased by about ten percentage points (up to 22 per cent). Between 2000 and 2014 Italy's manufacturing gross value added significantly declined, and a loss of 653,000 manufacturing jobs was recorded as a consequence of both the relocation of industries and the crisis (European Commission 2015, 7, 26). Between 2008 and 2014, moreover, manufacturing output declined by about 24 per cent, and Italy lost 13 per cent of its industrial capacity (European Commission 2014, 20). Such a contraction is unparalleled in all the main manufacturing producer countries and helps explain the still relatively high levels of unemployment in the country (11.8 per cent in February 2017; Eurostat 2015). Job losses in the manufacturing sector have reduced the numbers of the most protected and unionised jobs, contributing to the erosion of union density and collective bargaining coverage (Eurofound 2014).

Erosion along these lines has also been one of the main objectives of austerity policies and structural reforms in Italy. Since 2011, different labour reforms further liberalised temporary employment, enhanced the erosion of the system of collective bargaining and favoured the implementation of supply-side labour market policies, culminating in the Jobs Act (2014/2015). The latter generalised precarious employment relations by introducing open-ended contracts with graduated protection: it thus led to the growth of disciplinary layoffs: according to INPS (2017), these increased from 22,412 in 2014 to 32,317 in 2016. Labour market reforms, moreover, have extended voucher-based work to all sectors, leading to a 461 per cent increase in its use between 2011 and 2016 (the number of voucher-cheques grew from 23,813,978 in 2012 to 133,826,001 in 2016) (INPS 2017; UIL 2016).[4]

Adjustments in Italy also included a radical pension reform, reductions in public sector employment, tax increases, and decreases in social protection expenditure that were more pronounced than the EU15 average (Pavolini et al. 2015, 60). In addition, harshening immigration policies have intensified the racialisation of the Italian labour market (Pradella and Cillo 2015). The linking of residence permits with an employment contract and the criminalisation of undocumented immigrants (which began with the 2002 'Bossi-Fini Law') leave immigrant workers vulnerable to blackmail (Basso 2015).

These political economy factors have significantly weakened workers' bargaining power at the labour market level. The main trade unions in Italy have done very little to oppose these reforms. In the 2000s the main union confederations (CGIL, CISL and UIL) launched initiatives for the active recruitment of young, precarious and immigrant workers and created specific departments, categories and services; especially in the case of CGIL, these initiatives were also accompanied by forms of cooperation with social movements. These initiatives, however, coexisted with a process of institutionalisation, which led to the unions prioritising service provision rather than the conflictual representation of workers' interests. In the wake of the crisis, as in other countries (Bailey et al. 2016), the main unions increasingly subordinated bargaining to the interests of economic 'recovery' and competitiveness. They thus moved backwards in terms of involvement and representation of immigrant workers (Cillo and Pradella 2018). Even the traditionally more militant union, FIOM (the metalworkers' union within CGIL), has adapted to this new landscape of industrial relations. In the spring of 2016 its leadership disciplined shop stewards who organised independent strikes against compulsory overtime and labour intensification at the FIAT-FCA plants in Melfi and Termoli. In April 2016, Sergio Bellavita, the spokesperson of the internal opposition current 'Il sindacato è un'altra cosa' ('The union is something else'), which supported the strikes at FIAT, was removed from office (Sciotto 2016).

In this context, the logistics sector is swimming against the stream in economic terms and, as we shall see in the next section, in terms of mobilisation. Despite a decline in commodity circulation and a collapse in manufacturing production in 2009, between 2007 and 2013 the transportation and storage sector (TSS) registered a significant increase in production value (+5.6 per cent): an upward trend that is even more pronounced in comparison to 2005 (Eurostat 2015). Within this sector, contract logistics increased still more prominently: between 2009 and 2012 the total registered value increased from 71.2 to 77.3 billion euros (a 1.2 per cent increase in real terms). In 2015 the total registered value reached 81 million euros – a real term increase of 2 per cent if compared to 2013 (OCL 2014, 9, 10, 15, 83). Italy has thus become the fourth country in the EU for TSS production value, following France, Germany and the UK (Eurostat 2015).

This growth depends in the main on increased outsourcing of circulation activities (from the supply of materials to final distribution) linked to production outsourcing or contract logistics (Mariotti 2015; OCL 2014, 12). This growth is taking place despite the weaknesses of the Italian logistics model due to inadequate institutional planning and the strategies of Italian firms.[5] These weaknesses are clearly visible in container trade in ports. Despite their strategic position on the route between the Far East and Europe, Italian ports are not competitive with northern European ports because they lack adequate infrastructure for cargo ships with capacities exceeding 10,000 TEUs and fail to offer competitive logistics services to smaller ships. Intermodal transport services connecting the Far East–Europe route with Italy's neighbouring countries are still underdeveloped (Bologna 2013a, 2013b; Bologna, Curi and Stevanato 2013).

Moreover, logistics companies in Italy are highly fragmented. Almost 90 per cent of companies have less than ten employees; only thirty have more than one thousand employees. Micro-enterprises employ more than 27 per cent of employees in the transportation and logistics sector, while about half (53.3 per cent) of the one million employees work in SMEs (Forte and Miotti 2015, 3). In 2012, contract logistics included 103,751 companies: almost 79 per cent consisted of self-employed drivers, while about 15 per cent were 'drivers organised in capital companies' (OCL 2014, 9, 83). The latter include some of the major multinational third-party logistics providers, such as TNT, FedEx, DHL, Maersk, MSC and more. Within contract logistics there are 660 express couriers, 1,047 logistics operators providing integrated logistics services, 2,439 international shipping companies and 5,760 'warehousing' companies (OCL 2014, 11). The latter include many of the cooperatives to which big Italian and foreign companies (in manufacturing, retail and logistics) have outsourced the management of logistics activities. In 2013 within the TSS there were 4,185 cooperatives and 155 cooperative consortia, with a production value of 7,725.8 million euros and a total of 190,715 employees (Euricse 2015, 41, 44).

LABOUR CONDITIONS IN LOGISTICS

The cooperative system in Italy has changed profoundly since its beginnings: the organisation of work, internal structures and production objectives have fully adopted capitalist principles (Sacchetto and Semenzin 2014, 44). In order to be hired as cooperative 'associate workers', labourers pay association fees ranging from 2,000 to 15,000 euros, which contribute to investment or liability funds. Cooperatives thus shift business risks onto workers and further lower their indirect wages through systematic tax evasion (Benvegnù 2015; Massarelli 2014; Si Cobas and Adl Cobas, 2013). Workers are also pushed to lengthen and intensify their working day for the sake of profit sharing.

Working hours and wages in subcontracted logistics cooperatives are often unregulated, and workers are forced to put their own time at the full disposal of JIT production. As revealed by Massarelli (2014) and Si Cobas (Si Cobas and Adl Cobas 2013), it is common practice to let dozens of workers wait for hours in the store's locker room, using (and paying) them only when they are needed. This practice creates a reserve of on-call labour in the workplace. Alternatively, employees are forced to work up to twelve to fourteen hours a day by threats of being moved to other locations or having their wages reduced. Although most workers are on permanent contracts, their conditions are precarious: in many cases the opening or closing of cooperatives is planned in such a way as to allow the continuous wiping out of workers' accumulated seniority, the avoidance of paying salaries and arrears, and the sacking of workers who are unionised and/or mobilise against the companies (Massarelli 2014; Si Cobas and Adl Cobas 2013).

There have also been reports of frequent irregularities with regard to payrolls, noncompliance with national collective agreements, and failure to provide payments for holidays, illness, seniority and meal tickets (Ghezzi 2010). In the warehouses where struggles developed, these forms of wage compression were so prevalent that cooperatives were taking an average of 15,000 euros per year from each employee, paying monthly wages of about 700 euros. Although there are no unitary data for the whole sector, some enquiries (e.g., Massarelli 2014; Curcio 2014; Cuppini et al. 2015) and statistical studies (Bologna 2013b; Euricse 2014, 2015) show that immigrant workers are concentrated in the lowest-qualified tasks.[6] Workers from different nationalities are continuously replaced according to their propensity to engage in collective action.

Cooperatives impose these extremely exploitative working conditions both by threatening dismissals and through systematic intimidation and psychological and physical violence by supervisors, often of Italian nationality. Supervisors controlled

> the possibility of urinating by denying or delaying access to toilets. . . . They regulated the rhythm of the working day to the sound of curses and insults . . . [without calling] workers by name, but whistling or using nicknames linked to their countries of origin. (Massarelli 2014, 13)

In some cases, supervisors physically assaulted workers who claimed their rights or were less submissive (Massarelli 2014; Si Cobas and Adl Cobas 2013). By outsourcing to cooperatives, therefore, companies are able to meet JIT production imperatives, impose extremely precarious working conditions and reduce so-called labour costs. This is how Italian logistics can be competitive despite its technological and infrastructural weaknesses (Bologna 2013b).

In many cooperatives workers have tried to protect their interests by asking the main trade union confederations to intervene in company-level bargaining. The main unions, however, did not mobilise workers and often signed local agreements entailing worse conditions than the porters' national contract, in some cases without any authorisation by the workers. The main regions in which logistics activities are concentrated – Lombardy, Veneto and Emilia-Romagna – have a strong tradition of unionisation. In the cooperative model, however, the unions link cooperatives and business, and they play an important role in managing the workforce (Cuppini et al. 2015). Many cooperatives are directed by unionists formerly active in the confederations (Sacchetto and Semenzin 2014) and by local or regional Democratic Party leaders. In the Emilia Romagna region, for example, most cooperatives are part of the umbrella organisation Lega Coop, whose former national president was the current Labour minister Giuliano Poletti (Massarelli 2014). This helps to explain why the main union confederations aided cooperatives to meet the subcontracting companies' constant demands for lower labour costs (Massarelli 2014).

Italy's logistics sector, however, is a good example of the contradictory dynamics highlighted by Beverly Silver, where the labour market bargaining power of workers declines and the workplace bargaining power of those who are employed increases. The cooperative system of labour exploitation depends on the weakening of workers' labour market bargaining power as well as the main unions' increasing institutionalisation and willingness to make concessions to employers. Yet logistics workers in Italy are increasingly aware of their strategic position in global supply chains and of their potential for disruption. This awareness, together with the support of small rank-and-file unions – known together as Cobas (an abbreviation for 'Comitati di Base', or 'Base Committees') – and left-wing militants, gave them the confidence to improve their conditions. These factors help explain the success of the struggles that developed in Italy from 2008, beginning from one logistics centre of the Bennet supermarket chain in Origgio (Milan), spreading to the Centre-North of Italy and continuing today.

STRUGGLES IN LOGISTICS

The first logistics struggle was organised in 2008 by about 160 workers, employees of the Coop Leonardo cooperative at Bennet Origgio. Workers contacted the independent union SLAI Cobas (now Si Cobas[7]), asking for its support in achieving better working conditions and the right to unionise. The struggle at Origgio was radical from the very beginning: along with strike actions, pickets were organised over eight to nine months, blocking commodity flows from the warehouse to supermarkets in northern Italy. These pickets won the support of left-wing activists and social centres from Milan (Massarelli 2014; AngryWorkersWorld 2015).

Building on this successful experience, Si Cobas organised a large and growing number of workers in the logistics sector, reaching ten thousand members in 2014. Through a long struggle, Si Cobas and Adl Cobas[8] managed to achieve better working conditions in the cooperatives of the main logistics hubs in northern Italy (Milan, Piacenza, Bologna, Brescia, Padua and Verona), as well as Rome and Naples. The most important Italian and multinational companies subcontract their storage activities to cooperatives at these hubs: Bennett, Coop, Gigante, Granarolo and Esselunga in the fields of food industry and distribution, IKEA in retail, Yoox in online trade; GLS (the Italian subsidiary of Royal Mail), FedEx, DHL, Bartolini, SDA (the subsidiary of Italian Mail) and TNT in the logistics and shipping sectors.

As Aldo Milani, the national coordinator of Si Cobas, has pointed out, the struggles at Bennet Origgio prefigured what later became the essential characteristics of logistics struggles in Italy (Massarelli 2014, 93–108), starting from the combination of workers' self-organisation and independent trade union organisation. Workers, and immigrant workers in particular, have been the driving force behind these struggles. With this often being workers' first experience of struggle, they were supported by trade unionists and left-wing militants who had in many cases been active in the 1960s and 1970s, when the labour movement in Italy was at its peak. Similar to other countries (see Bailey et al. 2016), this allowed the sharing of organisational and political experiences between workers and political militants. Workers' self-organisation was also enabled by the awareness that fear was the 'real deterrent of the struggle, the best tactics to divide and enslave the people'; it was necessary to 'fight united' to defeat the blackmail based on individual and collective fear (Si Cobas delegate, in Massarelli 2014, 42).[9] Workers reclaimed their 'dignity'—not just economic dignity but also human dignity and respect.

Logistics struggles in Italy have also been characterised by a high level of radicalism and solidarity between workers. 'When a warehouse called for solidarity, workers [from other warehouses] rushed to help and together picketed the company'. Pickets also received active support from left-wing militants and organisations (Aldo Milani, in Massarelli 2014, 96). Si Cobas set up a resistance fund based on donations and a monthly fee from its members to support workers; in some cases, it also organised broader boycotts. Struggles for better working conditions or to stop layoffs have leveraged the enormous disruptive potential of local or national blockades. A one-day blockade at the IKEA store in Piacenza, for example,

> means that goods are not loaded onto trucks. These do not arrive on time for the ships, producing a delay in deliveries at destinations in Eastern Europe, the Middle East and North Africa. A one-day blockade blows up the organization of the entire process. . . . This means a big economic damage. . . . In a warehouse where fresh food is stored, a four-hour blockade means €2–300,000 lost. (Aldo Milani, in Curcio 2014, 376)

Si Cobas and Adl Cobas organised the first national strike of the logistics sector on 22 March 2013. The strike blocked the sector in the north of Italy, Rome and Naples. Workers mobilised in the thousands, not only regarding their individual claims but also for a platform of demands addressed to cooperatives as well as the main subcontracting companies (Si Cobas and Adl

Cobas 2013). They thus held both parties to their responsibilities. After this first national strike, two more national strikes led to a national agreement in February 2015 with some of the largest logistics operators in Italy (GLS, TNT, BRT and SDA). This agreement represented a significant improvement on the national logistics contract in terms of contract and wage conditions, including the obligation to hire workers already employed in warehouses in the case of contractual changes, the repeal of the status of 'associate worker' and the obligation for companies to employ workers directly.

Logistics struggles, however, have faced high levels of repression by both companies and the state. The most active immigrant workers were often threatened with expulsion. Besides facing repeated police interventions, arrests, legal charges and trials, several trade unionists were beaten and subjected to Mafia intimidation by cooperatives financed by organised crime (Scandalliato 2013). On 17 September 2016, Abd Elsalam Ahmed Eldanf, an Egyptian worker and father of five, was hit and killed by a truck while picketing a GLS delivery company in Piacenza with the independent union Unione Sindacale di Base (USB). According to witnesses, the company's managers incited the truck driver to charge at the pickets. Laws from the Fascist era have been applied to repress the struggles: during the strikes at the IKEA distribution centre in 2013, for example, Piacenza's police headquarters issued 'expulsion orders' for Aldo Milani and two other Si Cobas unionists. In the case of Granarolo, antistrike measures originally aimed at ensuring essential public services were extended to logistics, mainly to ensure the transport of perishable goods. State repression escalated in January 2017, when Aldo Milani was arrested during union negotiations with a cooperative subcontractor of food company Levoni. Milani was accused of extortion on the basis of fake proofs: thousands of logistics workers denounced his arrest as a strategy of repression and went on strike demanding his release. The magistrate eventually stated that Milani was not involved in the crime and released him from prison, but a mandatory residence order is still in place, making it impossible for Milani to participate in union activities.

These levels of repression can only be explained by the fact that logistics strikes blocked a sector central to capital accumulation and achieved tangible improvements in working conditions at a time of deep labour market restructuring and lack of significant trade union response. The success of logistics struggles may thus set a dangerous example for workers in other sectors. This explains why even CGIL local branches condemned these struggles in some cases (see, for example, Arci, CGIL and Libera 2014).

These struggles, moreover, expressed the need to move beyond the logistics sector, the trade union level and national borders. Logistics workers have participated in and organised mobilisations related to political issues, such as the repeal of the 'Bossi-Fini Law'. The important role played by immigrants from North Africa and the Middle East in the strikes also dealt a blow to institutional racism and Islamophobia in the country. In addition, logistics workers promoted a broader struggle involving workers in other sectors, seeking to unite their struggle with both unprotected workers in hotels and other services (Si Cobas 2015a), and with relatively better protected workers in other sectors, starting with the metalworking sector. Si Cobas has supported strikes in this sector since the second half of 2014, taking part in initiatives organised by FIOM and attempting to set up a common coordination (Si Cobas 2015b). A number of Si Cobas representatives and workers from Northern Italy joined the pickets during the successful strikes against compulsory overtime and the intensification of labour exploitation at the FIAT-FCA plants in Melfi and Termoli.

Si Cobas is also part of the 'Réseau Europeén des Syndicats Alternatifs et de Base', which includes some of the most important independent unions in Europe, such as the Union Syndicale Solidaire in France and Spain's Confederación General del Trabajo, and it has links to the Central Sindical and Popular Conlutas in Brazil. Si Cobas has also given solidarity and support to logistics struggles in other countries, including the struggles of Amazon warehouse workers in Germany. Since 2011, moreover, logistics workers have explicitly referred to the uprisings in North Africa and the Middle East, understanding their own struggles as part of a larger movement transcending national borders.

> After the January 25 Revolution, at TNT [Piacenza] we would always say: 'this is Tahrir Square too'. Ours, in fact, has been a minor revolution. No one would have bet on it a few years ago. We have shown that united we win. So, I have just one message for workers struggling in my country [Egypt]: you are the union. You don't need to follow anyone, just yourselves and your needs. You have to take your future into your hands, never looking at your personal, immediate interests. It's all of your interests taken together that must guide you, as it's only with unity and solidarity that you can win. (Mohammed Arafat, in Zerbino 2013)

CONCLUSION

This chapter grounds its discussion of alternatives to austerity in an analysis of global production transformations and migration as a factor of working-class recomposition. We start by questioning top-down IPE approaches, which rest on an a-relational conceptualisation of capital (and labour). This kind of approach leaves the links between the crisis in Europe, global dynamics of production restructuring, and workers' structural power untheorised. The struggles and social movements that emerged in response to the crisis are largely overlooked, as is the potential of immigration for the renewal of the labour movement in Europe.

Our analysis of the effects of the crisis in Italy points to a contradictory dynamic. Pronounced deindustrialisation, austerity and structural reforms are reducing workers' bargaining power at the labour-market level. But the growth of the logistics sector and its organisation along JIT principles increases workers' power at the point of production and their capability of disrupting highly integrated supply chains. While institutional trade union confederations have increasingly failed to organise workers in the logistics sector and to oppose the worsening of labour conditions through concerted bargaining, the combination of self-organisation and organisation by independent unions allowed logistics workers to exercise their power through blockades and strikes. This has empowered highly precarious and exploited workers, many of whom are immigrants.

These workers overcame the fears linked to their precarious legal statuses and working conditions. Although only some thousands of workers mobilised – a minority within the TSS and logistics cooperatives – these struggles involved the more important companies in logistics, a key sector for capital accumulation in Italy today. The consequences of blockades, strikes and mobilisations have been felt well beyond the individual companies and the logistics sector itself; they have affected entire supply chains. Logistics workers were thus able to hold both the cooperatives and the main subcontracting companies to their responsibilities, force the retraction of political layoffs and other repressive measures, and obtain improved agreements with some of the main logistics companies. Building on these achievements, Si Cobas and Adl Cobas were, as of April 2017, seeking to get their demands introduced in the new logistics national contract of employment. This would lead to improvements in the entire logistics sector, not only in companies unionised by Si Cobas, and could set an example for other sectors.

Logistics struggles thus entail a clear creative potential. They show that it is possible to successfully organise a collective response to the worsening of working and living conditions in the age of austerity. Their example of self-organisation and trade union organisation offers an alternative to resignation and passivity. In a context of increasingly generalised precarity, these struggles can inspire and strengthen broader sectors of the working class, as seen in the coordination between Si Cobas and FIOM shop stewards in the strikes at the FIAT plants in Melfi and Termoli. In order to prevent this coordination, the FIOM leadership removed the representative of the internal opposition 'Il sindacato un'altra cosa' from office. Several members of this current left FIOM and joined the independent union USB with the goal of relaunching a conflictual trade unionism able to mobilise the working class both within and beyond workplaces.

Although we cannot predict the outcome of these developments, they show that this is a turning point in the history of the workers' movement in Italy. Workers, and their unions, are facing major challenges and opportunities. The crisis and resulting austerity policies are making the conditions of workers in different sectors and with different contractual statuses more similar. In this context, the struggles in the logistics sector show that combining self-organisation and trade union organisation is crucial for workers to overcome fear and divisions, build solidarity and exercise their collective power at the point of production. Si Cobas's international links and the immigration status of most of its members, moreover, are a sign of the international projection of mobilisations in logistics. Because of logistics workers' central position in global processes of capital accumulation, the very logic of their struggles promotes a process of national and international class recomposition. There are many obstacles to this process, at both trade union and political levels. A lesson that we can draw, however, is that in order for this successful experience to be extended to other sectors and grow into a broader movement against austerity, workers need a political programme capable of breaking with the imperatives of national competitiveness and of addressing the international roots of the crisis.

NOTES

1. This chapter draws on Cillo and Pradella (2018).
2. Cowen (2010), Harney and Moten (2013), and Neilson (2012).
3. Ashton (2006), Bonacich and Wilson (2008, 123–30), Cowen (2014a, 191; 2014b, 100–113), and Mariotti (2015).
4. In Italy, employers use the system of 'vouchers for casual labour' (managed by Italy's National Institute for Social Insurance) in order to pay for casual work services. Vouchers confer workers no ability to bargain collectively; earn sick, maternity or holiday pay; or earn unemployment benefits.
5. Appetecchia (2014), Forte and Miotti (2015), and Ministero delle infrastrutture e dei trasporti (2012).
6. In some warehouses immigrant workers form 90 per cent of the workforce (Massarelli 2014). In 2012, in Padua province, about 5,774 workers were employed in the transportation and storage sector. About half of them (2,379 workers) held foreign citizenship: they were mainly employed as unskilled workers (1,617 foreign citizens out of 2,702 unskilled workers) and as semiskilled workers (605 foreign citizens out of 1,881 semiskilled workers) (Bologna 2013b, 11).
7. SLAI Cobas is a union present mainly in the metalworking sector; following an internal split, Si Cobas emerged as a new independent union able to channel the aims of logistics workers.
8. Adl Cobas is another independent union, mainly present in the logistics industry in the Veneto region.
9. 'In the warehouse fear was at home: if the bosses knew that a worker had family they had it in for him. The more common forms of intimidation were the blackmail on hours, the threat of dismissing you or not making you work for days' (Si Cobas delegate, Massarelli 2014, 42).

BIBLIOGRAPHY

Allen, W. Bruce. 1997. 'The Logistics Revolution and Transportation'. *Annals of the American Academy of Political and Social Science* 553: 106–16.

Amoore, Louise. 2006. 'Invisible Subject(s): Work and Workers in the Global Political Economy'. In *Poverty and the Production of World Politics*, edited by Matt Davies and Magnu Ryner, 14–37. Basingstoke: Palgrave-Macmillan.

AngryWorkersWorld. 2015. 'Ditching the Fear! Warehouse Workers Struggles in Italy and Their Wider Significance'. 12 July. Accessed July 20, 2015. https://angryworkersworld. wordpress.com/2015/07/12/ditching-the-fear-warehouse-workers-struggles-in-italy-and-their-wider-significance/.

Appetecchia, Andrea. 2014. 'Evoluzione del modello logistico italiano'. *Il lavoro nei trasporti – Mensile di informazione, cultura e documentazione* 2: 2–3.

Arci, CGIL, and Libera. 2014. 'Occorre che la rabbia e le legittime rivendicazioni rimangano all'interno del conflitto democratico'. 2 February. Accessed November 10, 2015. http:// www.cgilbo.it/flex/cm/pages/ServeBLOB.php/L/IT/IDPagina/565.

Ashton, Brian. 2006. 'Logistics and the Factory without Walls'. *Mute*, 14 September. Accessed November 10, 2015. http://www.metamute.org/editorial/articles/logistics-and-factory-without-walls.

Bailey, David J., Mònica Clua-Losada, Nikolai Huke, Olatz Rimera Almandoz and Kelly Rogers. 2016. 'Challenging the Age of Austerity: Disruptive Agency after the Global Economic Crisis'. *Comparative European Politics*. Accessed March 28, 2017. doi:10.1057/ s41295-016-0072-8.

Basso, Pietro. 2003. *Modern Times, Ancient Hours. Working Lives in the Twenty-First Century*. London and New York: Verso.

Basso, Pietro. 2015. 'Neoliberalism, Crisis and International Migration'. In *Polarizing Development*, edited by Lucia Pradella and Thomas Marois, 86–97. London: Pluto.

Benvegnù, Carlotta. 2015. 'Migrant Workers in the Logistic Sector in Padua: Exploitation and Unionization in the Cooperatives'. Paper presented at the conference 'Testing EU Citizenship as "Labour Citizenship"'. University of Padua, Italy, October 23.

Bologna, Sergio. 2010. *Le multinazionali del mare: Letture sul sistema marittimo-portuale*. Rome: Egea.

Bologna, Sergio. 2013a. *Banche e crisi: Dal petrolio al container*. Rome: DeriveApprodi.

Bologna, Sergio. 2013b. 'Lavoro e capitale nella logistica italiana: Alcune considerazioni sul Veneto'. Paper presented at the 40th Anniversario della costituzione di Interporto Padova Spa, Padua, Italy, March 15. Accessed November 10, 2015. http://it.scribd.com/doc/ 133176059/Bologna-Sergio-Lavoro-e-Capitale-Nella-Logistica-2013.

Bologna, Sergio, Sergio Curi and Danilo Stevanato. 2013. *Scenari dell'intermodalità: Studio per l'interporto di Padova*. Padua: Interporto Spa.

Bonacich, Edna, and Jake B. Wilson. 2008. *Getting the Goods: Ports, Labor, and the Logistics Revolution*. Ithaca: Cornell University Press.

Cafruny, Alan W. 2015. 'European Integration Studies, European Monetary Union, and Resilience of Austerity in Europe: Post-Mortem on a Crisis Foretold'. *Competition and Change* 19(2): 161–77.

Cillo, Rossana, and Lucia Pradella. 2018. 'New Immigrants' Struggles in Italy's Logistics Industry'. *Comparative European Politics* 16(1): 67–84.

Cowen, Deborah. 2010. 'A Geography of Logistics: Market Authority and the Security of Supply Chains'. *The Annals for the Association of American Geographers* 100(3): 1–21.

Cowen, Deborah. 2014a. 'Logistics'. In *The Routledge Handbook of Mobilities*, edited by Peter Adey, David Bissell, Kevin Hannam, Peter Merriman and Mimi Sheller, 187–95. London: Routledge.

Cowen, Deborah. 2014b. *The Deadly Life of Logistics: Mapping Violence in Global Trade*. Minneapolis: University of Minnesota Press.

Cuppini, Niccolò, Mattia Frapporti and Maurilio Pirone. 2015. 'Logistics Struggles in the Po Valley Region: Territorial Transformations and Processes of Antagonistic Subjectivation'. *The South Atlantic Quarterly* 114(1): 119–34.

Curcio, Anna. 2014. 'Practicing Militant Inquiry: Composition, Strike and Betting in the Logistics Workers Struggles in Italy'. *Ephemera* 14(3): 375–90.

Euricse. 2014. *La cooperazione italiana negli anni della crisi.* Trento: Euricse.

Euricse. 2015. *Economia cooperativa – Rilevanza, evoluzione e nuove frontiere della cooperazione italiana.* Trento: Euricse.

Eurofound. 2014. *Eurofound Yearbook 2013: Living and Working in Europe.* Luxembourg: Publications Office of the European Union.

European Commission, EC. 2013. *Competing in Global Value Chains: EU Industrial Structure Report 2013.* Luxembourg: European Commission DG Enterprise and Industry.

European Commission, EC. 2014. *Helping Firms Grow: European Competitiveness Report 2014.* Luxembourg: European Commission DG Enterprise and Industry.

European Commission, EC. 2015. *EU Structural Change 2015.* Luxembourg: European Commission DG Enterprise and Industry.

Eurostat. 2015. Industrial Production (Volume) Index Overview. Accessed July 20, 2015. http://ec.europa.eu/eurostat/statistics-explained/index.php/Industrial_production_(volume)_index_overview.

Forte, Ennio, and Delio Miotti. 2015. 'L'outsourcing, la terziarizzazione dei trasporti e delle logistiche nelle filiere traslog'. Paper presented at the 17th Annual Conference of SIET (Società Italiana di Economia dei Trasporti e della logistica), Milan, Italy, June 29–July 1.

Foster, John Bellamy, Robert W. McChesney and R. Jamil Jonna. 2011. 'The Global Reserve Army of Labour and the New Imperialism'. *Monthly Review* 63(6): 1–31.

Gambarotto, Francesca, and Stefano Solari. 2014. 'The Peripheralization of Southern European Capitalism within the EMU'. *Review of International Political Economy* 22(4): 1–25.

Ghezzi, Simone. 2010. 'The Fallacy of the Formal and Informal Divide: Lessons from a Post-Fordist Regional Economy'. In *Informal Work in Developed Nations*, edited by Enrico Marcelli, Colin C. Williams and Pascale Joassart, 114–31. London: Routledge.

Green, Jeremy, and Colin Hay. 2015. 'Towards a New Political Economy of the Crisis: Getting What Went Wrong Right'. *New Political Economy* 20(3): 331–41.

Harney, Stefano, and Fred Moten. 2013. *The Undercommons: Fugitive Planning and Black Study.* Wivenhoe: Minor Compositions.

Head, Simon. 2014. *Mindless: Why Smarter Machines Are Making Dumber Humans.* New York: Basic Books.

Huke, Nikolai, Mònica Clua-Losada and David J. Bailey. 2015. 'Disrupting the European Crisis: A Critical Political Economy of Contestation, Subversion and Escape'. *New Political Economy* 20(5): 725–51.

Istituto Nazionale Previdenza Sociale. 2017. *Osservatorio sul precariato. Report mensile. Gennaio-Dicembre 2016.* Roma: INPS.

Mariotti, Ilaria. 2015. *Transport and Logistics in a Globalizing World: A Focus on Italy.* New York: Springer.

Massarelli, Fulvio. 2014. *Scarichiamo i padroni: Lo sciopero dei facchini a Bologna.* Milan: Agenzia X.

Ministero delle infrastrutture e dei trasporti. 2012. *Il piano nazionale della logistica 2012–2020: Bozza finale.* Rome: Ministero delle infrastrutture e dei trasporti.

Neilson, Brett. 2012. 'Five Theses on Understanding Logistics as Power'. *Distinktion* 13(3): 323–40.

Ohno, Taiichi. 1988. *Toyota Production System: Beyond Large Scale Production.* Cambridge, MA: Productivity Press.

Osservatorio Contract Logistics, OCL. 2014. *Outsourcing della logistica: Tra falsi miti e creazione di valore.* Milan: Politecnico di Milano.

Pavolini, Emmanuele, Margarita León, Anna M. Guillén and Ugo Ascoli. 2015. 'From Austerity to Permanent Strain? The EU and Welfare State Reform in Italy and Spain'. *Comparative European Politics* 13(1): 56–76.

Pradella, Lucia. 2015. 'The Working Poor in Western Europe: Labour, Poverty and Global Capitalism'. *Comparative European Politics* 13: 596–613.

Pradella, Lucia, and Rossana Cillo. 2015. 'Immigrant Labour in Europe in Times of Crisis and Austerity'. *Competition and Change* 9(2): 145–60.

Pradella, Lucia, and Thomas Marois. 2015. *Polarizing Development: Alternatives to Neoliberalism and the Crisis*. London: Pluto.

Sacchetto, Devi, and Marco Semenzin. 2014. 'Storia e struttura della costituzione d'impresa cooperativa'. *Scienza & Politica* 26(50): 43–62.

Sassen, Saskia. 2007. *A Sociology of Globalisation*. New York: W. W. Norton.

Scandalliato, Maria Elena. 2013. 'Minacce, ricatti, una scia di sangue: Le mani delle cosche sui magazzini'. *La Repubblica*, 20 May.

Sciotto, Antonio. 2016. 'Il funzionario Fiom "licenziato" che ha tolto il sonno a Landini'. *Il manifesto*, 15 April.

Si Cobas. 2015a. 'Comunicato sindacale: Prosegue la tenace lotta delle 12 lavoratrici dell'Holiday Inn Express di Bologna Fiera. Comunicato'. 10 December. Accessed December 10, 2015. http://sicobas.org/notizie/ultime-3/2251-comunicato-sindacale-prosegue-la-tenace-lotta-delle-12-lavoratrici-dell-holiday-inn-express-di-bologna-fiera.

Si Cobas. 2015b. 'Per un coordinamento nazionale di lotta tra i lavoratori metalmeccanici'. 8 December. Accessed December 10, 2015. http://sicobas.org/notizie/ultime-3/2248-per-un-coordinamento-nazionale-di-lotta-tra-i-lavoratori-metalmeccanici.

Si Cobas and Adl Cobas. 2013. '22 marzo 2013: Grande giornata di sciopero'. 24 March. Accessed July 20, 2015. http://www.sicobas.org/categorie/96-ccnl-logistica/iniziative/1253-22-marzo-2013-grande-giornata-di-sciopero.

Silver, Beverly. 2014. 'Theorising the Working Class in Twenty-First-Century Global Capitalism'. In *Workers and Labour in a Globalised Capitalism*, edited by Maurizio Atzeni, 46–69. Basingstoke: Palgrave Macmillan.

Simonazzi, Annamaria, Andrea Ginzburg and Gianluigi Nocella. 2013. 'Economic Relations between Germany and Southern Europe'. *Cambridge Journal of Economics* 37: 653–75.

Timmer, Marcel P., Abdul Azeez Erumban, Bart Los, Robert Stehrer and Gaaitzen J. de Vries. 2014. 'Slicing Up Global Value Chains'. *Journal of Economic Perspectives* 28(2): 99–118.

Unione Italiana del Lavoro, UIL. 2016. '3° Rapporto UIL Voucher'. Roma.

Zerbino, Marco. 2013. 'La rivolta dei facchini immigrati: Intervista a Mohammed Arafat'. *La Repubblica*, 27 March.

Chapter Four

Resistance and Revolution

*Working-Class Intransigence, the Libertarian Tradition,
and the Catalan Crisis*

Stuart Price

> Bourgeois thought must come up against an insuperable obstacle, for its start-
> ing point [is] an apologia for the existing order. (Lukács 1971, 48)

> Democracy is not a political regime, but primarily an action, a modality of
> political agency, characterised by the irruption of the *demos*, or the people,
> onto the political stage. (Abensour 2011, xxiii)

> Certainly there is an irresponsible and destructive revolutionary spirit that
> must be held back. (Spender 1937, 165)

The primary goal of this chapter is to interrogate the material and ideological
practices associated with the notion of resistance (defined below) by revisiting a once formidable political tendency, the active recollection of which
provides a counterpoint to the conventional political wisdoms associated
with (1) liberal democracy; (2) the tradition known as state socialism; and (3)
contemporary calls for regional independence (in this instance, the secession-
ist current that has helped to create Spain's recent 'constitutional crisis').
Usually traced back to the anarcho-syndicalist, 'councilist', and libertarian
communist tradition (Pritchard et al. 2012), and especially to workers' self-
management during the Spanish Civil War (Mintz 2013), this alternative
current of thought advocates the communal seizure of productive resources
and regards state authority (of whatever stamp) as an imposition foisted on
an ideologically unified but federally organised working class (whether ur-

ban or rural) that would otherwise be free to exercise its own autonomous sovereignty (see Brinton 2004, 165).

Resistance, in this case, flows not from a defensive response to a particular attack, opposition to a specific government policy, or support for a 'single-issue' campaign but represents instead an absolute opposition to patriarchal capitalism as a socioeconomic condition. As such, theories of libertarian communism are bound to include antipathy towards the 'discourse and practice of austerity' (see the introduction to this book) but begin from a critical appraisal of social relations as a whole (the everyday regimen imposed on life and labour) under even the most 'benign' or 'stable' forms of paternalistic rule. It is therefore the hierarchical condition, rather than the specific injustices that it produces, that is the primary object of critique.

The challenge that usually arises in response to these assertions is: To what degree does the larger thesis provide a practical guide for positive social action? Describing the revolutionary precepts of anarcho-syndicalism, the Spanish historian Julián Casanova noted that, in the years before the Civil War of 1936–1939, this political current had become 'increasingly significant as *a social movement of protest* against the existing order', but 'it never went as far as to create a rational plan of action capable of being taken seriously as a real alternative' (2002, 401, my emphasis). Whatever the apparent shortcomings of libertarian practice in the past, and its particular role in the political culture of contemporary Spain (a country that encompasses so many regional, political, cultural, and historical variables), it is worth noting that, while the 'anti-authoritarian Left' incorporates a range of positions and behaviours,[1] it is motivated by the fundamental belief that social justice must be attained through attachment to a moral principle rather than the construction of a regime. In other words, Casanova's observation, though it provides an important corrective to revolutionary optimism, may not have addressed one of the fundamental assumptions of libertarian and syndicalist practice – that the expropriation of economic structures is accompanied by the dissolution of formal, centralised power. Here, in essence, is the strength, and yet the enduring difficulty, associated with this form of leftism – its reluctance to create an alternative form of state authority.

The notion, therefore, that the pursuit of libertarian doctrine is supposed to go hand in hand with a certain high-minded impracticality has always featured in critiques of its political stance. In the words of a long-standing Communist I once met in Andalusia, 'You libertarians are so good, you are good for nothing'.[2] When, by contrast, vocal political figures (irrespective of their precise party allegiance) attempt to create polities that draw upon the rhetoric of freedom and radical democracy, yet remain wedded to the economic structure of the bourgeois state, it is safe to say that they will reproduce the iniquities of the system they purport to oppose.

RADICAL POLITICS AND CONTEMPORARY SPAIN

This contradiction has been particularly noticeable in the most recent manifestation of public discontent in Spain – Catalonia's independence movement, in which the project of secession, despite its 'contextual' radicalism (offering a *Republican* and thus antimonarchical route to independence), cannot disguise the intractable economic divisions (Minder 2017, 17) that characterise not just this region but the nation as a whole. In contrast, the libertarian model attempts to sabotage all myths of statehood while combating the sectionalism that plagues the working class and (following the example of organisations like Mujeres Libres, active in the Spanish revolution) placing the liberation of women at the heart of its politics (Ackelsberg 2006; Nash 1995).

It is therefore distinct from, and acts in opposition to, the precepts of capitalist patriarchy, which in the current period is led by a political caste that allows its citizens to bear the brunt of financial retrenchment (in 2013, Spain had the highest percentage of unemployed workers in Europe,[3] while the much-vaunted economic recovery, announced in 2017, is dependent on a structural readjustment that promotes insecure forms of employment[4]). It is also hostile to the (now largely defunct) bureaucratic 'workers' state', which was responsible for the suppression of proletarian initiative in the Soviet Union (Read 1996; Murphy 2007; Pirani 2008) and, when the same totalitarian practices were exported to the Spanish Republic, for the gradual reversal of the revolutionary gains made in the early period of the Civil War (see below).

In addition, as already noted, the libertarian perspective treats all forms of nationalism and regionalism with suspicion (including 'leftist' variants that embrace the principle of secession), a point of view observed during a research project conducted in Barcelona in 2017,[5] and through recent statements made by groups like the CNT trade union, which noted that 'we are too aware of the old habit of nationalists of using the working class to fight their battles' (Pérez 2017). This emphasis on class provides, as suggested above, a universalist discourse, a moral touchstone for any utterance that makes an appeal for justice: it should not, however, elevate the consciousness and activity of 'the workers' beyond critique, nor should it portray their resistance as a 'spontaneous' reaction to the machinations of bosses and politicians – a mythical trope that is, as Flesher Fominaya points out, at once a convenient media dramatisation of 'intense visible protest' (2015a, 142) and a useful strategy for social movements that present their 'grievances and claims as the popular will of the people' (ibid., 143).

My argument is rather that any (supposedly 'unrealistic') demand, in whatever period, for direct workers' (and/or community) control of the economy – self-management as an engine of social transformation, rather than a

minor supplement within the capitalist system[6] – serves an important purpose, over and above the contentious issue of its 'practicality' as a mode of
rule. This is the fact that it highlights the burdensome nature of all 'officious'
structures (Appleton 2016), including the recent growth of 'authoritarian
neoliberalism' in nations, like Spain, that made a formal transition from
dictatorship but failed to 'break with the authoritarian structures of the state'
and, as a consequence, ended up with a form of 'arrested democracy' (Clua-
Losada and Ribera-Almandoz 2017, 31). Yet, despite the clear difference
between the positive vision of economic justice offered within those philosophies that advocate workers' expropriation of the economy and a system
where the most egregious examples of corruption, poverty and repression are
enacted within the frame of 'democratic' culture (Fisher 2013), the suggestion that state power should be replaced by a radical or even 'savage' form of
self-rule (Abensour 2011) remains a minority position.

Instead, various forms of 'apologia for the existing order' identified by
Lukács (1971, 48) continue to appear in the public rhetoric that underpins
bourgeois modernity and are particularly salient when regimes of austerity
are disguised by appeals to democratic principles or national pride. Once
again, this tactic is not the sole preserve of centralised state power, as regional politicians (like Catalonia's ex-president Artur Mas and his political de-
scendants) are equally capable of subsuming calls for economic justice in
general notions of progressive cultural identity (Minder 2017). It is impossible, however, to disguise the everyday reality that all hopes for a better life
depend on popular experience of economic opportunity. In October 2017, a
state-sponsored poll found that unemployment in Spain remained the chief
concern of 65 per cent of those surveyed, followed by corruption and the
political situation in general; by comparison, 25 per cent of the respondents
cited Catalan independence as the most pressing national difficulty[7] (Centro
de Investigaciones Sociológicas [CIS] 2017).

SPAIN: THE RHETORIC OF DEMOCRACY

The reproduction of a normative liberal narrative seems to depend on the
separation of references to political maturity and progress from the details of
economic failure that would otherwise cast doubt upon these supposed
achievements. So, for example, forty years after the 'restoration of democracy' in Spain, *El País* (2017) published an editorial in which the paper celebrated the 'deepest, most long-lasting democratic period in Spain's entire
recent history', based, it claimed, upon 'a very advanced Constitution that
reaffirmed the existence of the rule of law'. The list of principles used to
prove this assertion included the existence of 'one person, one vote; the
encoding of fundamental individual rights . . . the acknowledgment of collec-

Figure 4.1.   Riot police line the route of a march held by anarchists on Las Ramblas, Barcelona, 1 May 2017. Photo by Stuart Price.

tive identities and their corresponding linguistic and cultural rights', and 'the concepts of majority rule and respect for minorities'.

Besides the problems created by a limited form of devolution, in which 'central' state power in Spain still tries to standardise the political, cultural and linguistic behaviours of its regions (Martínez-Herrera 2002, 430), a number of other problems were relegated to the status of 'unresolved challenges', a list that encompassed 'the top-down attitude in government agencies', the 'increase in social segments subjected to miserable living conditions', and the growth of 'fuel poverty and . . . inequality' (*El País* 2017). Yet even the seemingly obvious benefits identified by *El País* are difficult to accept without qualification: arguing that an important feature of Spanish democracy was that it had 'established turns in power among various rival parties' (ibid.), the unacknowledged criticism is that this was exactly the complaint made for many years by citizens who objected to the sterile 'turns' taken between the governments of the right-wing Partido Popular (PP) and the ostensibly left-of-centre Partido Socialista Obrero Español (PSOE). The allegation was not only that this process represented the simple rotation of ruling groups that ran equally corrupt systems of patronage but also that this unhealthy relationship between the major parties was underpinned by the 'pact of silence' observed in connection with the crimes committed during the Franco era. The 'democratic' system was thus supposed to have helped reinforce the power of an elite that still refuses to confront the legacy of the cataclysmic event that created modern Spain – the Civil War of 1936–1939 (Sanz Sabido 2016).

The more than eighty years that have passed since the beginning of the war, and the forty that have elapsed since the 'transition to democracy', may suggest that there is now some considerable difference between the conditions that prevailed at these periods and the modern democracy that allows citizens to express what the *El País* editorial called their 'fundamental and individual rights' (2017). Yet if the *economic* regimen enacted by the neoliberal state continues to impoverish the working class while the *political* system guards against the proletarian autonomy described by Abensour (2011), the current order seems still to have much in common with both the failures of the 'democratic' Republican past and the evils of the Francoist dictatorship. If this is the case, then the historical continuity of certain resistance practices should come as no surprise.[8]

In this respect, it is interesting to note that during the 'illegal' Catalan referendum, leftist opposition to the brutal intervention of the Spanish state did not always draw upon the discourses and symbols promoted by the *independenistas*, but from exactly the contested recomposition of the anti-Fascist tradition. In one preelection event held in December 2017 by Catalunya en Comú-Podem (the Catalan version of Spain's Podemos), 'there was little nationalist sentiment on display at the meeting where, rather than the ubiquitous pro-independence flags, people carried the red, gold and purple flag of the second republic that was overthrown by General Franco in 1939' (Burgen 2017). Similarly, the recollections of those who lived through the war and the repression that followed testify to the powerful connection between past and present: interviewed by a CNN reporter in December 2017, ninety-five-year-old Rosario Caceres declared that the conflict between the Catalonian secessionists and the Madrid government was 'just like the Civil War but without the bombs' (Dewan 2017). The exact manifestation of opposition, therefore, draws upon both the contemporary political context and the inheritance and revivified memory of the militant past, in line with the observation that protest and resistance 'cannot be detached from that which preceded it' (see the introduction to this volume).

DEFINITIONS AND THEORIES OF RESISTANCE

In the physical sciences, the concept of resistance refers to the property of a particular substance or form that reduces or obstructs the effect of an external force. This can include conductive or semiconductive materials that, depending on their composition, offer varying degrees of opposition to an electrical current. Equally, resistance can refer to an object that interrupts the flow of air or fluids. In these cases, it is the nature and/or shape of the material that determines the extent to which a dynamic phenomenon is impeded or redirected. Resistance can be, therefore, an inherent quality at the molecular level and/or the product of the physical interface between a form that moves through or encounters the flow of another substance.

In political terms, resistance can also be seen as a 'natural' capacity that belongs to certain individuals or collectives, or as a form of stubbornness evident in the notion of 'passive resistance', a commitment to a form of inaction that is used to frustrate an aggressive or structurally dominant opponent. Resistance is more likely, however, to be described as the active, often physical production of an effect, although always in response to some power that intrudes, intentionally or otherwise, on the material interests, physical terrain or political consciousness of the victim. This means, in turn, that an individual or group can (usually correctly) interpret an intrusive action as an attack or imposition, while the authority responsible for marshalling or overseeing the forces that produce this impression regards its activities as no more than the routine pursuit of normative, judicious goals.

Entirely legal decisions that underwrite socioeconomic processes like, for example, the regular repossession by Spanish banks of people's homes (Flesher Fominaya 2015b; Sabaté 2016) are therefore produced as a matter of course, and it is only the determination of the victims to obtain some form of limited redress (Burgen 2016) that interrupts the systemic destruction of human lives. When, therefore, similar forms of state power are exercised within the framework of legality, it may seem as though we are witnessing exactly comparable forms of injustice. Yet some processes are embedded in routine procedure and have to be made visible through opposition, while others create public disquiet because they represent an extraordinary intervention. The most recent state imposition on a regional government took place in 2017, when Madrid imposed direct rule on Catalonia using Article

Figure 4.2.   Republican flag with red star, on Via Laeitana (during the Civil War, known as Via Durruti), Barcelona, 1 May demonstration, 2017. Photo by Stuart Price.

155 of the Constitution in response to the Catalan Parliament's ratification of an earlier, illicit Declaration of Independence (BBC News 2017). The violence unleashed by the National Police and the Civil Guard on voters who took part in the original vote (on 1 October) became a byword for oppression among the *independenistas* but, from the state's perspective, provided a useful dramatisation of the referendum's illegality.

In the light of even these examples, those approaches to the theory of resistance that deviate from the natural assumption that it is a response to an injury or an iniquitous condition would seem to ring a little hollow. These perspectives, many of which are drawn from the Foucauldian tradition, offer an interpretation of power relations that begins with the assumption that power is a 'medium of change' (Heller 1996, 83) and that it is a general resource rather than simply a weapon of the dominant class.

This 'postmodern' approach (Ebert 1991) serves as a reminder that the contest over economic goods, and the parallel battle to establish a hegemonic rationale for action, can be taken up with equal vigour by all sides in a dispute (though the relative strength of the combatants will differ). However, some commentators go beyond this idea and imagine resistance not as a necessity or a virtue but as one part of a 'mutually reinforcing' circuit of resistance and power (Bloom 2017, 3). This position is supported by two authors who argue that 'power and resistance are often indistinguishable' (Fleming and Spicer 2008, 305). Others believe that power can no longer be described as a mode of control since it is, supposedly, distributed throughout the social order (Bennett and Joyce 2010).

One of the major origins of the 'postmodern' perspective can be found in an interview given in 1984, when Foucault argued that 'if there was no resistance there would be *no relations of power*', and without resistance 'everything would be simply *a question of obedience*' (Caygill 2013, 8, my emphasis). This position should be treated with caution, since the first part implies that power as a social force depends on resistance (as an 'activity', or at least a state of mind), whereas power actually *subsists* within the structural modalities of capitalist patriarchy, ready to be animated and brought to bear by the implementation of a policy or practice. The successful manifestation of power does not depend on the creation of a counterforce ('resistance') but on the production of an intended effect, irrespective of how it is greeted or understood by the subjects or victims of the action. Obedience, in turn, is a symptom of the power relations that Foucault appears to deny.

If the unspoken suggestion is that resistance should cease in order to 'undermine' the logic of power, then this might fail to take account of the relative positions of the participants concerned, or of the importance of the issue that has caused dissension: in practice, therefore, the adoption of this position would simply allow the powerful to behave as they wished. It may well be the case that an entirely amoral struggle could occur between, for example, two or more opposing forces that represent equally repugnant so-cial cabals (such as the warring factions in corporate boardrooms, or rival groups within drug cartels), but the disputes between workers and the 'corpo-rate state' is of a different calibre. If, meanwhile, resistance is a necessary response to the imposition of an amoral authority, then revolution (at least in its libertarian form) is the determined pursuit of an agenda that seeks to end oppression altogether.

CRITIQUES OF REVOLUTION

On the rare occasions when a revolutionary transformation of the social order is described as a political objective rather than as a purely historical event, the beliefs and assumptions upon which it is founded are bound to be subjected to critical scrutiny. Besides the openly ideological opposition from a right wing that sees *any* kind of egalitarian campaign as the harbinger of disorder, the standard challenges to the theory and practice of self-management include the arguments that (1) sophisticated economic systems require managerial coordination from above; (2) the state is an 'extensive' or distributed phenomenon, meaning that there is no clear centre of power that can be undermined or captured by an insurgent movement; and (3) the class once designated as the driver of revolution no longer represents (if it ever did) a seamless, unified body capable of decisive action.

The first point is perhaps less than relevant for a political philosophy that sees its essential task as the dissolution of hierarchy and the immediate seizure of productive capital in each locality (sometimes even manifesting itself as a demand for efficiency),[9] but from a national and transnational perspective, a major reason for the relative weakness of the 'revolutionary scenario' can indeed be traced to the second problem – the structural complexity attributed to modern states. As noted above, they seem to have no fixed hub of oppression that can be attacked and dismantled, and, by the same token, their penetration into everyday life through modes of surveillance and the paternalistic intrusion of the 'welfare' system produces a less than absolute demarcation between lifeworld and the state (Jessop 2008). In addition, the 'strength in depth' of these invisible elites that maintain their dominance through a combination of coercion and consent (Hall 1994) points to the difficulty of establishing an independent, ideologically coherent opposition.

The third question, therefore, is central to the current discussion of agency, resistance and power. It is certainly true that, in the decades since the zenith of 'pure' class politics (exemplified in the sharp divisions witnessed in the 1930s), most sociological analyses of the subaltern condition do not subscribe to the concept of a cohesive body, drawing attention instead to the fragmentary or multilayered character of collective identity (Lockwood 1966; Roberts et al. 1977; Rueschemeyer 1986; Milner 1999). Although this does not mean that a coherent *position or outlook* is impossible to articulate (because collective class consciousness is constantly revived through economic attacks and the ideological assaults that accompany them), it does suggest that the use of broad generalisations and the narrow archetypes they engendered – such as the once dominant image of the male industrial worker who bears privation on behalf of a nuclear family (Hoel 1984, 106) – cannot provide a reliable template for making an appeal for mass action.

The complexities of class location have always, therefore, been a factor in the determination of political activity, but there are other barriers (besides the philosophical objections mentioned above) that reduce the chance of workers gaining the 'generative structural power' (Baumgartner et al. in Burns and Buckley, 1976: 253) required to control their economic destiny, and thus of reconfiguring the wider political landscape. Among the most significant of these developments is the fact that many employees are unable to appropriate the 'means of production' (as they did with some success, noted below, during the Civil War period) because they are *detached from a material base and concrete resource* that either is located elsewhere or does not exist. This is not peculiar to Spain, of course, but it is a general condition that must be considered. In the case of digital labour, for example, the privatisation of the Internet represents 'a form of material deprivation and enclosure' that 'separates individuals from the infrastructure that supports their communicative activities' (Andrejevic 2013, 155).

The casualisation of labour, meanwhile, where the employee is turned into a 'subcontractor' who has no formal relationship with the company (let alone any say in the operation of the business), is another of the techniques that prevents the attainment of collective solidarity, always easier when workers are directly and permanently employed and located in the same physical space. The precarious nature of work is of course nothing new. In 1930s Spain, 'tenant' farmers were controlled by the fact that their tenancy was granted only for short periods, meaning that any improvement they made to their plots benefitted the landowners when the property reverted to their exclusive control (Conze 1936, 10). In the modern era, on those occasions when precarious workers do manage to combine their energies to good effect, this, too, has its limits (because in many instances there is often nothing concrete to collectivise).

This was the case during the 2015 Telefónica occupation in Barcelona, when the (officially 'self-employed') technicians who invaded the company headquarters on the Plaça de Catalunya did so in the knowledge that the space they occupied (usually inhabited by sales staff and managers) did not contain the 'means of production' that could be turned to the workers' advantage (Sanz Sabido and Price 2016). For their part, employers often provide no 'tools' (other than linguistic training) and generate no discernible product, while relying on the use of workers who are temporally or spatially divorced from their colleagues. In effect, organisations and their resources are difficult to appropriate and socialise, although there is perhaps one property above all others that the militants of the 1930s valued and understood – what I would call the essential *collectivisation of consciousness*, reported in so many of the accounts that describe the fiercely moral attitudes of many Civil War militants (Ackelsberg 2006; Guillamón 2014). It is this intellectual and ideological task – the resurrection of basic solidarity between those who have become 'the subjects of austerity' – that answers, if only in part, the material challenges described above. Another force that drives the reconstruction of working-class identity is, of course, the inadvertent effects produced by neoliberal governments.

NEOLIBERAL POWER: UNINTENDED CONSEQUENCES

Despite the argument that power is decentralised, mechanisms of control seem to be ubiquitous. If, in reality, the apparent sophistication of the modern state seems to be underpinned by some rather crude techniques of repression (Tansel 2017), 'neoliberal' regimes have nonetheless employed the supposedly more benign instruments of oversight provided by the welfare state. 'Snooping' on the unemployed and claimants has always been a common practice, but the insult that accompanies this particular injury is the simultaneous removal or reduction of the economic support that was supposed to accompany this form of supervision. The poorest sections of the working-class face, therefore, a double bind: while employment practices are designed to maintain profitability (by suppressing wages, reducing staff numbers and atomising the consciousness of the workforce), the additional effect of austerity (the privatisation of public services and the reduction of benefits) locks individuals into a 'poverty trap' from which it is difficult to emerge. In Spain, the implementation of austerity led to 'severe cuts in health spending' and the 'privatisation of hospitals' (Liu 2015, 15), while Spanish banks were bailed out to the tune of 100 billion euros, provided by the European Union (ibid. 10). Police action against protesters, meanwhile, reminded the Spanish working class of exactly the kind of direct repression that characterised the actions of the dictatorship. At the heart of the neoliberal project, therefore, lies an inherent contradiction: the responsibilities of paternalistic government (always bathed in a nostalgic light that they do not deserve) are exchanged for the intrusive presence of disciplinary surveillance, but the absence or paucity of economic support forces communities once dependent on state aid to engage in forms of economic 'self-management' in order to survive (Azevedo and Gitahy 2010). Again, this process is not exactly unknown on the Iberian Peninsula. In his analysis of the Andalusian village of Marinaleda, Hancox notes that the community's 'struggle to create Utopia' began in the late 1970s 'from a position of abject poverty' (2015, 3).

Although, in one sense, the barriers to workers' control seem insuperable, a major risk facing the neoliberal project is that its own authoritarian agenda

Figure 4.3. Anarcho-syndicalist demonstration, Barcelona, 1 May 2017. Photo by Stuart Price.

reduces life to its most elemental condition, forcing the oppressed to 'go back to basics', inventing new democratic initiatives and producing the 'neoanarchist' behaviours (Gerbaudo 2017) associated with anti-austerity protesters in Spain and other European nations. Successful actions are not necessarily always pursued through the use of 'direct action', however: the attack on fixed minimum rate mortgages, which required evicted homeowners to maintain payments on properties they no longer owned, was pursued through the Spanish courts by fifteen thousand plaintiffs. Yet, as Charnock et al. note, in their analysis of overaccumulation in contemporary Spain, if the working class 'refuse[s] to acquiesce to their subordination to the social power of money', the logic of this resistance suggests that 'what first appears as a crisis of money can threaten *a political crisis of the state* itself' (Charnock et al. 2014, 106).

In other words, the neoliberal system generates, unintentionally, its own political opposition. I would argue, furthermore, that the relentless pursuit of austerity means that one of the major tenets of bourgeois democracy – the formal separation between political representation and the economic sphere, already noted above – is revealed as a barrier to the 'real' democracy demanded by groups like the Spanish *Indignados*, and this is a problem which cannot, ultimately, be solved through interventions such as that initiated by the radical electoral alliance Unidos Podemos (United We Can, formed on 9 May 2016).

Yet, despite the multiple drawbacks analysed above, the vision of a stateless, cooperative form of existence – the dream of autonomy – still resonates in the folk memories and social narratives (Price 2007) of those citizens whose countries have suffered dictatorship, endured labour discipline or, perhaps most relevant to the current chapter, undergone periods of revolutionary transformation. This is especially true where the 'masses' moved beyond their apportioned role as the obedient stage armies of the radical bourgeoisie and became (albeit briefly) the agents of history. The reproduction, therefore, of historic accounts of resistance allows us to feel again the strength of *proletarian intransigence* in response to the machinations of the bourgeois state, during a period in the 1930s when formal authority was openly nominated as the enemy of freedom and justice.

The next section deals with an event that seemed, for a short period at least, to promise the advent of a new, anti-authoritarian era. The forms of resistance that have developed in contemporary Spain, from the anti-eviction movement PAH (Plataforma de Afectados por la Hipoteca) to the protesters of Bebés Robados (the 'Stolen Babies' group[10]), have an organic link to (and indeed were produced by) this turbulent past: the wave of communal practices observed in Europe and beyond are not, therefore, unprecedented since, as Ainger notes, no revolution is entirely 'spontaneous' but is built on years of activity and struggle (Ainger in Price and Sanz Sabido 2016). The next section recalls the deep consciousness that forms the bedrock of 'identities of resistance' in contemporary Spain.

SPAIN, JULY 1936: REACTION, RESISTANCE AND THE BOURGEOIS STATE

Although a combative, highly politicised working class had been established on the Spanish mainland for decades, the immediate cause of the 'revolutionary insurrection' (Payne 2012, 24) that swept the nation in 1936 can be traced to the attempt by right-wing conspirators to end the limited social reforms enacted by a newly elected Republican government. Based in Spanish Morocco, reactionary generals from the Army of North Africa initiated a rising, ostensibly to save the country from (variously) Bolshevism, atheism, anarchy, Freemasonry and a mythical Jewish 'conspiracy'. Beginning on 17 July, the mutinous forces (led, after a period of indecision, by Francisco Franco) were brought to the mainland by aircraft and naval vessels provided by the German dictator Adolf Hitler. The core of the rebellion, made up of Legionnaires and Moorish divisions, was immediately reinforced by a substantial proportion of the Peninsular army, the Civil Guard, the paramilitary forces of the Carlist movement, and members of the far-right Falange (members of the latter reappeared during the Catalan crisis of 2017, sometimes thinly disguised as ordinary *unionistas*).

The leaders of the Republic, however, tried to deny the enormity of the dangers they faced. Fearing the power of radical working-class groups in their own camp, the authorities assured the population that the rising was of no consequence and had not spread to the Spanish mainland (Fraser 1986, 53). During an earlier civil war, in seventeenth-century England, there had been similar reluctance to invest trust in the common people when, as Wood observed, 'those who were defending the rights of Parliament against the Crown' faced the prospect that 'invoking popular sovereignty might open much more hazardous floodgates, endangering not only the state but the whole social order' (2012, 107). According to Wood, the question for authorities was whether 'the *right of resistance*' could be confined to trusted officials or extended to the populace as a whole (ibid., my emphasis).

The 'right of resistance' is usually arrogated exclusively by the state since it lays claim on the right to the legitimate exercise of violence (Bourdieu 2014). In 1930s Spain, however, alternative centres of influence existed alongside the established powers of the Catholic Church, the armed forces, the landowners and capitalists, and the civil authorities. These configurations of proletarian culture included militant trade unions, left-wing political parties, armed defence committees (Guillamón 2014), barrio collectives, and anarchist affinity groups, together with an independent radical press, providing the working class with access to a network of information, free from the interference of national or regional government.

Again, as Ainger has demonstrated, an upsurge in resistance is usually built on long histories of activism. In this case, the origins of libertarian politics ran deep: the first congress of the Spanish section of the First International had been held in Barcelona in 1870 (Leval 1975, 21). Spanish militants, despite the prevalence of an education system dominated (though not exclusively controlled) by the Catholic Church, had grown up within a milieu that was not only distinct from bourgeois culture but also actively opposed to the 'dominant value system' that it produced (Parkin 1972, 83). In command of their own sources of intelligence and embedded in organisations that gave them the 'means of legitimation' (83) that were usually the provenance of the elite, workers were unlikely to put much faith in official pronouncements. The negative experience of Republican state power, meanwhile, exemplified in the bloody suppression of the Asturias revolt in 1934, provided an object lesson for the working class (Sanz Sabido 2016).

Eyewitness recollections of the attempted coup provide insight into this fundamental distrust of the authorities. On 18 July, in Barcelona, the urban heart of Catalonia,[11] Abel Paz (then a newspaper vendor a month shy of his fifteenth birthday) saw the headline of *El Noticeiero Universal*,[12] which announced, 'in huge type', that 'the Spanish army stationed in Morocco had rebelled' (Paz 1997, 7). Reading the statement from the Ministry of War, which claimed that 'the government had the situation under control' (ibid., 8), Paz, as a member of the anarchist trade union Confederación Nacional del Trabajo (CNT), 'had been expecting [the rebellion] for days' (ibid., 8).

An almost identical tale is recounted by Ealham in his biographical introduction to José Peirats's analysis of the period. Peirats, a Barcelona brickmaker, had finished work at midday on Saturday, 19 July, and began to prepare for a shorthand class that would support his plans to develop a career as a journalist. Before he left for this appointment, a friend brought the dramatic intelligence that 'right-wing army officers stationed in Morocco had launched a coup' (2005, xxi). Ealham notes that 'the news would not have shocked José as CNT and anarchist circles had, for weeks, been appraised of a conspiracy' (ibid., xxi).

In some areas, preparations for the conflict were already being made. Another member of the CNT, Joaquín Pérez Navarro, testified to the state of readiness in the anarchist ranks when he recalled how 'in the two days before 19 July, every one of us in the confederal and anarchist defence groups in the city of Barcelona went without sleep', as the militants 'monitored and watched from every strategic point the comings and goings of thugs and evildoers' (2013, 77). According to the historian Agustín Guillamón, a raid organised on the evening of 17 July by Juan Yagüe, secretary of the CNT marine transport union, seized some 150 rifles from ships docked in the port of Barcelona (2014, 46) to prepare for the inevitable battle against the army.

On 19 July itself, working-class activists and forces loyal to the government (made up of Assault and Civil Guards), underpinned by the strategic initiative of the CNT, managed to overcome the immediate threat posed by the rebellion. The numbers of armed left-wing combatants in the city had not, however, been particularly overwhelming. According to Manuel Cruells, one of those who took part in the fighting, the distinction between committed militants and the bulk of the working class was noticeable: the masses had appeared on the evening of 19 July, he recalled, when the conflict was over, and they 'seized victory for themselves' (Fraser 1986, 107).

Felix Carrasquer, a member of the FAI (Federación Anarquista Ibérica, an association formed to keep the CNT on the anarchist path) corroborated this view when he noted that 'where there were 2,000 of us libertarians who rallied to put down a fascist coup – not, let me stress, to make a libertarian revolution – by 8 a.m. the next day there were 100,000 in the streets' (ibid., 107). The fact that Carrasquer took care to underline this aspect of the resistance again demonstrates the essential benefits of solidarity between relatively small groups, the need for painstaking preparation, and the importance of giving a lead to a larger movement – this was not, however, accomplished through the centralisation of power, an option that leading CNT militants refused to take when the fight was over, preferring instead to build a militia force capable of taking the fight to the Nationalists and to begin the task of organising the economy.

Although the consolidation by the working class of a triumph achieved by its most dedicated fighters is a cause for celebration, it also highlights the problems created by armed actions that force the bulk of the population into the role of passive bystanders. Meanwhile, the fact that the battle was never intended to produce a revolutionary coup attests both to the moral 'superiority' of the anarchist tradition (wary of imitating 'bolshevik' methods) and to its inherent weakness as an instrument of libertarian communist power.

If the legitimate government, overtaken by events, had to cede the initiative to those most determined to resist the advance of a voracious enemy in order to prevent the victory of the Right, then this situation demonstrated that the authority of the administration had been (albeit temporarily) undermined. It was also apparent that many of those who had risked their lives in the struggle against the insurgents had no intention of returning to the miserable conditions that had prevailed under successive governments. If the anarchists had decided not to 'go for broke' and create a libertarian communist revolution, the militant groups and unions did, nonetheless, take over public buildings, seize and collectivise the land, turn capitalist enterprises into collectives and begin to take production and services into their own hands. The external, dramatic evidence of this upheaval was perhaps easier to notice, at first, than the deeper decentralisation of economic authority, and it is the 'spectacular' phenomenon (painted in vivid colours by foreign visitors) that is most often circulated in the popular imagination.

THE SPECTACLE OF REVOLUTION: VISITORS TO BARCELONA, 1936

In the early stages of the struggle, it seemed that the formal authority exercised by the Generalitat (Barcelona was the seat of administrative power in Catalonia) had evaporated. This assumption proved to be misleading: in the weeks and months that followed the right-wing revolt and the determined resistance of the Left, the bourgeois social order proved more resilient than it had appeared. Yet, in the first flush of victory – and indeed for some months afterwards – foreign enthusiasts were drawn to Barcelona because of its apparent transformation into a leftist citadel. A number of these visitors produced material that reflected the revolutionary hopes of a generation. Shortly after the workers' triumph, Mary Low, a twenty-four-year-old Surrealist poet and member of the Fourth International,[13] arrived in the city.[14] Accompanied by her companion and fellow Trotskyist, the Cuban Jean Breá, she began to record her impressions (which appeared in an account of the period called *Red Spanish Notebook*, published a year after the upheaval).

The anticlericalism of the revolutionaries, which led to a considerable toll on priests who suffered extrajudicial execution, was immediately apparent. The US military attaché, Colonel Fuqua, reported to his superiors that 'all churches in Barcelona have been burned; the city is more or less in the hands of the communistic groups and the government is slowly losing the little control it now has' (Report 6383, July 24, 1936). When they reached the Cathedral, Low and Breá found entry to the building denied: militiamen at the gate explained that the structure would be turned into an educational facility and thus 'put to a decent use at last' (Low and Breá 1937, 19). Unable to gain access, they explored the narrow streets that radiated from the Ramblas, Barcelona's main thoroughfare. In many places, they noticed large sheets of paper, 'hastily scrawled with big initials in red', that had been pasted over the nameplates of businesses and shops (ibid., 20). These crude signs were intended to mark a change in managerial control, showing that the properties concerned had been transferred from private ownership to the jurisdiction of militant left-wing parties or trade unions.

As Low noted in later sections of the jointly written memoir, the devolution of economic power to political organisations or syndicates is not the same as the establishment of universal working-class control, nor could it be mistaken for the overthrow of capitalist social relations.[15] Yet, along the Ramblas itself, Low and Breá discovered further symbolic evidence of the general social upheaval. Low observed that the facades of the buildings were 'alive with waving flags in a long avenue of dazzling red', while 'the air was filled with an intense din of loudspeakers' carrying political speeches interspersed with snatches of the 'Internationale' (ibid., 20). Standing in groups beneath the trees, the citizens of Barcelona had gathered to listen to the revolutionary rhetoric of the militants. From the point of view of hostile (though supposedly neutral) observers, the situation was out of control.

Meanwhile, intrigued visitors continued to arrive in the city. On August 5, at around eleven at night (less than a month after Low and Breá had arrived in Spain), Franz Borkenau (a left-wing refugee from Nazi Germany who had become disillusioned with authoritarian communism) turned a corner into the same wide boulevard – he called Las Ramblas 'the chief artery of Barcelona' – and immediately received 'a tremendous surprise' (Borkenau 1937/1963, 69). There, 'in a flash', was the 'overwhelming' spectacle of the revolution, which made Borkenau feel as though he had 'landed on a continent different from anything I had seen before' (ibid., 69). He watched the 'armed workers . . . wearing their civilian clothes', sitting on benches or walking along the pavement with rifles on their shoulders (ibid., 70). A few of the barricades from the fighting of 19 July, he noted, were still intact, with armed proletarians crouching behind them, but for the most part these had disappeared. The anarchists, meanwhile, recognisable by their 'badges and insignia in red and black', had the overwhelming number of adherents (ibid., 70).

Other political visitors recorded a similar impression. August Thalheimer, a leading member of the 'Brandlerite' Communist group, the KPO, arrived on 20 August, a full month after the coup had been defeated. 'The Ramblas', he observed, 'is crowded with people until late at night', while the 'cafés and bars are full' (Richardson 1992, 271). 'You get the impression', he wrote, 'that the town is thoroughly controlled by proletarian elements' (ibid., 271). The appearance of revolutionary activity was still impossible to ignore. 'The houses are plastered with posters from the CNT, FAI, POUM and PSUC', Thalheimer noted, while 'there are a lot of milicianos [militia volunteers] in leather or silk jackets, and countless workers' patrols carrying weapons' (271).

Lois and Charles Orr (two left-wing Americans who worked with the POUM) reached the city on 17 September. They had been delayed for two days in Figueras because they had no papers and had fallen under suspicion. Taken to the Republican police organisation, the Investigació Social, they had managed to convince their captors that they were 'good comrades' and were given leave to proceed to Barcelona (Horn 2009, 69). In a jointly written letter to Lois's family, they noted, 'We never were in a more interesting situation, where one can see tremendous change at a visible pace', and celebrated the 'spirit of the people' which was 'at a high pitch' (ibid., 70).

A comparable, yet obviously more famous, account was given by the English novelist George Orwell, who at the time of his arrival in the city (December 1936) had begun to establish his credentials as a writer.[16] In *Homage to Catalonia*, he testified that, arriving directly from England, 'the aspect of Barcelona was something startling and overwhelming' (Orwell 1986, 2). He, too, heard the loudspeakers on Las Ramblas, 'bellowing revolutionary songs night and day' (ibid., 3), and saw that 'practically every building of any size had been seized by the workers' and was draped with 'red flags or with the red and black of the Anarchists' (ibid., 2). 'Every shop and café', wrote Orwell, 'had an inscription saying it had been collectivised' (ibid., 3), while 'the revolutionary posters [flamed] from the walls in clean reds and blues' (ibid., 3).

The appearance of working-class power was therefore still evident less than nine months after 19 August. The underlying reality, however, was that proletarian organisations and their achievements were beginning to come under increasing pressure from the Republican authorities, which issued decrees to turn the militias into a regular army, while starting to erode the 'dual power' that was evident in revolutionary centres like Barcelona. The culmination of this trend was in May 1937, during the armed attempt by Catalan police to return the central telephone exchange – the Telefonica, administered in those days by the UGT and CNT trade unions, but dominated by the latter – to government control. The consequence was an internecine struggle between the forces of bourgeois reaction lined up behind the Generalitat (supported by its Assault Guards, the PSUC, the Communist Party, and the supposedly 'neutral' CNT government ministers) and the more militant sections of the CNT (reinforced by the POUM, the Libertarian Youth, and anarchist militants belonging to the Friends of Durruti). The eruption of this struggle (known as the 'May Days') still divides opinion on the Left, between (on the one hand) the adherents of state socialism and the more reformist wing of anarchism and (on the other) those libertarians and revolutionaries who interpret the event as lasting evidence of working-class intransigence in the face of state power (see, for example, Aguzzi 1938; Orwell 1986; Souchy et al. 1987; Bolloten 1991; Gorkin 2001; Aguilera 2012).

RIGHT- AND 'LEFT-WING' STATES

For students of class resistance, the enduring practical lesson of May 1937 – despite its historical obscurity, its decidedly regional character within Spain, and in the face of the germane but occasionally sterile debate over the precedent that 'anti-fascist war' is supposed to take over 'social revolution' – lies in the reappearance of independent working-class initiative. This impulse was called forth, as it was in July 1936 (see above), by the *intrusion* of a form of power that the militants of the CNT and their allies regarded as illegitimate. Yet working-class self-organisation is supposed to *expose the chasm between Right and Left*, not between 'factions' of the Left.

While the Right of the political spectrum is accused of equating rebellion with an existential threat to the social order, it is assumed that the Left will always welcome working-class dissent. This, however, is not necessarily the case: on those occasions when 'leftist' factions have assumed formal control of the state apparatus and have sought to maintain capitalist social relations, they have come into conflict with those more radical groups that still adhere to socialist principles and, even more significantly, must confront the inevitable dissension of working-class organisations that the patriarchal capitalist order constructs as its natural enemies. Rueschemeyer argued that the 'power of workers' begins with the 'ineradicable element of discretion' that is present in all forms of labour (1986, 75). If this is the basis for economic class interest, then those who have to perform a particular task will do so without necessarily needing guidance from above. Although hidden from view, 'major and recurrent conflicts between workers and employers over the organisation of work' (ibid., 71) provide the basis not only for industrial strife but also for the general reconstruction of a politics of resistance that encompasses all those who produce social and economic value but have no control over its use.

While 'radical' administrations might imagine that they will retain the support of their base, the economic needs of workers will often trump political sentiment or party loyalty. Among the numerous examples of this phenomenon, both historical and contemporary, are the conflicts that arose in the early years of the Bolshevik regime in Russia, noted at the beginning of this chapter (Read 1996; Murphy 2007; Pirani 2008), the disputes between workers' organisations and Republican administrations in 1930s Spain, and the groundswell of opposition to Syriza in Greece as it began to depart from its original principles in favour of 'neoliberal' policies (Gelis 2014; Ovenden 2015). The general point is that, when true class autonomy is exercised, deep faultlines are revealed between the positions occupied by the various groups that lay claim to the legacy of socialism.[17]

FROM AN 'AUTHORITARIAN' TO A 'LIBERTARIAN' HYPOTHESIS

In recent years, certainly since the financial downturn, one counter-discourse to austerity has achieved some intellectual success. This is Badiou's 'communist hypothesis' of 2010, which attacks contemporary imperial powers for their repressive rule. Badiou's argument is that the West 'is in the grip of a truly historic crisis', forcing it to 'fall back on its "democratic" pretensions' (2010, 4). Yet, in recognising that much more openly coercive mechanisms are now used to ensure the success of the system, Badiou leads his readers to suspect that the crisis has damaged the democratic consensus itself: if so, the notion of a general retreat into democratic posturing becomes no more than a transparent fiction.

The 'citizens' of the world are thus presented with the semblance of a global social order that they recognise as brutal and dysfunctional – one that they know is never democratic in its socioeconomic practices – while at the same time they are offered a narrative that draws attention to supposedly more threatening conditions (such as the spectre of terrorism or the 'anarchy' identified in the right-wing press during the English riots of August 2011). This does not mean that democracy is no longer 'the contemporary stamp of political legitimacy' (Fierlbeck 2008, xiii), but rather that it is articulated as a separate and specialised mode of address, noted above. The point therefore is not to be 'anti-democratic' in an authoritarian manner, leading to an attempt to impose perspectives on the subaltern, but to distinguish between formal systems or regimes of democracy and a model of grassroots solidarity.

None of the remarks above are meant to suggest that a theorist like Badiou is entirely insensitive to spontaneous forms of organisation, nor that he is unaware of recent modes of rebellion, as one of his books (*The Rebirth of History*, 2012) attests. It is rather that his allegiance to an authoritarian perspective should be opposed. Although, for example, there is much to be said for studying Bolshevik tracts as tactical interventions, it seems odd to ignore the host of critical works that identify Lenin's policies (rather than their Stalinist 'perversion') as the original inspiration for the growth of the 'Soviet' autocracy, a position that is articulated in a host of critical works (Luxemburg 1961; Brinton 1970; Schapiro 1977; Maximoff 1979; Andrew 1981; Rousset 1982; Weil 1987; Berkman 1989).

If we turn to the historical models employed by Badiou to substantiate his point of view, we learn still more about his attachment to particular models of socialist practice. He cites the French Revolution (1792–1794), the Chinese Revolution (1927–1949), the 'Russian (Bolshevik) Revolution' (1902–1917), and the 'Great Cultural Revolution' (1965–1968) as a way of exemplifying the greatest pinnacles of social and political transformation, but he does not mention the Spanish Revolution of 1936–1939. This omission speaks volumes about his assessment of revolutionary success and failure, as well as his attitude to the anti-authoritarian tradition. This chapter offers, therefore, an alternative proposition – the beginnings of a *libertarian communist* hypothesis. This point of view, drawing on a mixture of socialist and feminist perspectives once popularised in texts like *Beyond the Fragments* (Rowbotham et al. 1979), attacks the hierarchical principle as it manifests itself in all institutions, whether of the Left or the Right, and expresses a positive attachment to models of working-class 'self-activity'.

CONCLUSION

The growth of austerity as a general condition, and the concomitant spread of precarious employment from the periphery to the centre of economic life (Lorey 2015) has given rise to fresh perspectives on resistance, labour, class and the meaning of democracy, a political system that 'designates both the form through which power is legitimated and the manner in which it is exercised' (Agamben 2011, 1). While Lorey notes that the 'possibilities for organising in factories or occupational groups' have been eroded by the growth of individualisation (2015, 6), she also points to an opportunity to

Figure 4.4. Sticker depicting the dictator Franco as a member of Ciudadanos, the 'centre-right' party that contested the December elections, Barcelona, 21 December 2017. Photo by Stuart Price.

'invent new forms of political agency' (ibid., 9). Gerbaudo, examining the same challenges, draws attention to the resurgence in 'the discourse of the people' (2017, 90) that, while not necessarily expressed in terms of class power, nonetheless indicates the resurgence of a radical imaginary, the first step in the reconstruction of self-management and grassroots control that is in effect both communal and economic and that points the way to new social formations.

This chapter has focused, therefore, on *proletarian intransigence*, identifying an elementary resistance to forms of power that, whatever their formal political composition, are recognised as inimical to the integrity of a working class, the identity of which is constantly re-created in practice. The libertarian position, though conscious of the divisions within the ranks of the oppressed, as well as the need to return to the models of individual and collective liberty that sustained the Spanish militants of 1936, must always confront the same accusation that is levelled at the 'state socialists': that tampering with the established order is inherently dangerous, and may produce consequences that, even where unintended, could entail various forms of physical or psychological violence. One well-known counterargument, to the effect that the 'system' itself is relentlessly violent in all its undertakings, is an insufficient riposte to the 'liberal' critique.

I would argue instead that a 'reconstituted' libertarian Left may well be forced to respond to a variety of attacks, physical or ideological, but that its immediate task is the circulation of a social vision that begins with a positive reassessment of communal/economic activity. During the Spanish Revolution and Civil War (1936–1939), a form of 'proletarian democracy' (Mulholland 2012) was brought into being, one that still offers an unparalleled practical insight into the productive nature of class-based resistance. An act of violent subversion provoked a defensive response that led, in turn, to the widespread seizure of land and capital. In effect, a revolutionary condition grew within the confines of the bourgeois state. As the Civil War progressed, the divisions in the ranks of the loyalists provoked another crisis. If the conflict in August 1936 was fought between, broadly speaking, the combined forces of the Left and the transnational fascistic Right, the argument that came to a head in May 1937 served to demonstrate the stark differences between proletarian intransigence and the restless aggression of the state.

There are, of course, vast differences between 1930s Spain and the neoliberal social order that now holds sway, just as there seems to be a considerable gulf between the theoretical positions adopted during that period and the supposedly more nuanced treatment of power, class and resistance associated with contemporary academic analysis (noted above). The point, however, is to learn from those periods when the 'brutal opposition between the people and the *grandees* of the day' produced 'a revolutionary situation' (Abensour 2011, xxiv). If we can deepen our understanding of the distinction between the modern state as an extensive, 'social' phenomenon and the 'core' of the 'repressive state apparatus' used to defend economic inequality, then we may be able to feel the true force of Abensour's analysis: 'If the State is inextricably linked to submission, conversely the democratic revolution is inseparable from the destruction of State power' (95).

NOTES

1. In the past, its goals and precepts have included anti-Statism, collective ownership and individual equality (Fontenis 1954, 18), economic self-management, democratic practices based on federalism, support for progressive/autonomous social movements, opposition to homophobia, support for antiracist and anti-imperialist initiatives, and a model of political conduct that draws on socialist feminism, including an insistence on practical measures such as mobilising working-class and trade union support for women's rights (Berry 2008, 118).

2. Santiago Campos, a resident of Arroyomolinos de Léon, then in his eighties, repeated this saying, which was used by a relative of his in the 1930s when mocking the politics of *Cenetistas*. Campos died in 2015 (for further information, see Sanz Sabido 2016).

3. See Scharpf (2013, 118) in Schäfer and Streeck.

4. See, for example, Jones, 'Eurozone's Strange Low-Wage Employment Boom', in *Financial Times* online, 5 July 2017; Consoli and Sánchez-Barrioluengo, 'Polarization and the Growth of Low-Skill Employment in Spanish Local Labour Markets', Utrecht University, October 2016; and Myant and Horwitz, 'Spain's Labour Market Reforms: No Solution to Its Employment Problems', LSE Blog, 15 June 2015.

5. I followed the Catalan crisis from May to December 2017, which included four visits to Barcelona, to witness: the May Day *manifestacion*, the illegal referendum vote, the declaration of independence, and the regional election of 21st December.

6. See, for example, the distinction made in Wallis, in Ness and Azzellini's *Ours to Master and to Own* (2011).

7. The results of this questionnaire need to be treated with a little caution, since the first few enquiries posed in the survey referred explicitly to the economy, leading perhaps to the emphasis discovered by the pollsters.

8. 'Old' forms of militancy are supplemented by the use of social media to coordinate militant activity. Describing the contemporary resistance to mine closures in Asturias, Sanz Sabido describes the production of articles and other material on 'dedicated social media accounts and websites', specifically produced in order to 'raise awareness and inform other activists and followers' of the progress and of the campaign (2016, 149).

9. The fact that programmes of collectivisation during the Spanish Revolution produced a more efficient economic order can be explained because of the low productivity that obtained in the years leading up to the Civil War, but it may also suggest that contemporary capitalist enterprise is inherently wasteful and could be run more effectively.

10. The 'Bebés Robados' or 'Ninos Robados' group was formed to draw attention to the theft of children under the Franco dictatorship, when Nationalist couples without offspring were given the children of poor or Republican families, who were told by nuns, doctors and priests that their sons and daughters had died. See, for example, Adler 2011, 'Spain's Stolen Babies and the Families Who Lived a Lie', in *BBC News* online, at http://www.bbc.co.uk/news/magazine-15335899 (accessed 27 June 2017). Accompanied by my colleague Ruth Sanz Sabido (author of *Memories of the Spanish Civil War: Conflict and Community in Rural Spain*, 2016), I first encountered this group by accident, when it held a demonstration in Madrid in May 2013. During a short trip dedicated to the study of events organised by 15-M and associated groups, we came across protests by municipal workers, Bebés Robados, and a group calling for the legalisation of cannabis, which moved through side streets under a massive haze of marijuana smoke.

11. Catalonia, a region that had a troubled relationship with the central government in Madrid, was and is one of the main industrial centres in Spain.

12. Paz gives the date of this incident as the afternoon of Friday, 17 July 1936: as the rising in Spanish Morocco took place on this day, it is possible that Paz, like Peirats, learned of the rebellion on Saturday, 18 July.

13. The Fourth International was the revolutionary organisation founded by Leon Trotsky. Anarchist and libertarian criticism of his role in the suppression of the Kronstadt revolt of 1921 is entirely justified, but Trotsky's antipathy to Stalinism and his critique of the political shortcomings of the Spanish revolutionary Left produced some insightful comments on the practices known as war and revolution.

14. Low and Breá had travelled from Belgium, making the final leg of the journey by train from the Gare d'Orsay in Paris, before reaching Port Bou and thence forward to Barcelona.

15. This theme, that the shift of ownership was not necessarily as deep-seated or radical as it might at first have seemed, is echoed in Franz Borkenau's analysis of these events, while the brief duration of workers' power in its spectacular form is famously discussed in Orwell's *Homage to Catalonia*.

16. Orwell had read and reviewed the work of Low and Breá, and in addition Borkenau's book: echoes of their perceptions and language occur in minor details throughout his analysis.

17. A number of notable authors celebrate working-class resistance to the Nationalist 'coup' in August 1936, but many of the same individuals regard the events of May 1937 as a form of treachery. The most obvious and reasonable explanation for this difference is that the two conflagrations occurred within quite different circumstances: the first can be presented as a nationwide struggle on behalf of a democratic government, while the second was initiated by a 'legitimate' central authority. My point, however, is that these periods of dissension should, in their different ways, be regarded as examples of 'class' resistance versus 'state' power.

BIBLIOGRAPHY

Abensour, Miguel. 2011. *Democracy against the State: Marx and the Machiavellian Moment*. Cambridge and Malden: Polity.

Ackelsberg, Martha. 2006. *Free Women of Spain: Anarchism and the Struggle for the Emancipation of Women*. Oakland: AK Press.

Adler, Katya. 2011. 'Spain's Stolen Babies and the Families Who Lived a Lie'. *BBC News*. Accessed 27 June 2017. http://www.bbc.co.uk/news/magazine-15335899.

Agamben, Giorgio. 2011. 'Introductory Note on the Concept of Democracy'. In *Democracy in What State?* edited by Giorgio Agamben, Alain Badiou, Daniel Bensaïd and Wendy Brown, 1–5. New York: Columbia University Press.

Aguilera, Manuel. 2012. *Compañeros y Camaradas*. Madrid: Actas.

Aguzzi, Aldo. 1938. 'Anarchist Volunteers in Spain and the Events of May 1937'. In *L'Adunata dei Refrattari* 33, 13 August, reprinted in *Pages from Italian Anarchist History*, 2005. London: Kate Sharpley Library.

Ainger, Katharine. 2016. 'The Social Fabric of Resilience: How Movements Survive, Thrive or Fade Away'. In *Sites of Protest*, edited by Stuart Price and Ruth Sanz Sabido, 37–56. London: Rowman & Littlefield International.

Andrejevic, Mark. 2013. 'Estranged Free Labor'. In *Digital Labor: The Internet as Playground and Factory*, edited by Trebor Scholtz. London and New York: Routledge.

Andrew, Edward. 1981. *Closing the Iron Cage: The Scientific Management of Work and Leisure*. Black Rose Books.

Appleton, Josie. 2016. *Officious: Rise of the Busybody State*. Alresford: Zero Books.

Azevedo, Alessandra, and Leda Gitahy. 2010. 'The Cooperative Movement, Self-Management, and Competiveness: The Case of Mondragón Corparación Cooprativa'. *Journal of Labor and Society* 13(1): 5–29.

Badiou, Alain. 2010. *The Communist Hypothesis*. London and New York: Verso.

Badiou, Alain. 2012. *The Rebirth of History*. London and New York: Verso.

Baumgartner, Thomas, Walter Buckley, Tom R. Burns and Peter Schuster. 1976. 'Meta-Power and the Structuring of Social Hierarchies'. In *Power and Control: Social Structures and their Transformations*, edited by Tom R. Burns and Walter Buckley. Beverly Hills, CA: Sage.

BBC News. 2017. 'Catalans Declare Independence as Madrid Imposes Direct Rule'. *BBC News*, 27 October 2017. Accessed 1 January 2018. http://www.bbc.co.uk/news/world-europe-41780116.

Bennett, Tony, and Patrick Joyce. 2010. *Material Powers: Cultural Studies, History and the Material Turn*. London and New York: Routledge.

Berkman, Alexander. 1989. *The Bolshevik Myth*. London and Winchester, MA: Pluto.

Berry, David. 2008. 'Change the World without Taking Power? The Libertarian Communist Tradition in France Today'. *Journal of Contemporary European Studies* 16(1): 111–30.

Bloom, Peter. 2017. *Beyond Power and Resistance*. London and New York: Rowman & Littlefield International.

Bolloten, Burnett. 1991. *The Spanish Civil War: Revolution and Counterrevolution*. Chapel Hill: University of North Carolina Press.

Borkenau, Franz. 1963. *The Spanish Cockpit: An Eye-Witness Account of the Political and Social Conflicts of the Spanish Civil War*. Ann Arbor: University of Michigan Press.

Bourdieu, Pierre. 2014. *On the State: Lectures at the Collège de France, 1989–1992*. Cambridge and Malden, MA: Polity.

Brinton, Maurice. 1970. *The Bolsheviks and Workers' Control*. London: Solidarity.

Brinton, Maurice. 2004. *For Workers' Power: The Selected Writings of Maurice Brinton*. Edited by David Goodway. Oakland, CA, and Edinburgh: AK Press.

Burgen, Stephen. 2016. 'Spanish Consumers Win Victory over Mortgage Payments'. *Guardian*. Accessed 27 June 2017. https://www.theguardian.com/business/2016/apr/08/spanish-consumers-win-victory-over-mortgage-payments-barclays-santander-class-action.

Burgen, Stephen. 2017. 'Catalan Left Seeks Socialist Coalition as Crucial Election Looms'. *Observer*, 17 December 2017. Accessed 30 December 2017. https://www.theguardian.com/world/2017/dec/17/catalan-elections-leftwing-coalition-new-start.

Casanova, Julián. 2002. 'Anarchism, Revolution and Civil War in Spain: The Challenge of Social History'. *International Review of Social History* 37(3): 398–404.

Caygill, Howard. 2013. *On Resistance: A Philosophy of Defiance*. London and New York: Bloomsbury.

Centro de Investigaciones Sociológicas. 2017. *Estudio no3191. Barómetro de Octubre 2017*. Madrid, Spain: CIS.

Charnock, Greig, Thomas Purcell and Ramon Ribera-Fumaz. 2014. *The Limits to Capital in Spain: Crisis and Revolt in the European South*. London and New York: Palgrave Macmillan.

Clua-Losada, Mònica, and Olatz Ribera-Almandoz. 2017. 'Authoritarian Neoliberalism and the Disciplining of Labour'. In *States of Discipline: Authoritarian Neoliberalism and the Contested Reproduction of Capitalist Order*, edited by Cemal Burak Tansel, 29–46. London: Rowman & Littlefield International.

Consoli, Davide, and Mabel Sánchez-Barrioluengo. 2016. 'Polarization and the Growth of Low-Skill Employment in Spanish Local Labour Markets'. *Papers in Evolutionary Economic Geography*. Utrecht University, October 2016.

Conze, Edward. 1936. *Spain Today*. London: Martin, Secker and Warburg.

de Souza, Marcelo Lopes, Richard J. White and Simon Springer. 2016. *Theories of Resistance: Anarchism, Geography, and the Spirit of Revolt*. London: Rowman & Littlefield International.

Dewan, Angela. 2017. '"Like the Civil War without the Bombs": Catalonia's Messy Vote'. *CNN news online*. Accessed 25 June 2017. https://edition.cnn.com/2017/12/15/europe/catalonia-election-independence-spain-intl/index.html.

Ealham, Chris. 2005. 'The Life and Struggles of José Peirats'. In *The CNT in the Spanish Revolution, Volume 2*, edited by José Valls Peirats. Hastings: Christie Books.

Ebert, Teresa L. 1991. 'Writing in the Political: Resistance (Post)modernism'. *Legal Studies Forum* XV(4): 291–303.

El País. 2017. 'The Making of Modern Spain'. Accessed 25 June 2017. http://elpais.com/elpais/2017/06/15/inenglish/1497535821_308499.html.

Fierlbeck, Karl. 2008. *Globalising Democracy: Power, Legitimacy and the Power of Democratic Ideas*. Manchester: Manchester University Press.

Fisher, Rebecca. 2013. *Managing Democracy, Managing Dissent*. London: Corporate Watch.

Fleming, Peter and André Spicer. 2008. 'Beyond Power and Resistance: New Approaches to Organisational Politics'. *Management Communication Quarterly* 21(3): 301–9.

Flesher Fominaya, Cristina. 2015a. 'Debunking Spontaneity: Spain's 15-M/*Indignados* as Autonomous Movement'. *Social Movement Studies* 14(2): 142–63.

Flesher Fominaya, Cristina. 2015b. 'Redefining the Crisis/Redefining Democracy: Mobilising for the Right to Housing in Spain's PAH Movement'. *South European Society and Politics* 20(4): 465–85.

Fontenis, Georges. 1954. *Manifesto of Libertarian Communism*. London: Anarchist Communist Editions.

Fraser, Ronald. 1986. *Blood of Spain: An Oral History of the Spanish Civil War*. New York: Pantheon Books.

Gelis, V. N. 2014. *Syriza in Greece: Neo-Liberals in Disguise: Is Tsipras the EU's Last Chance? Eyewitness Reports: Volume 3*. CreateSpace.

Gerbaudo, Paolo. 2017. *The Mask and the Flag: Populism, Citizenism and Global Protest*. London: Hirst.

Gorkin, Julián. 2001. *Contra el Estalinismo (Vol. 82)*. Barcelona: Laertes SA de Ediciones.

Guillamón, Agustín. 2014. *Ready for Revolution: The CNT Defense Committees in Barcelona, 1933–38*. London and Berkeley, Oakland and Edinburgh: Kate Sharpley Library and AK Press.

Hall, John A. 1994. *Coercion and Consent: Studies on the Modern State*. Cambridge and Oxford: Polity Press.

Hancox, Dan. 2015. *The Village against the World*. London and New York: Verso.

Heller, K. J. 1996. 'Power, Subjectification and Resistance in Foucault'. *SubStance* 25(1): 78–110.

Hoel, Marit. 1984. 'The Female Working Class'. In *Patriarchy in a Welfare Society*, edited by Harriet Holter. Oslo, London and New York: Universitetsforlaget.

Horn, Gerd-Rainer. 2009. *Letters from Barcelona: An American Woman in Revolution and Civil War*. Houndmills and New York: Palgrave Macmillan.

Jessop, Bob. 2008. *State Power*. Cambridge and Malden, MA: Polity.

Jones, Claire. 2017. 'Eurozone's Strange Low-Wage Employment Boom'. *Financial Times*, 5 July 2017. Accessed 31 December 2017. https://www.ft.com/content/63b19fd8-5b1f-11e7-9bc8-8055f264aa8b.

Leval, Gaston. 1975. *Collectives in the Spanish Revolution*. London: Freedom Press.

Liu, Larry L. 2015. *The Austerity Trap: Economic and Social Consequences of Fiscal Consolidation in Europe*. Charleston: Liu.

Lockwood, David. 1966. 'Sources of Variation in Working Class Images of Society'. *Sociological Review* 14(3): 249–67.

Lorey, Isabel. 2015. *State of Insecurity: Government of the Precarious*. London and New York: Verso.

Low, Mary, and Juan Breá. 1937. *The Red Spanish Notebook: The First Six Months of the Revolution and the Civil War*. London: Martin Secker and Warburg.

Lukács, Georg. 1971. *History and Class Consciousness*. Pontypool: Merlin Press.

Luxemburg, Rosa. 1961. *The Russian Revolution and Leninism or Marxism?* Ann Arbor: University of Michigan Press.

Martínez-Herrera, Enric. 2002. 'From Nation-Building to Building Identification with Political Communities: Consequences of Political Decentralisation in Spain, the Basque Country, Catalonia and Galicia, 1978–2001'. *European Journal of Political Research* 41: 421–53.

Maximoff, Gregory Petrovich. 1979. *The Guillotine at Work: Volume One, the Leninist Counter-Revolution*. Sanday, Orkney: Cienfuegos Press.

Milner, Andrew. 1999. *Class*. London, Delhi and Thousand Oaks: SAGE Publications.

Minder, Raphael. 2017. *The Struggle for Catalonia: Rebel Politics in Spain*. Hurst: London.

Mintz, Frank. 2013. *Anarchism and Workers' Self-Management in Revolutionary Spain*. Oakland, CA and Edinburgh: AK Press.

Mulholland, Marc. 2012. *Bourgeois Liberty and the Politics of Fear: From Absolutism to Neo-Conservatism*. Oxford: Oxford University Press.

Murphy, Kevin. 2007. *Revolution and Counterrevolution: Class Struggle in a Moscow Metal Factory*. Chicago: Haymarket Books.

Myant, Martin, and Laszlo Horwitz. 2015. 'Spain's Labour Market Reforms: No Solution to Its Employment Problems'. *LSE Blog*, 15 June 2015. Accessed 31 December 2017. http://blogs.

lse.ac.uk/netuf/2015/06/15/spains-labour-market-reforms-no-solution-to-its-employment-problems/.

Nash, Mary. 1995. *Defying Male Civilisation: Women in the Spanish Civil War*. Denver: Arden.

Navarro, Joaquín Pérez. 2013. *One Man's War in Spain: Trickery, Treachery and Thievery*. Hastings: Read and Noir, Christie Books.

Ness, Immanuel, and Dario Azzellini, 2011. *Ours to Master and to Own: Workers' Control from the Commune to the Present*. Chicago: Haymarket Books.

Orwell, George. 1986. *Homage to Catalonia*. London and New York: Penguin.

Ovenden, Kevin. 2015. *Syriza: Inside the Labyrinth*. London and New York: Pluto Press.

Parkin, Frank. 1972. *Class Inequality and Political Order*. St Albans, Granada Publishing Limited: Paladin.

Payne, Stanley G. 2012. *The Spanish Civil War*. Cambridge: Cambridge University Press.

Paz, Abel. 1997. *The Spanish Civil War*. Paris: Pocket Archives, Éditions Hazan.

Peirats, José Valls. 2005. *The CNT in the Spanish Revolution, Volume 2*. Hastings: Christie Books.

Pérez, Miguel. 2017. 'CNT Statement re: Catalonia Events'. *Raddle*. Accessed 31 December 2017. https://raddle.me/f/Anarchism/8004/cnt-statement-re-catalonia-events.

Pirani, Simon. 2008. *The Russian Revolution in Retreat, 1920–24: Soviet Workers and the New Communist Elite*. London and New York: Routledge.

Price, Stuart. 2007. *Discourse Power Address: The Politics of Public Communication*. Burlington, VT, and Aldershot: Ashgate (republished by Routledge, 2016).

Price, Stuart, and Ruth Sanz Sabido. 2016. 'Introduction: Sites of Protest'. In *Sites of Protest*, edited by Stuart Price and Ruth Sanz Sabido, 1–14. London: Rowman & Littlefield International.

Pritchard, Alex, Ruth Kinna, Saku Pinta and David Berry. 2012. *Libertarian Socialism: Politics in Black and Red*. Houndmills & New York: Palgrave Macmillan.

Read, Christopher. 1996. *From Tsar to Soviets: The Russian People and Their Revolution, 1917–21*. London and New York: Routledge.

Richardson, Al. 1992. *The Spanish Civil War: The View from the Left*. Monmouth: Merlin Press & Socialist Platform.

Roberts, Kenneth, F. G. Cook, S. C. Clark and Elizabeth Semeonoff. 1977. *The Fragmentary Class Structure*. London: Heinemann.

Rousset, David. 1982. *The Legacy of the Bolshevik Revolution: Volume One*. London and New York: Allison and Busby.

Rowbotham, Sheila, Lynne Segal and Hillary Wainwright. 1979. *Beyond the Fragments*. London: Merlin Press.

Rueschemeyer, Dietrich. 1986. *Power and the Division of Labour*. Cambridge and Oxford: Polity Press.

Sabaté, Irene. 2016. 'The Spanish Mortgage Crisis and the Re-Emergence of Moral Economies in Uncertain Times'. *History and Anthropology* 27(1): 107–20.

Sanz Sabido, Ruth. 2016. 'Echoes of the Spanish Revolution: Social Memories, Social Struggles'. In *Memory in a Mediated World*, edited by Andrea Hajek, Christine Lohmeier and Christian Pentzold. London and New York: Palgrave Macmillan.

Sanz Sabido, Ruth, and Stuart Price. 2016. 'The Ladders Revolution: Material Struggle, Social Media and News Coverage'. *Critical Discourse Studies*, Discourse and Protest Events 13(3): 247–60.

Schapiro, Leonard. 1977. *The Origin of the Communist Autocracy*, 2nd edition. Cambridge, MA: Harvard University Press.

Scharpf, Armin. 2013. 'Monetary Union, Fiscal Crisis and the Disabling of Democratic Accountability'. In *Politics in the Age of Austerity*, edited by Armin Schäfer and Wolfgang Streeck. Cambridge and Malden, MA: Polity.

Souchy, Augustin, José Peirats, Burnett Bolloten and Emma Goldman. 1987. *The May Days: Barcelona 1937*. London: Freedom Press.

Spender, Stephen. 1937. *Forward from Liberalism*. London: Left Book Club Edition, Victor Gollancz.

Streeck, Wolfgang, and Armin Schäfer, eds. 2013. *Politics in the Age of Austerity*. Cambridge and Malden, MA: Polity.

Tansel, Cemal Burak. 2017. *States of Discipline: Authoritarian Neoliberalism and the Contested Reproduction of Capitalist Order*. London: Rowman & Littlefield International.

Wallis, Ivan. 2011. 'Workers' Control and Revolution'. In *Ours to Master and to Own: Workers' Control from the Commune to the Present*, edited by Immanuel Ness and Dario Azzelini, 10–31. Chicago: Haymarket Books.

Weil, Simone. 1987. *Formative Writings*. London: Routledge and Keegan Paul.

Wood, Ellen Meiksins. 2012. *Liberty and Property: A Social History of Western Political Thought from the Renaissance to Enlightenment*. London and New York: Verso Books.

Worth, Owen. 2013. *Resistance in the Age of Austerity: Nationalism, the Failure of the Left, and the Return of God*. London and New York: Zed Books.

Chapter Five

From Social Movement to Labour Protests

The Case of the Sans Papiers *in France*

Heather Connolly and Sylvie Contrepois

The *sans papiers* movement in France has become an internationally symbolic case of self-organisation among undocumented immigrants (Freedman 2008; Iskander 2007). This movement first emerged in the form of a community-based social movement involving mainly Malians (Jounin 2014) and focused on claims for French citizenship, before evolving into a more institutionalised form of labour protest through trade union organisations (Meardi 2013). This chapter discusses in detail how the shift from social movement to trade union cause occurred, mainly focusing on the period from the mid-1990s to 2016. We examine the political significance of undocumented workers as a space for action within the Confédération générale du travail (CGT), the second-largest trade union confederation in France, and explore the organisational innovations put in place by this confederation in response to the struggles of the *sans papiers* workers.

Our argument is that the shift from social movement to trade union cause corresponds to the dialectical transition from a strategy of survival for the *sans papiers* workers to a disruption of trade union practice and then to the development of a new space and cause for labour protest within the CGT. The survival phase corresponds to the organisation of forms of community and informal solidarity in order to survive in clandestinity on a daily basis, which are well documented in the book by Delphine Coulin, *Samba pour la France*, published in 2011 and adapted into the film *Samba*, released in 2014. From the mid-1990s until the early 2000s, faced with the hardening immigration policy, immigrant community solidarities crystallised in the form of a citizen movement (Freedman 2008; Iskander 2007). Following mainly community-based action, there was a shift to a disruptive phase within the trade unions from 2006, which continued for several years, at which point undocumented workers turned to the trade unions for support in the workplace. The political decision taken by the CGT union to dedicate sustainable support to undocumented immigrants opened up a new phase from around 2014, at which point undocumented workers became a more integral part of French trade union action.

The case study presented here is based on data collected during research on industrial relations in multilingual working environments (Contrepois 2016, 2017a) and field work, in the form of interviews and participant observation, conducted as part of a joint comparative research project on trade union representation of immigrants in the UK and France (Connolly and Contrepois 2016). In the first part of the chapter we introduce the French political context surrounding immigration before examining the initial stages of the *sans papiers* movement as a community-based social movement from the mid-1990s. We then set out how the *sans papiers* movement became a more significant part of trade union action from 2006 onwards. The remainder of the chapter presents in more detail how the unions have organised and mobilised undocumented workers since 2014 and how these workers have become more embedded within the trade unions. We finish by reflecting on the extent to which this movement represents *real* resistance and whether the movement is something new and sustainable.

THE POLITICAL CONTEXT OF IMMIGRATION

France has long been a country of immigration, and from its colonial past large numbers of immigrants came from the colonies and were recognised as French citizens. France has considerably reduced the number of immigrants entering the country over the last two decades. Restrictive immigration policies were introduced from the beginning of the 1970s onwards. The early effects of the economic crisis in the 1970s, which proved particularly severe, then favoured the emergence of the National Front, whose first candidates in the 1973 parliamentary elections won 0.4 per cent of the vote. The following year, the 1974 Act restricted migratory flows to family reunification, encouraged immigrants to return to their country of origin, set up a series of measures aimed at better integrating those staying and prohibited illegal immigration. It was estimated that undocumented immigrants represented 82 per cent of the foreign workforce at the time.[1]

During the 1980s and 1990s, further changes were made to immigration legislation, especially regarding the right to enter and stay on French soil. A number of laws were aimed at improving immigrants' integration into French society. In 1984, a ten-year residency permit, not linked to the beneficiary's employment situation, was introduced. In 1989, the Haut Conseil à l'Intégration was set up, followed ten years later by the Commissions départementales d'accès à la citoyenneté (CODAC). The *Pasqua* laws were introduced in 1993 as the centrepiece of the centre-right government's 'zero immigration' policy. The legislation created a new set of requirements for all persons filing a request for legal status. The requirements included proof of uninterrupted housing and employment for renewal of visas, for example. These requirements for regularisation were often insurmountable for immigrants, and the legislation produced a growing category of immigrants, according to Iskander (2007, 313): 'Immigrants who had been denied legal status, despite the fact that many had at one point held legal resident permits, but who could not be legally expelled – immigrants who would thus remain *sans papiers* on French soil indefinitely'. The *Pasqua* laws also led to the crackdown on undocumented immigrants, and the police were given powers to verify the legal residence status of anyone who appeared 'foreign-looking' and detain for up to three months anyone who could not provide proof of legal status. Aiding and abetting undocumented immigrants became a criminal offence, and in 1996 twelve thousand undocumented immigrants were deported by the French government (ibid., 313).

Legislative activity on immigration then further accelerated from 2002 onwards, prompted by the European-level framework decision to combat irregular immigration and human trafficking, and in a context where the far-right leader, Jean-Marie Le Pen, reached the second round of the French presidential elections. The acts passed in 2003, 2006 and 2007 particularly restricted naturalisation. As a result, the number of expulsion orders for 'unlawful' residence rose from 14,901 in 2005 to 16,653 in 2006. Between 2007 and 2011, under President Sarkozy, immigration-control policies were further strengthened. This government had three main objectives relating to immigration: managing migratory flows; encouraging development activity in sending countries; and promoting the integration of immigrants wishing to settle in France through the *Contrat d'accueil et d'intégration* (welcome and integration contract).

In 2008, in order to reduce legal immigration to the strict needs of the labour market, the Interior and Labour Ministries drew up an initial list of 150 occupations that were open to non-EU workers, which was further reduced to seventy in 2011. Furthermore, from 2009 onwards, international (or bilateral) agreements between France and African countries (Gabon, Tunisia, Senegal, Benin) were passed in order to 'rationalise' immigrant flows (Bussat and Archias, 2013). Finally, the Act of 16 June 2011, the last from the Sarkozy era, tightened the conditions for immigrants who wanted to stay in France by weakening the 'right of soil' (*droit du sol*).

Since the early 1990s the issue of undocumented workers has become a particularly sensitive political issue. It is estimated that there are between three and four hundred thousand undocumented immigrants in France (Barron et al., 2016). They are often presented in the media as taking advantage of a system of universal rights guaranteed by the French state to its citizens. [2] In the mid-1990s – alongside the restrictions on immigration and legal status introduced by the *Pasqua* laws and responding to the political tension generated by high unemployment figures – the government sought to crack down on industries using high levels of informal and undocumented immigrant labour. The Ministry of Labour concentrated on the garment industry, the construction industry, janitorial services and restaurants (Iskander 2007). Given the hostile context facing undocumented workers during the early 1990s and the prospect of being unemployed, undocumented and without legal residency papers, it is unsurprising that these workers, who had often lived and worked in France for decades in some cases, began to protest as a strategy for survival.

THE ORIGINS OF THE *SANS PAPIERS* SOCIAL MOVEMENT

The *sans papiers* movement began in 1996 when a group of mainly undocumented Malian immigrants occupied the St Ambroise Church in northern Paris. In the context of the recent introduction of the anti-immigrant *Pasqua* laws mentioned above, a growing number of immigrants had seen their multiple administrative appeals for legal work and residence permits rejected and fell into undocumented status. The group, all based in the same low-income housing complex in a suburb of Paris, was mainly made up of single men who had come to France in search of work and political refugees and families with French-born children who had been in the country for many years. The group occupied the church and refused to leave, attracting press and media attention, which brought in more undocumented protesters hoping for regularisation as an outcome of the protests. Five days after the *sans papiers* took over the church, the government forcibly evicted them from the space and made a number of arrests. The number of protesters increased, and they moved to occupying different public spaces, but eventually further arrests were made, and fifty-seven Malian immigrants detained during the protest were deported back to their country of origin.

The peak of this phase of the movement happened in mid-June 1996, when undocumented immigrant protesters occupied the St Barnard Church in the north of Paris. After two weeks of occupying the church they began a hunger strike – a tactic used by immigrant workers against restrictive immigration measures in 1973, 1980 and 1992, which at these times resulted in changes to immigration policy and amnesty programmes. The hunger strikes at St Barnard provoked solidarity protests from the public and left-of-centre political parties and trade unions, and a coalition of renowned writers and performers all urged the government to negotiate with the immigrants. The centre-right government held firm, and on the forty-ninth day of the protesters' hunger strike, a police force of 1,500 was sent in to the church to round up the three hundred immigrants, some of who were eventually deported back to their country of origin. The brutality of the action provoked street protests and public outrage and arguably resulted in the Socialist Party's electoral victory against the Right later in the year. The St Bernard occupation inspired a number of copycat actions in cities throughout France, where undocumented immigrants made public demands for residence and work permits, and if these failed, they occupied a public space, usually a church, and went on hunger strike. This wave of immigrant protests continued for the next four years and eventually forced the hand of the government to grant legal status to around 150,000 undocumented immigrants, or around one-third of the estimated total population of undocumented immigrants at the time in France (see Iskander 2007 for further analysis on this phase of the movement).

FROM SOCIAL MOVEMENT PROTESTS TO LABOUR PROTESTS

From the mid-2000s the *sans papiers* movement began to develop into workplace strikes and actions targeting employers. This development occurred in a legislative context that allowed only limited forms of economic immigration. Legislation introduced in 2006 reinstated 'salaried' residency cards for immigrants hired on permanent or long-term contracts. Under this same legislation, 'temporary worker' cards were also to be issued to immigrants hired on short-term contracts. In 2007 legislation was introduced on the control of immigration, integration and asylum, which opened up the possibility for employers to proceed to the regularisation of an undocumented worker on the basis of the worker having an employment contract and on condition that the job was included on the national shortage occupation list.

From 2006 to 2010, several thousand undocumented workers went on strike with the support of the trade unions (CGT, CFDT, Solidarity, CNT, FSU and UNSA) and associations defending the rights of immigrants (Droits devant!!, le Réseau éducation sans frontiers [RESF], Femmes Égalité, la Cimade, Autremonde and la Ligue des droits de l'homme). The majority of these undocumented workers were African and working in the hotel-catering, cleaning and building sectors. Below we summarise the main stages of this movement, drawing on interviews with key actors in the strikes and in organising the *sans papiers*, as well as on the work of researchers who have closely studied the movement (ASPLAN 2010; Barron et al. 2011; Veron 2010).

The first of these mobilisations started in 2006 when a group of undocumented workers from a small industrial laundry company in Massy (in the south of the Ile de France region) turned to the CGT regional office for help. They were threatened with dismissal and had gone out on strike. The trade union appointed several of its representatives to assist these workers. It turned out that their employment rights could not be recognised without them being regularised. Thus their regularisation became the key demand of the strike. Their regularisation was obtained within a few weeks on the basis of residency certificates; no work documents were requested by the authorities at this point.

The following year, in June 2007, a similar strike was launched in the restaurant chain Buffalo Grill. The prefecture (the local governor) adopted a different solution this time by regularising only those employees who were being kept on by the company. Only twenty workers out of the sixty-three strikers were regularised, through residency permits with rights to a 'private and family life',[3] but with no mention of their status as workers. A third strike broke out on the thirteenth of February 2008 at the restaurant La Grande Armée, near the Arc de Triomphe in Paris. Nine undocumented chefs were demanding regularisation. Seven chefs were regularised after one week, and the two others a few months later. Although chefs are not on the shortage occupation list decided by the government, the residency cards they received for the first time in this series of strikes mentioned the status of 'worker'.

In the following months hundreds of undocumented workers contacted the CGT. Alongside the association Droits devant!!, the CGT organised a well-supported day of action in April 2008. That day, three hundred undocumented workers from sixteen companies went on strike. They were joined by more than a thousand additional undocumented workers in the weeks that followed. In total, some sixty companies in the Paris region were affected by these strikes. At this stage, the undocumented workers who participated in these actions were those who were the least precarious of the undocumented workers' movement: they were all declared full-time permanent employees by their employers, paid social security contributions and were hired directly by the company that they worked for. Their situation with regard to the regularisation criteria at that time was indisputable and gave credibility to the movement. The more precarious undocumented workers, the most vulnerable and certainly the most numerous still remained in the shadows.

Yet, on 2 May 2008, members of the Coordination parisienne des collectifs de sans-papiers (CSP75), who were mostly precarious undocumented workers not meeting the criteria for regularisation, decided to occupy the Bourse du travail, making the demand that the CGT also take into account their cases for regularisation and take them to the prefecture of Paris.

Mobilisations accelerated during the second half of 2008. Nearly 2,000 undocumented workers went on strike, while 1,500 others were having their regularisation files processed by the CGT. The CGT gradually became the key intermediary in the process for regularisation of undocumented workers. Alongside the strikes there were numerous workplace occupations including restaurants, company headquarters and the headquarters of the cleaning company employers' organisation (Maison de la propreté, Villejuif). The main demands of these actions were to require employers to complete two official forms as part of the regularisation file. The first of these forms attests their commitment to pay the *Anaem* tax, which is paid by employers in France when employing foreign workers. The second form (the *Cerfa*) sets out the terms of the proposed employment contract. Employers are also required to sign a certificate for undocumented workers who have worked in the company under one or more fake identities – those using forged documents. This is to certify that the employee in question corresponds to the person on the payroll and in the employment contract.

At the end of the strike wave in 2008, around two thousand regularisations of undocumented workers were obtained. However, these regularisations still concerned mainly those whose situations were the least precarious. The rest—temporary workers, fixed-term workers and agency workers—remained largely excluded from the successes of the movement.

The end of 2008 was marked by a tightening of European migration policy. In October 2008, the Directive RETOUR and the European Pact on Immigration changed the conditions for detaining foreigners and the conditions for the return of foreigners to their country of origin. There were strong reactions from associations working in this area, and they organised a countersummit in Vichy in November 2008 in response to a European summit of interior and immigration ministers. Many demonstrators were stopped along the way, and the demonstration organised in Vichy was violently repressed.

A few months later, however, a national day of action was organised by a number of associations to protest the increased penalties in Article L622-1 of the legislation on the rights of entry and stay of foreigners (CESEDA). This article, a first version of which was introduced under the Daladier government in 1938, states that 'anyone who, through direct or indirect assistance, has facilitated or attempted to facilitate the entry, movement or residence of an alien in France will be punished with ten years' imprisonment'. Important rallies took place in front of the courthouses, with one primary motto: *La Solidarité n'est pas un délit!* (Solidarity is not a crime!).

In July 2009, the CSP75, mentioned above, was expelled from the Bourse du Travail in Paris, which had been occupied for fourteen months. They moved to a building in the eighteenth arrondissement of Paris and founded the Ministry of the Regularisation of all the undocumented (le Ministère de la Régularisation de tous les sans papiers). During this period, the 'Labour union/non-status' work group was set up, bringing together trade union representatives and undocumented workers. One of its main achievements was the publication of a four-page brochure stating the list of workers' rights and the existing criteria for regularisation (Carrère 2009).

A second wave of major strikes took place at the end of 2009, with the aim of obtaining standardised criteria for regularisation to cover the diversity of employment situations of all undocumented workers. Around 1,200 people went on strike, mainly employees of small and medium-sized enterprises, temporary workers or informal workers. They were supported by a group of trade unions and associations known as the groupe des Onze (group of eleven), which consisted of the trade unions CGT, CFDT, FSU, Solidaires and UNSA and the associations Droits devant!!, the RESF, Femmes Égalité, la Cimade, Autremonde and la Ligue des droits de l'homme.

Taking advantage of the highly dispersed picket lines and the precarity of the strikers' employment status, the employers challenged the workplace occupations more systematically and radically than previously. They successfully challenged the strikes in the courts in a large number of cases, including the case of temporary workers who had declared they were on strike while not working on any temporary contracts. Thus, running parallel to a legal battle around the definition of a 'striker', the groupe des Onze decided to give strike cards to protect undocumented workers in the case of any police controls, and in case they were dismissed by their employer. These numbered strike cards included the logo of the CGT, the name and surname of the worker, possibly his or her alias (the identity under which he or she was working), phone number, signature and photograph, as well as the name, the address and sector of his or her employer and finally the name of the person responsible for his or her picket line. This information was reproduced in two parts, with one being handed over to the striker, while the other was kept at the headquarters of the CGT in Montreuil, which regularly submitted updated lists of strikers to the Ministry of Labour.

During 2009, the CGT counted nearly 7,000 strikers, and around 1,500 undocumented workers were regularised. In April 2010, a decision by the Paris Court of Appeal finally recognised that temporary workers should be considered on strike by recognising that they were 'regularly employed', in the case of those workers who carried out regular contracts for the same agency.

The CGT continued its action while the CSP75 organised a march from Paris to Nice for undocumented workers in May 2010. At the end of 2010, thousands more workers were regularised, from a decision made by the Ministry of Interior benefiting a large number of the strikers. Finally, in May 2011, a national day of action against racism and migration policy, and for the regularisation of the undocumented, was organised by the collective D'ailleurs nous sommes d'ici!, the CGT, left-wing parties and the Ligue des droits de l'homme. Demonstrations took place in about twenty cities, with the demonstration in Paris bringing together around eight thousand people.

At the end of these strikes at least 1,500 undocumented workers joined the CGT (Meardi 2013), and some became leaders. Trade union mobilisation and lobbying eventually led to two new laws (*circulaires*) in 2010 and 2012, clarifying the processes and establishing criteria for the regularisation of undocumented workers. The *circulaires* allowed a link to be established between the worker's real identity and his or her fake identity in order to reassign rights to the former. They also designated the number of pay slips that were needed, depending on the length of time in the country. This legislation was a significant win for the *sans papiers* movement, and the shift from community-based social movement to a labour protest movement gave them access to institutional power resources through the trade union movement.

EMBEDDING THE *SANS PAPIERS* CAUSE IN UNION ACTION AND ORGANISATION

The production of the *circulaires* in 2010 and 2012 facilitating the regularisation of undocumented workers established a new phase in the organisation and representation of undocumented workers in the CGT. In order to guarantee the application of the *circulaires*, the CGT made informal links with undocumented workers to begin the regularisation process and then opened a weekly surgery (*permanence*) in September 2014. Beyond assisting the undocumented workers in their regularisation process, the objective for the CGT has been to identify any circumvention of labour law by employers and to combat social dumping. Strike movements have continued in parallel with this legal activity. The leader of the *permanence* explained:

> Once we had won the criteria in 2010 and the *circulaire* on 28 November 2012, we had to of course continue to fight to win better. But at the same time, the criteria in the *circulaire* had to be applied. There was considerable pressure from undocumented employees to determine whether the criteria could be applied to their case. From the end of 2012 to 2014, workers were already being received, but nothing was organised. Now, there were many people, people were received as they presented themselves. I felt that we had to organise something, with the difficulty that we do not want to turn into a service industry. We are more in the conquest of new rights than in the enforcement of rights. It is an important political subject, it is a debate. I think one does not prevent the other. What is done corresponds somewhat to the role of the workplace representatives, a concrete response to concrete needs. I think you cannot just tell people 'come to the demons'.

For the CGT, the main issue beyond regularisation is advancing the ideas of a free movement of people not subject to the diktats of the market and respecting national and international labour standards. According to the confederation, the *sans papiers* case reveals situations and practices that can only last if they are hidden. An important part of trade union action is therefore dedicated to shedding light on these practices of social dumping by employers and trafficking of papers. Alongside mobilisation and servicing the *sans papiers*, trade union officers are also dedicating a lot of time sharing key information and advising state institutions.

> We are working with the Ministry of Labour and the Interior to improve the labour market. It is not a question of blaming irregular workers but of regularising their situation. At our last meeting with the Ministry of Labour, I brought in 5 files of people whose employers refused to draw up pay slips. We worked on the criteria for their regularisation. The five were finally regularised, but above all the examination of these cases made it possible to refine the criteria and the requests for proofs. We have also asked that the presumption of 6 months of work which is applied by labour inspectors for the payment of URSAFF[4] contributions when they discover an unregistered worker is also used to establish the corresponding number of pay slips. (CGT trade union official responsible for the *sans papiers*)

This political approach that labour should be treated like a valued contribution to society instead of being used as a commodity is not new in itself, but it gives the *sans papiers* fight a universal dimension. By responding to the demands of the most vulnerable and excluded people, the CGT is addressing the core of the labour exploitation system in a capitalist economy, based on the minimisation of labour costs.

Undocumented workers who hear about the *permanence* – usually through word of mouth – and are looking for regularisation go to CGT headquarters in Montreuil, where the surgery takes place and where they can establish contact with the organisation. The undocumented workers are asked to become members at the initial meeting. For the CGT, joining the trade union means these workers are not only members but also potential activists. As members they are regularly invited to specific and general initiatives and are also encouraged to help with the surgery. One of the main obstacles to retaining undocumented members is the particularly high level of occupational and geographical mobility. As a consequence, the CGT has considered creating a new section for these workers, where they would remain until they become established in a particular company or economic sector (Contrepois 2016). In March 2016, the temporarily established Migrant Union directly affiliated to the confederation had around one thousand fee-paying members, with a further five thousand supporters.

During the time of our research, around seventy to eighty *sans papiers* attended the *permanence* each week. The treatment of regularisation cases was organised in several stages. The first step was very brief, with the intention of establishing contact with the worker. The second step, which could mean several further appointments at the *permanence*, was aimed at putting together the regularisation file for the worker. The third step was the monitoring of the situation towards regularisation of the worker. The workers are asked to become members of the CGT systematically at the first stage, which then opens up the support for the second and third stages. The majority of workers accept becoming members, and the contributions requested vary between three and ten euros depending on individual resources and circumstances. In 2016, the CGT had approximately six thousand members among the undocumented workers, whom it invited regularly to its initiatives by text message. As a result of this involvement and the different stages of dealing with their case, many undocumented workers became more familiar with the organisation, and some became activists as part of the team to help service and organise the *sans papiers*.

The physical location of the *permanence* for the undocumented workers took place in the CGT headquarters in part of the main hall, in a semi-enclosed space. Appointments were sent out by text message to workers who had previously filled out an application form. There were around twenty individuals seen by members of the CGT team per hour. Two CGT activists, some who were *sans papiers* themselves, were seated at a table in the hall to take the appointments. For one of the *permanence*, we observed that one of the activists spoke English and Bambara in addition to French.

The first contact with the union is extremely brief and relatively standardised. It is essentially a question of verifying identity cards, the date of arrival in France, the immigration status (asylum application or other), employment status, occupation and the names of the employers, the existence of pay slips and any documents that may prove useful in the process of regularisation. A second appointment is then given to these workers to pick up their CGT membership card and a letter indicating that the regularisation file is being processed by the CGT. The worker can then show these documents to the police in case of arrest and to his or her employer to show that the worker is in the process of applying for authorisation to work with the *prefecture* (the local governor).

Interviews with CGT activists and undocumented workers revealed that the interaction between the undocumented workers and the activists was relatively limited due to a number of factors: a short appointment time, the undocumented worker's lack of knowledge of the French system, and above all a linguistic barrier that can be relatively significant in the case of non-French-speaking workers. One of the Bangladeshi workers at the surgery said, 'They asked me only my name, my nationality and how long I have been in France. They told me they would call me if there was a meeting. I did not ask too many questions, there were a lot of people waiting'. One of the people in charge of the CGT reception confirmed:

> Many of them manage in French in terms of general communication, but as soon as certain questions arise, they do not understand too much. The Malians speak mainly Bambara, which is a language of traders that is found in much of Africa. Some also speak Soninke, but they can understand the Bambara. As for the Bangladeshi people, those who have just arrived do not understand French at all, so always speak to them in English. Some who are here for a long time and who may have done some courses know how to say little things in French. But otherwise, they cannot understand, especially when there are complex things in their file. You have to speak to them in English. Sometimes they do not understand French or English, and there is an interpreter among them who can speak to them in their local language.

In light of the vulnerable circumstances of undocumented workers, membership of the CGT is on the whole a pragmatic solution to gaining regularisation rather than a gesture of support for the union. One of our female interviewees explained, 'It's better than going to a lawyer because the lawyer is expensive – 1000 euros – and does not actually handle your file. Already, it's hard to live in France and earn money. You do not have to pay lawyers. At the CGT, the contribution is 5 or 10 euros depending on your case and they actually deal with your file'. However, the progressive integration of this young woman in the organisation, for example, shows a possible evolution of the meaning given to membership as files are processed.

At the end of the first appointment, the files are processed by the activists of the *permanence*. Workers who already or nearly fulfil the conditions for regularisation are identified and called for a series of individual interviews so that their regularisation file can be prepared. At this stage, therefore, it appears that most of the *permanence* focuses on the *least* vulnerable of the undocumented workers, those who have been able to obtain a regular job enabling them to obtain a sufficient number of payslips to obtain a work permit.

However, the arrival of a large number of Bangladeshi workers who have been working in the labour market for several years and who are unable to produce the required pay slips has raised the question of a specific action to defend the rights of workers in the 'itinerant' trade. No specific decisions had yet been taken at the time of the research.

The situations presented by the workers raise extremely complex legal problems due to the clandestine nature of these workers: the use of names that can change over time, the absence of a pay slip or fake pay slips, the companies where people have worked, with a multiplicity of intermediaries blurring the identity of the employer.

The case of one young worker who came to the *permanence* illustrates the difficulties: He stated that he worked for a building company to mount scaffolding. He did not know his employer and explained that he was brought to work in France by someone from his own country. He went to his interlocutor, of whom he knew almost nothing, to ask for his pay slips. The interlocutor provided him with pay slips and continued to pay him in cash. On examining his file during the *permanence*, it appeared that these pay slips had the name of a cleaning company in the hotel sector, not in the building sector, which meant the pay slips were forged.

The kinds of situations being brought to the CGT were often extremely complex and difficult to follow because of the fragmented nature of the undocumented workers' transitions. Three main factors contribute to this fragmentation: ignorance of the legal requirements for regularisation, the mental state that undocumented workers are most often found in after years of mistreatment by employers and the linguistic barrier. Faced with these obstacles, activists who are not specifically trained to take charge of these groups of workers mobilise all their resources to put together acceptable files for the *prefecture*. When the language barrier is too much, interpreters are called in to help.

The surgery has been an important space for the integration of undocumented immigrant workers within the CGT. One of them evokes his journey:

> I participated in several strike movements with the CGT since 2009, I was working for a temporary agency. I assisted the movement on the basis of my knowledge of the law and defended my comrades in court. It was with the arrival of the Bangladeshi workers that the head of the permanence asked me to be part of the group. They had a hard time understanding this population because they do not understand French, they speak English. I volunteered because I speak English. Also, I thought that having an experience as an undocumented striker could be of interest to those in charge of the *permanence*. I try to accommodate the Bangladeshis as I can explain to them correctly.

It was mainly because of their language skills and their status as go-betweens with the host communities that these workers were called upon to take on increasing responsibilities within the organisation. At the time of the research, several undocumented activists were working for the CGT reception, processing of files and organisation of strike movements.

Once they have been regularised, the workers are better able to integrate into French society. The CGT follows them through their efforts to enforce their rights as employees and until they are better integrated into the trade union. Further research is needed to follow up on the effectiveness of the integration of these undocumented workers in the trade union (taking up representative and executive positions, for example), but from the continuing campaigns and mobilisations by the CGT to support undocumented immigrants we can argue that there has been a creation of a more formalised space for action for these workers in recent times.

DISCUSSION

In this chapter we explored to what extent the *sans papiers* movement is something new and sustainable in the French social movement landscape. We examine how the actions of the CGT and the *sans papiers* went beyond questions of survival and towards the development of a space for resistance for the regularisation and improvement of living and working lives of undocumented immigrants. The majority of undocumented immigrants from our research had come to France to escape poor economic conditions and/or dangerous political contexts. They had often been in France for decades, and up until recently they had been able to find work either using a fake identity or with employers willing to take them on without papers. The workers' arrival in France was determined by several 'pull factors' like ease of access, social welfare, linguistic proximity, characteristics of the labour market, existing networks and more. Migration is thus in itself a survival strategy for these workers, and for a long time the regularisation of their situation was not necessarily a pressing issue, as long as they could find work.

With the hardening of immigration laws and employers being increasingly subject to sanctions when employing irregular workers, undocumented immigrants' situations have deteriorated progressively since the 1990s and then very rapidly since 2010. Those who had strong networks, like the Chinese, and a command of the French language, like North Africans, were still able to access the labour market. However, they were subject to increasing exploitation and strong pressures from mafias and gangs.[5]

For some immigrant groups – like Bangladeshis, for example – who have more recently migrated to seek refugee status, and who have not had preexisting networks in France, the situation is even more complicated, as they are virtually unable to access the labour market. These differing but equally precarious situations produced enormous distress among the different populations of undocumented workers, who saw their strategies for survival suddenly collapsing. This has been the trigger in many cases for a collective response, either by contacting trade unions directly or by responding to a call to strike. The immigrants' principal demand was to regularise their situation so they could access the labour market officially.

On the trade union side, we noticed that universalism remained the key principle to which French trade unions continued to adhere when dealing with immigrants' rights. Universalism is the assumption that all workers are confronted by the same capitalistic exploitation irrespective of cultural differences and variety of capitalism (Chibber 2013). French trade unionism is based on a 'republican egalitarianist model' of integration, built on the principles of the 1789 Revolution, which is mainly assimilationist and rejects any form of distinction based on ethno-racial elements in the name of national unity (Dechaux 1991; Bertossi 2007; Bertossi and Duyvendakb 2012). In contrast to the Anglo-American model, in which taking provisions to accommodate 'difference' – whether of sexuality, religion or disability – is tolerated or even prized, 'accommodating difference' in France is seen as a form of sectarianism and a threat to the republic. Significantly, the word *immigrant* is virtually absent from the trade unions' official vocabulary, which only acknowledges differences between 'workers' in terms of their status – 'precarious workers', 'posted workers', 'agency workers', 'permanent workers' – or in terms of their occupation – 'railwayworkers', 'metalworkers', 'teachers' and more (Contrepois 2017b). Immigration policies are basically regarded as consequences of capitalist exploitation, and trade unions are clearly reluctant to acquiesce on them, focusing only on the aspects that weaken workers' positions in the labour market. If and when specific actions are envisaged, these are aimed above all at combatting the various forms of exploitation at work. Irregular situations, precarious contracts and discriminatory situations are all perceived as elements in the same mechanism that instigates competition between workers in order to lower labour costs. They are resisted as processes that could happen to any worker in a capitalist labour market. The refusal to consider the intrinsic characteristics of the most exploited – their culture, religion, language or beliefs – is a rejection of any differential treatment, which is perceived as potentially detrimental to human rights.

There is a double challenge for trade unions acting as a force for integration for socially excluded workers. First, immigrant and minority workers tend to work either on the margins or not at all, which means that trade unions find it difficult to access and represent them. Secondly, the denial of ethnic and racial differences means that structural and institutional forms of discrimination and exclusion are ignored or not explicitly addressed, which can easily lead to a lack of engagement with the trade union movement on the part of workers who feel they have to suppress their core identities. The CGT have had to reflect on whether there needs to be some form of response and/or organisation of the *sans papiers* based on the more specific issues that they face in the labour market and in society more generally.

We argue that the better integration of the *sans papiers* within the structures and actions of the CGT demonstrates a shift in trade union 'logics of actions' (Connolly et al. 2014) – namely, the basic drives around which union discourse and policies are built in trade unions – and leads to a questioning of the mainly assimilationist model of trade unionism. Yet the representation of undocumented workers has posed a challenge for the confederation mainly around issues connected with cultural and institutional adaptation towards this group of workers. More specifically, French trade unions have had to confront fundamental features of their identity. For trade unions, the inclusion of undocumented workers' actions in their strategy has necessitated adaptation mainly in three areas: strategy, structures of the organisation and cross-cultural communication.

Regarding strategy, first, the treatment of undocumented workers has been the subject of numerous debates within the CGT, notably concerning the nature and extent of trade union action, but also the integration of these workers into the organisation's structures. Concerning the nature and scope of trade union action, the debate between the proponents of a purely industrial unionism and those of a more pragmatic trade unionism are not hesitating to engage in the field of service to the members where this can make effective the implementation of the rights obtained.

The second feature of identity is the dual representation structure, where members are attached by occupation to their industry federation through their local union branch and by location through a regional interprofessional structure. This type of structure, adopted at a time when occupational and regional affiliation played a key role in the formation of militant groups, has strongly influenced the integration of new members up until recently. The undocumented workers represent a highly mobile workforce, both geographically and occupationally. They constitute, par excellence, a good part of the contingent of precarious labour that trade union organisations struggle to integrate into their ranks.

Then, regarding structures, it soon appeared that it was a challenge to organise undocumented workers within the existing 'syndicats' as their extreme precariousness meant that not only were they changing occupations regularly, but they were also very geographically mobile. Therefore, the only way to organise them appeared to be through national organisations. In the CGT, up until the 2016 national congress, the *syndicat national* was called *le syndicat des travailleurs migrants*. It was led by a French national trade union officer in charge of immigrant workers and clandestine work.

As far as the integration of these workers into the structures of the organisation is concerned, the case of the *sans papiers* reactivates the numerous debates that may have taken place during the history of trade unionism on the appropriateness of specific organisations and the dangers of ghettoisation it presents. The first is the principle of *laïcité* (secularism), which presupposes the separation of the state and religious organisations and the neutrality of the state.[6] The principle is held by most of the trade union confederations from their foundation – apart from the Confédération Française des Travailleurs Chrétiens (CFTC). The French notion of *laïcité*, dating back to the Revolution, actively blocks religious interference in affairs of state and public manifestations of religious identity in public spaces, including workplaces. From this, certain religious expressions within the *sans papiers* movement (particularly prayers) appeared to be problematic in the eyes of the French activists who were leading the movement.

Finally, cross-cultural communication is a more difficult aspect as French trade unions proved to have difficulties integrating newly arrived immigrants, for reasons linked to language and culture, as seen above. The massive movement of *sans papiers* meant that trade union officers had to put in place quick solutions in order to overcome language barriers in the first instance. A number of undocumented workers thus became translators to help organise their fellow workers and were given union responsibilities. This empowerment of a few gave undocumented workers a way to make their voices heard within the union.

Two of the main issues, though, are the role played by the interpreter/leader – to what extent his discourse reflects the collective position of his fellow workers – and the management of religious expression within trade union ranks. Both of these issues need further research. Our assumption is that adjustments were made which questioned the assimilationist culture and encouraged greater internal democracy. Another consequence would be an evolution of the logic of action (Connolly et al. 2014). French trade union identity has traditionally been based on representing workers' class interests and forwarding their social rights. However, in representing immigrant workers, particularly undocumented immigrants, the unions have been confronted with sets of more specific interests that challenge traditional logics of actions.

The successes of the *sans papiers* campaign show that trade unions can organise in sectors with high concentrations of immigrants and minority workers and can demand labour rights for those working and living on the margins of society. By offering a service to undocumented workers, in spite of its service-based appearance, the union aimed to identify and call out employer practices and force them to apply regulations. The broader political goal was to fight 'illegal' work and prevent social dumping and to encourage self-organising and future mobilisations of *sans papiers* workers. The union also hopes for the greater integration and involvement of the *sans papiers* within the wider union. Whether trade unions are able to build and sustain this kind of solidarity and action and whether the *sans papiers* 'find a home' within the trade union remain key challenges, but they are important ones in such uncertain times.

NOTES

1. Les travailleurs immigrés en France en 1971, documentaire audiovisuel du 23 décembre 1971, Fiche INA n°01064. http://fresques.ina.fr/jalons/fiche-media/InaEdu01064/les-travailleurs-immigres-en-france-en-1971.html.

2. http://www.lefigaro.fr/actualite-france/2017/03/29/01016-20170329ARTFIG00292-faux-papiers-16852-documents-contrefaits-saisis-en-un-an-par-la-police-aux-frontieres.php.

3. https://www.service-public.fr/particuliers/vosdroits/F2209.
4. French body managing social security payment and funds.
5. https://blogs.mediapart.fr/terrains-de-luttes/blog/031114/du-travail-dissimule-la-traite-d-etres-humains; http://www.liberation.fr/france/2017/01/08/sans-papiers-a-visages-decouverts _1540006.
6. http://www.gouvernement.fr/qu-est-ce-que-la-laicite. Secularism is based on three principles and values: the freedom of conscience and the freedom to manifest one's convictions within the limits of respect for public order, the separation of public institutions and religious organisations, and the equality of all before the law, whatever their beliefs or convictions. Secularism guarantees believers and nonbelievers the same right to freedom of expression of their convictions. It ensures the right to have or not to have a religion, to change or not to have any more. It guarantees the free exercise of cults and freedom of religion, but also freedom from religion: no one can be compelled to respect religious dogmas or prescriptions. Secularism presupposes the separation of the state and religious organisations. From this separation is deduced the neutrality of the state, territorial collectivities and public services, not of its users.

BIBLIOGRAPHY

ASPLAN. 2010. 'La grève des sans-papiers au miroir de la précarité'. *Plein droit* 2010/1 (84): 33–36. DOI 10.3917/pld.084.0033.

Barron, Pierre, Anne Bory, Sébastien Chauvin, Nicolas Jounin and Lucie Tourette. 2014. '68. Les grèves de travailleurs sans papiers (2006–2010)'. In *Histoire des mouvements sociaux en France: De 1814 à nos jours*, edited by Michel Pigenet and Danielle Tartakowsky. Paris: La Découverte.

Barron, Pierre, Anne Bory, Sébastien Chauvin, Nicolas Jounin and Lucie Tourette. 2016. 'State Categories and Labour Protest: Migrant Workers and the Fight for Legal Status in France'. *Work, Employment and Society* 30(4): 631–48.

Barron, Pierre, Anne Bory, Lucie Tourette, Sébastien Chauvin and Nicolas Jounin. 2011. *On bosse ici, on reste ici! La grève des sans-papiers, une aventure inédite*. Paris: La découverte.

Bertossi, Christophe. 2007. 'French and British Models of Integration. Public Philosophies, Policies and State Institutions'. Working Paper No. 46, University of Oxford.

Bertossi, Christophe, and Jan Willem Duyvendakb. 2012. 'National Models of Immigrant Integration: The Costs for Comparative Research'. *Comparative European Politics* 10(3): 237–47.

Bussat, Virginie, and Philippe Archias. 2013. *Fight against Racism and Discriminations: The French Political, Economic and Social Context (2003–2012), National Report for the European Research Project*. Project CRAW – Challenging Racism at Work: Case Studies. Paris: Association Travail Emploi Europe Société (ASTREES).

Carrère, Violaine. 2009. 'Derrière le sans-papiers on découvre le travailleur'. *Plein droit* 80(1): 27–31.

Chibber, Vivek. 2013. *Postcolonial Theory and the Specter of of Capital*. New York: Verso.

Connolly, Heather, and Sylvie Contrepois. 2016. 'British and French Trade Unions' Efforts to Integrate Undocumented Migrants'. 10th International Labour and Employment Relations Association, European Regional Congress. Milan, Italy, 8–10 September 2016.

Connolly, Heather, Stefania Marino and Miguel Martinez Lucio. 2014. 'Trade Union Renewal and the Challenges of Representation: Strategies towards Migrant and Ethnic Minority Workers in the Netherlands, Spain and the United Kingdom'. *European Journal of Industrial Relations* 20(1): 5–20.

Contrepois, Sylvie. 2016. *Language Diversity in France, Practices and Perspectives. Case Studies*. IR-MultiLing Project Report for the European Commission, DG Employment and Social Affairs, London Metropolitan University.

Contrepois, Sylvie. 2017a. *Industrial Relations in Multilingual Environments at Work, a Six Countries Comparative Study*. IR-MultiLing Project Comparative Report for the European Commission, DG Employment and Social Affairs, London Metropolitan University.

Contrepois, Sylvie. 2017b. 'France, the Assimilationist Model Called into Question'. In *Trade Unions and Migrants Workers, New Contexts and Challenges in Europe*, edited by Stefania Marino, Judith Roosblad and Rinus Penninx, 138–57. Cheltenham: Edward Elgar.

Dechauffour, Laetitia. 2014. 'The Role of French Unions in the Civic Integration of French Workers'. Accessed 5 April 2016. https://www.ilr.cornell.edu/mobilizing-against-inequality/post/role-french-unions-civic-integration-immigrant-workers.

Dechaux, Jean-Hugues. 1991. 'Les immigrés et le monde du travail: Un nouvel âge de l'immigration?' *Observations et diagnostics économiques: Revue de l'OFCE* (36): 85–116.

Denis, Jean-Michel. 2009. 'Dans le nettoyage industriel, on ne fait pas du syndicalisme comme chez Renault!' *Politix* 2009/1 (85): 105–26.

Freedman, Jane. 2008. 'The French "Sans-Papiers" Movement: An Unfinished Struggle'. In *Migration and Activism in Europe since 1945. Europe in Transition*, edited by Wendy Pojmann, 81–96. The NYU European Studies Series. New York: Palgrave Macmillan.

Iskander, Natasha. 2007. 'Informal Work and Protest: Undocumented Activism in France, 1996–2000'. *British Journal of Industrial Relations* 45(2): 309–34.

Jounin, Nicolas. 2014. 'Aux origines des "travailleurs sans papiers". Les spécificités d'un groupe au service d'une identification généraliste'. *Revue européenne des migrations internationales* 3(1): 131–52.

Meardi, Guglielmo. 2013. 'Unions between National Politics and Transnational Migration: A Comparison of Germany, UK and France'. Society for the Advancement of Socio-Economics (SASE) Annual Meeting. Milan, Italy, 27–29 June 2013.

Mouriaux, René, and Catherine Wihtol De Wenden. 1987. 'Syndicalisme français et islam'. *Revue française de science politique* 37ᵉ année (6): 794–819.

Veron, Daniel. 2010. 'Sans-papiers: d'un quotidien tactique à l'action collective'. *Variations*. 13/14. Accessed 30 September 2016. http://variations.revues.org/182.

Chapter Six

Beyond Water, Beyond Folk Politics?

Lessons from Greece for an Irish
Socialist Governmentality

Nicholas Kiersey

The cycle of Occupy Wall Street protests of 2011 and 2012 arguably constitutes the high-water mark of left-horizontalist strategy in recent decades. Triggered by the collapsing credibility of neoliberal economic management, the emergence of new communications technologies, but also arguably by a change in popular consciousness about the possibilities within contemporary politics (Mason 2012), the years following the 2008 financial crisis saw unprecedented numbers of young people taking to the streets around the world. While not necessarily identifying with the formal intellectual history and traditions of anarchism, their actions nevertheless suggested an affinity for radically democratic anarchist values and practices. They were demanding a better future but, importantly, under the banner of 'the 99%', they intended to achieve this goal via *prefigurative* means – that is, via a self-directed and radically inclusive mobilisation of the mass of ordinary, common people (Graeber 2009; Day 2005).

The protests were not without controversy, however. A number of sympathetic voices on the Left expressed concerns about the libertarian undertones of the movements (Dean 2012a; Henwood 2011). To an extent, these criticisms evoked older debates between Marxism and anarchism (Kiersey and Vrasti 2016). On the one hand, Marxists worried that contemporary anarchism harbored a naive and unquestioning nostalgia for folk politics, wherein everyday people are imagined as 'the locus of the small-scale, the authentic, the traditional and the natural' (Srnicek and Williams 2015). Thus, these critics warned, the movements appeared to prioritize a politics of 'meeting the people where they're at', focusing on tactical expressions of already existing common sense, as opposed to the strategic work of changing consciousness and building power. This substitution of tactics for strategy, the critics claimed, undermined the potential institutional depth of the movements, defanging them in the face of complex global challenges, like neoliberal financialisation or global warming. On the other hand, those of a more anarchist persuasion expressed suspicion of a return to some sort of sanitized history of vertically integrated Marxist praxis, and suggested the debate might better be reframed in terms of a search for common ground and the possibilities for *convergence* between the two traditions (Prichard and Worth 2016).

This chapter explores these debates in the context of recent developments in Irish politics and the cycle of social movement activity that emerged in 2014 as a response to government plans for privatisation of the public water system. It is often remarked that 'the Irish don't protest' (Cox 2013; Mercille 2013; F. O'Connor 2017), and it is indeed the case that austerity has proceeded in Ireland without much fuss; in the 2008–2013 period, as social movements were 'kicking off' (Mason 2012) in Greece, Spain and a host of other countries, the response of the Irish movements was weak enough that Greek anti-austerity protesters felt justified in chanting, 'We are not Ireland, we will resist' (Finn 2011, 37). However, with the onset of economic recovery in 2013, a new passion for protest appeared to be waking in the country (Adshead 2017, 7). Indeed, 2014 saw a spate of seemingly spontaneous, neighborhood-level expressions of resistance to the installation of household water meters. While these dispersed expressions lacked a coherent national force, they were of a scale beyond anything that could have been contrived by the organized Left. Later that year, however, a number of unions and other leftist political organisations combined resources in an attempt to give these disparate expressions an institutional integrity. 'Right2Water', the result of this effort, called a national day of action for October 11, 2014, where as many as eighty thousand people showed up at a number of events around the country. Next, on December 9, a march in Dublin drew one hundred thousand people, more than 2 per cent of the Republic's 4.5 million population (all figures from O'Connell 2015). Similar protests took place throughout 2015 and arguably played a very significant role in the lead-up to the 2016 election.

As the chapter will explore, however, the Irish Left has largely failed in the task of converting these nascent energies of resistance and protest into an effective counterpower to financialized global capitalism. Arguably, one of the main reasons for this failure is the persistence of a naive faith in folk politics among the movements and a belief in the redemptive potential of an authentically expressed Irish people. Right2Water frequently drew on the ambiguous signifier of the Irish as a 'risen people', a notion that widened the discursive frame of the struggle against austerity to encompass a much longer-running story of the nation's historical struggle for democracy (Hearne 2014, 2015). This identification of a continuity in Ireland's historical struggles enabled the movement to become much more inclusive by offering a familiar discursive repertoire around which feelings of solidarity among the movements could easily be articulated (Trommer 2018). Problematically, however, the 'risen people' signifier also inevitably evoked an anticolonial history, thereby downplaying specific transnational aspects of the European Union's austerity agenda. In this sense, arguably, it misled the movements into thinking that the problems that confronted them were such that they could be addressed only through a recovery of Irish sovereignty.

A further issue is the fact that the Irish parliamentary Left did little to focus or direct these popular energies. The 2016 election saw historic gains for a number of leftist parties, including the traditionally nationalist Sinn Fein (SF), and a host of independent candidates opposed to austerity. As I will detail below, however, the election nevertheless marked a disappointing conclusion to the 2014 cycle of struggles. Considering the unprecedented scale of the protests and the significant spike in support for Independents in the 2016 election, the moment was one clearly ripe with the potential for a significant rearticulation in Irish politics. Problematically, however, in 2015, divisions had emerged among the left-wing parties. On the one hand, SF presented an argument that the parties should put power before principle and, if need be, enter into coalition with Fianna Fáil (FF) or Fine Gael (FG), the two main socially conservative parties that have constituted the primary cleavage of the Republic's post–civil war politics, as junior partner. The Anti-Austerity Alliance (AAA), on the other hand, responded that the Right2Change campaign had become a 'prop' for SF, and refused to form a government with SF full stop. As a result, the 32nd Dáil convened as something of a *zombie parliament*. Founded on an arrangement that most Irish voters would previously have thought unthinkable – a 'confidence and supply' pseudo-coalition between FG and FF (Kelly 2016), wherein FF would prop up a weak FG parliamentary majority (which included a fluctuating number of Independents) – it was likely to endure only until such time one or the other of the two main parties believed itself to be ready for another election.

Could the Irish parliamentary Left have fared any better with a unified front? It is hard to say. But what is clear is that the 2014–2016 cycle of struggles revealed a number of problems amongst the Irish Left. In this chapter, I elaborate on the nature of these problems and their ramifications for the debate over Left convergence. The first section begins with a brief discussion of the historic weakness of the Irish Left before making some remarks on the grip of folk politics in popular and academic commentary on contemporary Irish social movements, and how it invokes anticolonial memories in order to naturalize the state as the essential terrain of its struggle. It also examines the difficulty Irish Left parties have faced in providing focus and direction to the movements. Then I turn to the 2015 Greek 'Oxi' vote, and contributions made to public debates in that time frame relating to Foucault's concept of 'socialist governmentality'. Specifically, I explore whether or how these contributions might offer insights on the construction of more mutually affirming relationships between parties and movements, and avoid the pitfalls of folk politics.

The purpose of the second section is not to suggest that an exact apples-to-apples comparison of the plight of the Irish and Greek Lefts is possible, or even desirable. It is, however, to suggest that the debates from Greece provide something of a 'conceptual toolbox' that might be productively applied to the Irish scenario. Thus, the third section develops this frame of socialist governmentality, and argues that an effective strategic orientation of the Irish Left at this point will presuppose a hybrid form of political engagement, drawing on a theoretical framing of the movements as embodying a politics of the multitude and of the parties as embodying a more hegemonic politics of the people. The main upshot, following Hardt and Negri (2017), is that Irish Left strategy should not content itself with the naive defeatism of the folk-political position. While Hardt and Negri can in many ways be interpreted as advocates of radically democratic politics, their project resists the representation of the people as the sole necessary terrain of politics. As we shall see, Left strategy is for them less a question of the struggle for an authentic democratic form and more a question of creating the material conditions of possibility for the development of what they call the multitude.

As the Greek case will suggest, however, time is not an unlimited quantity for countries subjected to the yoke of austerity. Protracted encounters with austerity create fertile environments for right-wing political energies. This in mind, the chapter concludes with an argument that an effective socialist governmentality must attend to two urgent tasks. First, accepting the current nonexistence of the conditions of possibility for a pure communism in global capitalism, it must pose the question of vertical strategy, or hegemonic socialism (Prichard and Worth 2016, 7). Secondly, as Foucault reminds us, actually-existing socialisms have tended to succumb to the temptations of sovereign exceptionalism and have acted to constrain the field of democratic engagement. In future, therefore, socialist governmentality must refuse the temptation to name a class enemy (Foucault 2003, 262). Critically, however, work towards the fulfillment of these two tasks must take place *simultaneously*. This is because each strategy contains within it the potential to fundamentally compromise the efficacy of the other. The left-hegemonic approach, on the one hand, is ultimately a project of representation; it possesses the ability to wield the power of the state, giving it a strategic advantage in terms of addressing the nondiscursive or 'asignifying' (Christiaens

2016) elements of contemporary capitalist power. Yet its tendency to fetish-
ize democratic representation renders it vulnerable to the naive defeatism of
folk politics. The multitude approach, on the other hand, possesses a capacity
for viral, network-based auto-generation that the hegemonic model is lacking
(Arditi 2008), but, as the Greek case attests, it cannot sustain itself in times of
austerity without some form of rearguard action vis-à-vis the state (Panitch
2015). Accordingly, some form of compromise between the two approaches
must be achieved. However, if this analysis holds, and the common self-
governance of the movements is a necessary incubator of anti-capitalist subjectivity today, then it is equally necessary to acknowledge the absence of
strong autonomist communities in Ireland. For this reason, commentators on
Irish social movements may want to moderate their fixation on anticolonial
critique; a meaningful resistance to Irish austerity is one grounded less in the
struggle for emancipation of an authentic Irish people and more in the promotion and development of a global anti-capitalist praxis.

THE RISEN PEOPLE? AUSTERITY AND THE IRISH LEFT

It is not controversial to say that the people of Ireland have suffered extraor-
dinarily under austerity (Molloy 2012). Surprisingly, however, and as many
have remarked, the government's cutbacks have not provoked much by way
of social unrest (Lewis 2011; Mercille 2013). Indeed, as Minister of Finance
Brian Lenihan felt compelled to note, in the early phases of the government's
fiscal adjustment program, 'our partners in Europe . . . are amazed at our
capacity to take pain. In France, you would have riots if you tried to do this'
(Finn 2011, 34). Equally, albeit from a different political perspective, it is
reported that anti-austerity protesters in Greece could frequently be heard
chanting, 'We are not Ireland, we will resist' (34). However, as Adshead
explains, if the 'narrative of the crisis' was captured by 'conservatives' at the
outset, things began to change as the economy entered into recovery (Adshead 2017, 7). While the preferred frame of elite discourse pitted public-
sector and private-sector workers against each other, she notes, it became
clear over time that the austerity program really had 'hit everyone'. In this
sense, as awareness grew, there came a point where 'large-scale antipathy'
was reserved solely for bankers and property developers (8).

Critically, some observers of Irish social movements have been keen to
point out the existence of anti-austerity movements prior to 2014. These
scholars point to a variety of micro-resistances in everyday scenes of Irish
political life, such as the Ballyhea protests and squatting campaigns connected with Occupy Dame Street in 2011 (Szolucha 2014b; Szolucha 2014a),
as evidence of the effervescence of an already ongoing Irish resistance. Indeed, Cox (2017) poses the 2014 protests as the harvest of more than five

decades of community-based resistance, forging an urban working-class consciousness in the crucible of the resettlement of inner-city populations to newly developed suburban neighborhoods. In the context of these struggles, says Cox, new movements emerged, often led by women waging campaigns against drug addiction and the imposition of municipal waste-disposal charges, and demanding better basic public services. Yet while it would be hard to deny the significance of these examples of quotidian resistance, not least as incubators of future militant subjectivity, it can hardly be said that they constituted an effective counterpower to Irish capitalism, or even compelled any major shifts in government policy. To the contrary, as Francis O'Connor (2017) observes, many of these earlier protests were beset by 'nationalist narratives of oppression' and were marked 'a refusal to take a specific ideological stance'.

A variety of theories have been offered to explain the history of Irish complacency when it comes to the pursuit of economic justice. Some of the factors cited are bound up with the country's idiosyncratic political history, while others appear to be of more recent provenance, connected to the vicissitudes of life in austerity capitalism itself. First, while the Irish have no affinity for extreme Right ideologies, it cannot be said that they are an especially left-wing people (Mair 1992, 384–89). Breaking with Continental European traditions, the primary cleavage in Irish politics is grounded in the country's civil war origins and its two dominant, socially conservative political parties, FF and FG. Labour, as a smaller, third party, has traditionally enjoyed a nominal identification with the Left. Yet it has also suffered from what Puirséil (2007) terms an inverse relationship with the fortunes of FF, which has traditionally appealed to poorer, agricultural and less anglicized segments of the population – famously, Labour decided to sit out the 1918 election, a moment that some historians identify as 'the real foundation of contemporary Irish politics' (Adshead 2015, 8).

This historic anemia of the Irish Left is compounded by a number of factors, some material and some arguably more psychological. First, in the late 1980s, under the moniker Social Partnership, a centralized national bargaining structure was introduced. This model was applied to Labour, but it spread quickly to encompass a range of groups and movements in the so-called Community and Voluntary Pillar. Linking access to government funds to participation in Social Partnership, as Francis O'Connor points out, a significant amount of civil society action was channeled into 'a unilateral relationship that operated on the state's terms' (2017, 12). A second reason, as Ferriter (2013) posits, is that high rates of emigration have long served as a kind of safety valve for the country's social ills, especially in times of economic hardship. Third, as noted by Allen and O'Boyle (2013), is the widespread perception of ineffective union leadership, with union density in the private sector dropping from 55 to 20 per cent in the space of just a few decades. A fourth reason, in the contemporary context, and as cultural psychologists Power and Nussbaum (2014) contend, is that the Irish seem to have internalized the narrative that they are 'partly responsible for their own misfortune and are prepared to reap what they sowed'. Fifth and finally, it could be that the economic circumstances of the context of the Great Recession had had a material-disciplinary effect on Irish daily life, constraining 'political entrepreneurs' who might otherwise be inclined to organize and lead protests (Adshead 2017).

These factors are all plausible in explaining why the Irish response to austerity was so unimpressive, especially when contrasted with the scenes of resistance that occurred in Greece and Spain. In 2013, however, there appeared to be the beginning of a change in the political status quo. This was the year that the Troika made its last visit, and the nation appeared to enter into the early phases of a recovery. Now, that a political 'awakening' might occur under such circumstances is consistent with what social scientists term *relative deprivation*, a theory that poses the notion that economic inequality tends to become more visible when an economy begins to recover from recession (see Gurr 2015). Indeed, as Finn (2015) contends, it is likely that talk of a recovery in Ireland was a decisive factor motivating the protests. If the 'emergency' was now over, those who had suffered most under austerity could now speak out without fear of being accused of 'rocking the boat'.

Yet perhaps the greater catalyst came in 2014, when the Irish government had announced plans to institute a new tax on water. To that point, payment for most domestic water charges had been embedded in general taxation. Yet the 2010 Memorandum of Understanding with the Troika included language about achieving 'full cost-recovery in the provision of water services' (cited in Finn 2015). Critically, it was already known in 2014 that this memorandum had been signed under immense pressure from the ECB (Hirst 2014) and that the EU was putting pressure on the Italian, Greek and Portuguese governments to privatize their water services (Boylan 2016). Equally, however, as Trommer (2018) observes, it can't be gainsaid that domestic elites had already long been expressing a preference for 'market-environmentalist reforms' to water provision. It can be surmised, therefore, that on this particular provision, the government would have submitted somewhat willingly.

Branded as a water conservation strategy, then, the government's 'National Recovery Plan 2010–2014' made it clear that moving water costs out of the general taxation column would be a priority. However, as the concrete plans were announced, it became clear that the new charge would amount to a regressive form of double taxation (Kerrigan 2015). Charges would range from €176 to as much as €500 per household, depending on its size (Fleming 2014). Moreover, there were a number of troubling revelations about the new semistate vehicle, Irish Water, that was to implement them. First, in order to cover the expected costs of repairing Ireland's aging water grid, it was clear that the firm would have to seek external private investment, thus linking the performance of a public utility to the speculative edicts of global financial markets (Bresnihan 2015). Second, it emerged that the firm had allocated €85 million of its total setup costs to consultancy fees. Third, information appeared suggesting that the company had been established specifically with a view to an eventual privatisation (O'Connell 2015). For significant numbers of Irish people, this was the final straw. On October 11, 2014, the 'Right2Water' umbrella group organized a national day of action, where as many as eighty thousand people showed up at a number of events around the country. Next, on December 9, a march in Dublin drew one hundred thousand people, more than 2 per cent of the Republic's 4.5 million population (O'Connell 2015). Similar numbers would turn up at protests throughout 2015.

The scale of the protests was impressive and, even with the 2016 election still quite far off, it became clear through 2014 and 2015 that the political mainstream was starting to fear for its Left flank. Assisted by well-known voices in the media, the coalition parties attempted to stoke fears of 'hard-left Trotskyite' factions (Collins 2015) among the movements and suggested that the Right2Water movement was a 'sinister fringe' led somehow by a 'small group' of 'elite' and 'fascist' pied pipers, with 'expensive phones' (Howlin 2016; Kerrigan 2015). As O'Toole noted, this frame was somewhat predictable – with the worst of the financial woes now in the past, it made sense for the government to present the election as a choice between 'stability or chaos' (O'Toole 2015). Similarly, for Irish political blogger Richard McAleavey (2015), this fearful discourse was motivated to no small degree by the recent electoral success of Syriza in Greece, and the worry that it might inspire a comparable anti-austerity movement in Ireland.

Critically missed in the government's 'pied piper' characterisations was the spontaneous, neighbourhood-level nature of the movement itself, which was of a scale beyond anything that could have been contrived by the organized Left. At the community level, people were working together to obstruct the independent contractors sent to install meters near their homes (Kerrigan 2015). There were reports of a mysterious 'water fairy' phenomenon taking place, likely motivated by an instructional video on YouTube (https://youtube/2PTIV2GNF-g) that demonstrated an easy method for sabotaging the meters. Moreover, registration rates were low, and as many as 70 per cent of households were refusing to pay the charge at all (Tierney 2015). Despite media characterisations, then, this was no fringe movement. For many, it was evidence that, in Ireland, a new mode of 'active citizenship' was 'kicking off' (Hearne 2014; Maleney 2014).

Ultimately, the water protesters achieved at least a partial victory. In their refusal to pay, and in their sabotaging of the water-metering system, the protesters increased the material costs of implementing the government's program to a point where the financialisation of the Irish water system was no longer economically viable. To disperse the movements, the government attempted a number of capitulations to protesters' demands, including moving back the due date for the bills several times and offering households a one-time €100 'conservation grant' in exchange simply for registering with the system. In July 2015, however, the EU's statistics agency, Eurostat, declared that these capitulations were of such a degree that Irish Water was acting effectively under government control and could no longer be considered an independent market entity (Kerrigan 2015). In setting Irish Water up as a semistate agency, the government had been hoping to keep the costs off the national books, but the Eurostat declaration had revealed these hopes to be aspirational at best.

The victory of the movements over water cast a significant shadow over the government's election prospects. In 2011, FF had been nearly eliminated as an electoral force, with FG and Labour installed in their place. Importantly, however, both FG and Labour had campaigned on broadly anti-austerity platforms, criticising the preceding FF-Green coalition for its refusal to impose losses on bondholders. Once in office, however, they had actually intensified the implementation of austerity, targeting those on lower income scales in particular (Finn 2015). By contrast, the results of the 2016 election suggested a seismic shift in the nation's post–civil war consensus. Having overseen five of the country's eight years of austerity to that point, FG support decreased precipitously, with a loss of more than twenty seats, while Labour suffered the worst election performance of its history, returning just seven seats (Adshead 2017, 15). FF, for its part, regained some of the ground lost in 2011 but did nothing to reverse its longer-term decline.

The significance of this electoral shift cannot be gainsaid. Occurring on the one-hundred-year anniversary of the 1916 Easter Rising, commonly regarded as a major inflection point in the struggle for national independence, the election radically transformed the distribution of power in the national parliament. Yet it was a transformation that remained as yet incomplete. Among the big winners, SF gained nine seats, though not enough to lead a coalition, while an ideologically mixed group of non-party-affiliated independent candidates took a shocking twenty-three seats. For most Irish voters, the idea of any sort of coalition between FF and FG would be completely unthinkable. Nevertheless, FF agreed to a 'confidence and supply' (Kelly 2016) arrangement, thereby securing a parliamentary majority for FG (which also included the support of a fluctuating number of Independents). As such, it is no understatement to say that the 32nd Dáil convened as something of a zombie parliament.

For some commentators, the almost total defeat of Labour, and the only slight increase for FF, meant that the electorate had 'swung to the centre'; a survey at the time showed that 60 per cent of Independent voters classified themselves as 'centrist' (O'Malley 2016). This conclusion was problematic, however. In terms of actual votes cast, the increase in support for candidates with positions to the left of Labour (i.e., the combined increase in votes for SF, the Anti-Austerity Alliance/People Before Profit, and the self-identifying left 'Independents 4 Change' group) was approximately 111,000, not far off the 24.3 per cent 'swing' (126,200 votes) towards FF (all figures are from https://en.wikipedia.org/wiki/Irishgeneralelection, 2016). It was quite certain, in this sense, that Labour had been outflanked on the left by a coalition of committed anti-austerity parties, all of whom had mobilized against the water charges.

Nevertheless, the election was something of a missed opportunity for the Irish Left. While left-wing parties have never performed well in Ireland, the large spike in support for Independents in the 2016 election indicated something of the potential for a major rearticulation of the Irish political horizon. In 2014 and 2015, Right2Water had achieved an unprecedented degree of success, mobilising large numbers for an unquestionably leftist cause. One of the reasons for its success, no doubt, was that it considered itself more a 'platform' than a movement; interestingly, where Ireland's 'Occupy Dame Street' had explicitly prohibited the use of ideological language (see Kiersey 2014), Right2Water was emphatic in its 'inclusivity' (Right2Water 2015), allowing a combined participation of trade unions and political parties, on the one hand, and a multitude of diffuse, local-level initiatives to become involved, on the other.

Equally, however, it is clear that the movement was steeped in the language of anticolonial struggle. Demonstrators at the marches regularly invoked the symbols and mythology of the 1916 Easter Rising and linked 'water charges in the austerity era to issues of self-determination and sovereignty' (Trommer 2018, 8). Equally, commentators in the media, both friendly and critical, regularly invoked the notion of 'the risen people', recalling Ireland's historical struggle for independence from British colonialism (see, for example, Taft 2015; Clifford 2014; Holland 2015). For Trommer, critically, this rhetoric gave an aura of familiarity and accessibility to the protests. Thus, she notes, regardless of whether they associated Irish Water with an EU conspiracy to usurp Irish democracy or a financialized global capitalism run amok, or they simply felt they couldn't pay their bills, a wide range of protesters could feel welcome within the movement. Equally, however, the embrace of nationalist symbolism also suggested that 'success' was not the primary metric by which the movements were measuring the effectiveness of their participation. To the contrary, such symbolism evoked a sense of the nation's long history of continuous rebellion against 'overwhelming force', where failure was 'normal' (2008, 11).

The semiotic toolkit of nationalism thus at least partly explains the success of the movements in generating solidarity on the streets. Arguably, however, it also risked the substitution of a virtuous 'feel good' defeatism in the place of an actual politics. This tendency towards defeatism among the movements became apparent when, despite the fact that the Left was enjoying a historically unprecedented electoral momentum (Finn 2011, 58), Right2Water decided not to field candidates of its own. Instead, it published a platform document called Right2Change (2015), containing a number of principles to which parties could commit themselves if they so chose. In response, the traditionally more nationalist SF unilaterally announced a vote-transfer pact with the other Right2Water-affiliated parties for the upcoming election. Problematically, however, two of the parties were not in a position to reciprocate, because SF would not rule out a coalition with FF, FG or Labour as junior partner. Moreover, the AAA argued that the rebranded Right2Change campaign had become a 'prop' for SF (Kelly 2015) and refused to form a government with SF full stop, on account of the cutbacks it had implemented as part of the government of Northern Ireland. With SF thus putting power before principle, and the AAA putting principle before power, it might be argued that the Irish parliamentary Left failed to present the electorate with a convincing united front.

Despite its success in generating rebellious solidarities, then, the Right2Water movements may ultimately have been confused as to the most appropriate scale for their resistance against European austerity. Now, in the wake of the 2016 election, it would seem that the movement has been effectively dispersed, at least to the extent that it might provide a cogent force in the struggle against European austerity. This is regrettable because, while the Dáil suspended water charges in July 2016, the European Commission moved quickly to advise Ireland that the creation of Irish Water had changed the nation's 'established practice' for the recovery of the costs and that, therefore, the exemption from domestic water charges, secured under Article 9.4 of the EU's 2000 Water Framework Directive, was no longer available (Bardon 2016). Thus, at the time of writing, the water question remains unresolved.

In the winter of 2016, disruptive resistance picked up again, briefly, around the issue of Dublin's chronic homelessness problem (for background, see Holland 2015; Duncan 2014; and O'Byrne, 2016). At this time, a number of activists, trade union craftsmen and homeless people entered a disused National Asset Management Agency (NAMA) building named Apollo House, beginning what would become a month-long occupation. Operating under the title Home Sweet Home, the group sought to draw attention to the plight of Ireland's record-breaking six thousand homeless people, and the poor quality of available emergency accommodation (Steward 2017). It received the support of a number of well-known Irish media personalities and frequently drew large crowds of supporters (Cullen 2016). Its success, however brief, suggested that Irish movements remained available for mobilisation. Again, the movements appeared to be coming together on an openly ideological basis, but there was little evidence in their actions that they were connecting these local expressions of the logic of austerity to any sort of wider strategy for tackling the unevenness of European power relations.

GREECE AND SOCIALIST GOVERNMENTALITY

If Irish social movements have resorted to folk-political discourse in order to build their sense of solidarity against austerity, movements elsewhere appear to have embraced a politics rooted more in anti-capitalist strategy. One impressive example of this comes from the context following the 2015 Greek general election, and what many now see as Prime Minister Alexis Tsipras's betrayal of the movements in capitulating to the Eurogroup's demands. In this time frame, a vibrant public debate took place on the question of whether the country should have embraced 'Plan B' and departed immediately from the Eurozone in order to save its sovereignty, or accepted that the future of the nation's democracy was bound to its economic survival and that 'buying some time' was the order of the day (Duggan 2015).

Navigating the tension between these two courses in a noncontradictory manner has been a central challenge for Syriza as well as its sister party in Spain, Podemos. In the Spanish case, indeed, the movements have been referred to as the 'political engine' of the party, the source of its values, holding it accountable and pushing it to go even further. As much is reflected in Podemos's 'Constituent Process', a two-month nationwide debate that occurred in the autumn of 2014, and which established the party's 'ethical, political, and organizational' framework. Critical to this process was the careful study by Iglesias, among others, of the various congresses supporting electoral reform over the last two decades, in Venezuela, Ecuador and Bolivia. According to German Cano of Podemos's Latin American relations team, the party has come to embrace a kind of constitutional suppleness in order to be able 'to articulate demands that in the first instance don't appear to fit with already constituted identities' (Seguín 2015). Bringing this model home to Spain, Podemos relied on some nine hundred nationally distributed circles to create a 'participative' election manifesto, which was then voted for online.

The Constituent Strategy of Podemos appears in some ways therefore to resemble the populist strategy of the Irish movements. As in Ireland, the Spanish movements were also antipolitical, to some extent; one of the Indignados' slogans was 'We are neither right nor left, we are coming from the bottom and going for the top' (Hancox 2015). This makes sense because, as is now commonly acknowledged, the political projects of both Podemos and Syriza are heavily influenced by the arguments of Gramscian political theorists Ernesto Laclau and Chantal Mouffe (Hancox 2015; Errejón 2014). In the idiom of Laclau and Mouffe, these parties have been playing a 'game called hegemony' (2001, 193). Here, the measure of a good theory of hegemony is that it should refuse to presume the horizon of possible subjects 'given' in social relations. Thus, whereas Marxist theories tend to posit human subjects, and the social structures they inhabit, as somehow endogenous to the history of material antagonism, for Laclau and Mouffe there is no automatic correspondence between one's position in the material relations of production and one's political ideology. For this reason, leftist demands cannot be articulated with the expectation that they will reflect objective interests. Instead, the movements should deprioritize the use of anti-capitalist rhetoric, which both dictates the kinds of subjects we find in social antagonism and presumes to speak objectively on their behalf, in order to be able to articulate a more vague, or floating, master signifier to which all segments of the people might express loyalty. Prioritising a radically democratic ethics over the cause of socialism, therefore, Laclau and Mouffe argue that hegemony must be founded on the surplus or excess meaning of the heterogeneous demands of the diverse movements and the subversion of the 'differential character' of these demands, via the floating signifier, into 'a chain of equivalence' (Arditi 2008, 27).

Problematically, however, this prioritisation of inclusiveness bespeaks a kind of folk-political naiveté in its own right. Preoccupied as it is with the question of the form of the movements, as opposed to any specific ideological content, the theory of hegemony substitutes the achievement of pluralism for concrete liberation; because hegemony is erected on a field of contingent, emerging demands, the question of objective social structures is moot. Yet, as Arditi suggests, it is important not to confuse our 'desire to identify the hegemonic form of politics with its verification' (Arditi 2008, 27). That is, we ought not become so seduced by the ideal of a pluralistic hegemony that we forget, for example, capitalism's long record of successfully playing identity groups against each other in the name of profit. Capitalism's control is certainly partially ideological, but it is also material. To neglect this dimension in our efforts to construct a Left-political program is, ultimately, to render that program 'ideologically hollow' (Prichard and Worth 2016, 7).

Yet, while the influence of the thinking of Laclau and Mouffe on Podemos is obvious, it is worth pausing first to note the strategic significance of its mere existence as a party, marking as it does an institutionalized effort to overcome the dispersed and transitory nature of horizontalist power by giving institutional integrity to the memory of the movements, and by allowing them to plan ahead and to take on much bigger structural forces. Pablo Iglesias of Podemos, for example, has been openly critical of the idealism of folk politics: 'Our aim today . . . is not the withering away of the state, or the disappearance of prisons, or that Earth become a paradise. But we do aim, as I said, to make it so that all children go to public schools clean and well-fed'

(2015). The critical distinction here with folk politics is the recognition that the democratic form of the movements is not itself enough; activism is an activity pursued under conditions of perpetual insecurity, and especially so in the context of a financial crisis. Acquiring a more vertical form, then, a major goal of Podemos has been to try to mitigate such insecurity, and to provision for the continuity of the movements by raising funds for the creation of various online resources, including various 'Web-TV' media streams, online forums (principally, the so-called Plaza Podemos) and 'transparency web-sites' (opening its expenses to public scrutiny), but also funding candidates and campaign workers for elections.

For Podemos, real change comes from below, but, equally, there appears to be a recognition that a 'grand strategy' based solely on the equivalence of the people's demands is unlikely to provide a sufficient basis for victory in conditions of globalized capitalism. Thus, in contrast with the Irish case, Podemos appears to have made strides in prioritising vertical integration as a way of building a national counterpower to European austerity. In their actions, that is, they have demonstrated their strategic commitment to a material provisioning for their model of hegemony and, in so doing, arguably, they have distanced themselves from the tactics-first populism of Laclau and Mouffe. For this reason, some have characterized this distancing or modification as a kind of 'Latin-Americanisation of southern European politics' (Errejón 2014).

Meanwhile, in Greece, the case of Syriza offers a further example of the need to prioritize a provisioning for the movements. During the 2015 Greek general election, voters were presented with a dilemma. On the one hand, they had to recognize the fundamental limits to its agency that any government under global capitalism must suffer. On the other, they had to reckon with the urgency of supporting and sheltering the movements as a hedge against rising right-wing sentiment. The revolutionary-leftist Antarsya coalition performed poorly in the election (just 0.6 per cent), compared to the victorious Syriza. However, refusing calls from Antarsya, and even from within the ranks of its own so-called Left Platform, for an immediate, all-or-nothing 'Grexit' from the Eurozone, Alex Tsipras attempted instead to use his electoral victory, and the results of a positive 'Oxi' referendum in June, as leverage for a better deal in his negotiations with the Eurogroup. Understandably, many 'Plan B' supporters decried this tack as capitulation or, worse, betrayal (Lordon 2015; Ali 2015). For others, however, such declarations were far too simplistic, ignoring the considerable political and technical problems that a Grexit would likely raise, and not just in the immediate term.

Critically, on the political side, polls at the time continued to show an overwhelming degree of support, including 66 per cent of Syriza supporters, for remaining in the Eurozone, even after the signing of the Third Memorandum (Gindin and Panitch 2015). Such support notwithstanding, the technical feasibility of an actual Grexit was highly questionable; it would face real obstacles, including the relative weakness of the country's bank deposits. Moreover, outside of the Eurozone, a Greek government in default would not be able to expect much by way of help from Europe's already wrathful elites. Thus, given the likelihood of economic obliteration, the great pain this would inflict on the very same subjects the party is sworn to defend, and the possibility that these same subjects might in turn come to rationalize a rightward political turn, capitulation was really the only viable strategy (Panitch 2015). As Gourgouris (2015b) observes, the desire under such circumstances to pursue a strategy of 'abandoning the Euro no matter the cost', a strategy ultimately no more guaranteed to succeed than the strategy of remaining within it, amounted to little more than an inverted 'fetishism' of the euro. Faced with such a false choice, then, Tsipras chose finally to respect the wishes of the Greek electorate.

Suffice to say, the Greek situation after the signing of the Memorandum was a highly idiosyncratic one. In Gourgouris's terms, it was a situation where 'the field of historical action . . . exceeded the theoretical armory'. Ultimately, in deciding not to press for Grexit, it appears that Tsipras was guided by a sense of this impossibility of the choices before him. On the one hand, leaving would likely have been incredibly risky and had no guarantee of success. On the other, as Bratsis (2015) argues, the Greek social movements were as yet not fully constituted or ready for the task of pressuring Europe's financial institutions. While they achieved phenomenal success in organising '30 plus general strikes and many more demonstrations', they were ultimately unable to prevent passage of the Memorandum. Therefore, beyond being the more democratic option, Tsipras's decision contained a twofold element of realism. Balibar and Mezzadra express the logic of this realism succinctly, declaring the decision a victory in terms of 'time and space' (Watson 2015). Time, that is, for the composition of new militant subjectivities elsewhere in Europe and, hopefully, some electoral victories, but, equally, space for a broader political engagement with Greece's public institutions, where clientelism and corruption remain rampant.

In highlighting this Greek debate, the goal is not to suggest that an exact apples-to-apples comparison with the plight of the Irish Left is possible, or even desirable. However, a survey of the debates from the Greek case does suggest something of a 'conceptual toolbox' that might be productively applied to the Irish scenario. On the one hand, as Foucault famously framed it, the goal of cutting off 'the king's head' (2001, 122) in our own minds is surely one of the most cherished values of the horizontalist Left. On the other, it is also clear that given the conditions facing the anti-austerity movements in Greece, they could not afford to abandon their state. In Surin's terms, 'a minimally functioning state apparatus' (Surin 2014, 9) had to be hitched to the movement's interests. But how minimal, exactly? And how might one advocate such a 'realism' in this context, without effectively re-attaching the king's head? That is, without becoming trapped in a left-rationalisation of what is really the logic of sovereign exceptionalism?

Breaking with writers like Agamben and Badiou, for whom the political is always necessarily exceptional, Gourgouris answers these questions with a call for what he terms *left governmentality* (2015b). This is a term he derives from Foucault, who claimed once that all actually existing socialisms have had to borrow their vision of governance from other, more explicitly political governmentalities, like liberalism or totalitarianism. Declaring 'I do not think there is an autonomous socialist governmentality' (2008, 92), Foucault suggested that while socialism expresses clear historical and economic values, it has no theory of its own 'way of governing' (2008, 94). For this reason, he concluded, a real Left governmentality has yet to be 'invented' (2008, 94). As to what such a governmentality might look like, however, Foucault did not say much. He merely pointed out two criteria. First, that it should be focused on the 'transformation of economic conditions'. Second, that it should eschew the temptations of sovereign power and refuse any dangerous romanticisations of its own historical purpose with notions like 'class enemy' (2003, 262).

Taking up this challenge in the Greek context, Gourgouris (2015a) argues that the first step in inventing an authentic leftist governmentality is to draw a distinction between the movements, which constitute the self-organising engine of leftist transformation on the basis of their 'autonomous critical imagination' and the instrumental power of institutionalized government, which is bound to 'make clear and timely decisions in particular historico-political conditions and limitations it inherits'. Under Left governmentality, then, the two remain heterogeneous to each other, neither subservient to the other, but each nevertheless 'responsible for each other' (2015b). Critically, Gourgouris here appears to be drawing on two distinct traditions of contemporary left-wing theory. The first, derived from Gramsci, is the hegemonic model, which engages in a 'war of movement' (for discussion, see Worth 2013) within society in order to leverage the power of the state and thereby gain a better foothold against the disciplinary, 'asignifying' powers of contemporary global capitalism (Lazzarato 2014). The second is that of the 'post-hegemonic' model, often associated with Hardt and Negri's concept of the multitude. Here, it is recognized that the skills and capacities gained from use of new technologies of production and communication have enabled new powers of the crowd for self-composition, thus making possible what Hardt and Negri term *exodus* (Hardt and Negri 2008), or the strategic defection of humanity from the antidemocratic normative hierarchies of capitalism.

We will return to the finer points of Hardt and Negri's contributions to this debate, below. For now, however, the point is that Syriza's first obligation as a party would have been to represent its voters and, so far as it is able, to act on the international stage to preserve the conditions of existence of the movements from which it derives its primary strength. For the movements, however, the task is to hold Syriza to its values. That is, to demand that it become a force for democratising the country's flawed institutions, from the municipal level and up. To demand, equally, that it engage with the nation's impressively capable volunteer economy, to strengthen it so that it might better be able to help those who are suffering under austerity, and to increase the powers of the crowd for self-governance (Gindin and Panitch 2015). To demand, furthermore, that it take full advantage of its legal options within the EU, as Yanis Varoufakis (2016) has repeatedly called for, and work with allies in other austerity-stricken European countries to expose and obstruct the Troika's agenda. Of course, in the time since Syriza's capitulation, we can say that the party's performance on these goals has been less than satisfying and, if anything, that it has become a relay for the imposition of the very agenda it set out to oppose (Lapavitsas 2016). Compounded by the effects of a burgeoning refugee crisis, there is no doubt that, under Tsipras, the government has made some poor choices and that the country is today facing a massively difficult situation.

The lesson of the Greek experience, therefore, is that a selective turning towards the state apparatus can furnish an essential counterpower for the movements in their struggle for equality and justice. Such talk does not necessarily constitute a starry-eyed nostalgia for vertically integrated socialisms of the past or reject fully the democratic idealism of folk politics. Nor is it complacent about the need to criticize Syriza's apparent lack of willingness to maneuver in the margins left to it, insofar as they existed, and exist yet, in the wake of the EU's disciplinary edicts (DiEM25 2017). What it does suggest, however, is that the principle of exodus is served only when the multitude has time and resources to experiment. Faced with austerity, socialist governmentality represents a necessary convergence, or compromise, between hegemonic and multitudinal modes of leftist strategy. So long as the embrace of hegemony is based on an awareness of the flaws of folk politics, and recognizes that the principle of exodus, or the autogeneration of the multitude, must be a core value, there is no reason to think it can't provide opportunities for continued experimentation in nonhierarchical forms of government, and strengthen the promise that a break with the politics of austerity is possible.

DEFENSE OF AN IRISH DIRTBAG?

Addressing the pathways available to the Left in countries like Greece, where the movements are relatively advanced in their development, the above would appear to be a very productive debate. We should concede, however, that the prospects for socialist governmentality in a country like Ireland are infinitely dimmer. On the one hand, as discussed above, leftist political parties in Ireland already display a propensity to engage in a kind of purity politics, waging turf wars over the moral priority of nation and class in their nationally oriented struggles. On the other hand, it is clear that the movements themselves have a poor grasp on the nature of their strategic situation. As discussed in the last section, the key guiding voice of left-hegemonic strategy is Gramsci. In Ireland, however, the movements are strongly influenced by the folk-political style, so it may be more accurate to say their guiding spirit is a certain, narrowly interpreted Gramsci. Like Laclau and Mouffe, they appear to be guided by a Gramsci stripped of his Marxism, and exhibit a deep suspicion of the 'ideological language' of anti-capitalist organisations and institutions. As Coulter (2015) observes, no small portion of the blame for this can be laid at the feet of the Republic's progressive intellectual class, who were largely preoccupied by a 'cultural turn' in their research, during the Celtic Tiger years. Guided by instincts that ring significantly more of liberal than Marxist categories of analysis, Left intellectuals in Ireland frequently draw on 'postcolonial theory', situating the power relations of the many identity-based hierarchies of privilege that cross modern Irish society in imperial genealogies. Thus, during the Celtic Tiger, topics such as the Republic's uneven distribution of wealth, or its complicity in empire via various indirect forms of participation in the global War on Terror, tended not to feature in academic research. Indeed, even among the handful of more well-meaning critics who did take on economic themes, there was a tendency to see the Republic as a passive victim of a core-periphery model and, therefore, to deny the genuine advances in material prosperity that the Celtic Tiger had wrought (Coulter 2015, 30–31).

The hegemony of this cultural approach to the critique of Irish politics has fragmented somewhat since the collapse of the Celtic Tiger, and a variety of sophisticated, materialist analyses are now emerging (Nagle 2015; Byrne 2016). Such voices remain marginal, however, as can be seen clearly in those cases where it has dared to challenge the core assumptions of the cultural left. To pick a relatively high-profile example, on May 19, 2017, Dublin novelist Frankie Gaffney (Gaffney 2017) published an editorial in the *Irish Times* wherein he argued, from an inner-city, working-class position, that identity 'activists' had achieved such a dominant status in Irish society that they had actually become an obstacle to the cause of equality. Gaffney was responding to a controversy concerning Dean Scurry, a founding member of the Home Sweet Home movement, discussed above, who had recently launched a podcast called 'Pow Wow with Dean'. Someone had challenged Scurry on Twitter, arguing that the name of the podcast was ill conceived, as the term *pow wow* belonged to 'First Nations Culture'. For Gaffney, the case was part of an alarming trend in Ireland's increasingly online Left culture. Identity activists, he suggested, were behaving increasingly like a kind of virtue police, perpetually cross-checking and 'calling out' the privileged speech of poor, white, working-class men, regardless of their position in class-based terms. This maneuver, Gaffney complained, was patronising to working-class white men who, under austerity, have suffered increasingly from poverty, violence, addiction, and many other symptoms of a nonprivileged existence.

Gaffney's contribution was not only germane in the Irish context, of course. In the United States, in the wake of Bernie Sanders's popular 2016 campaign for nomination as presidential candidate of the Democratic Party, similar voices, of the so-called Dirtbag Left (Semley 2017), have come under sustained criticism for an alleged tone-deafness on questions of gender and race. Despite the fact that many of their leading voices are women, they have been accused of 'brocialism', and of complicity in the undermining of Hillary Clinton's bid to become the first female president of the United States (Zamora 2016). However, while the American Socialist Left has seen something of a resurgence since the election, attested not least by the massive popularity of podcasts like *Chapo Traphouse* and the greatest surge in membership in organisations like the Democratic Socialists of America since the 1960s (Locker 2017), parallel phenomenon have yet to find any expression among the Irish movements. Voices like Gaffney's thus remain quite marginal. Nevertheless, his article kicked off a heated online debate among the Irish Left, triggering a number of posts on popular blogs on the Irish Left scene as well as a lengthy debate on Twitter. On May 25, a piece called '#CopOnComrades: Statement from feminists based in Ireland' appeared on the blog *Feminist Ire* (Redmond 2017). It was signed by a group of 350 women, from a variety of backgrounds, but including relatively high-profile Irish academic feminists like Mary McAuliffe, lecturer in Gender Studies at University College Dublin and former president of the Women's History Association of Ireland (WHAI), along with Linda Connolly, director of the Social Sciences Institute at Maynooth University.

The authors conceded that working-class men do face disadvantages but suggested that Gaffney's argument had drawn on 'language and narratives that have been made popular by men's rights activist (MRA) groups and the alt-right'. In so doing, they claimed, Gaffney had aligned himself with a problematic view of the world, wherein 'straight white men' were now considered 'the new most oppressed group'. In this sense, Gaffney had made himself complicit in a strategy of 'erasure', silencing the victims of masculinist violence. The authors were also keen to respond to Gaffney's point about 'call-out culture'. This, they claimed, was an increasingly common topic on the Left but its function ultimately was to excuse an unwillingness to address 'the complexities of gender, race, ethnicity and sexual orientation in our political organizing'. Gaffney thus embodied a kind of identity-autistic Left, which wanted the struggle of women and other minorities to take a back seat in the struggle for economic justice. And the #CopOnComrades post was by no means a solitary example; similarly critical arguments were issued by well-known leftist performance artist Andrew Galvin (2017) and political blogger Richard McAleavey (2017), and the controversy was also debated in an hour-long episode of an *Irish Times* podcast (Sheridan 2017).

Among Gaffney's critics, the common refrain was that, in order for white males to be considered adequate as 'comrades', they must learn to accept that, because they can have no direct experience of gendered oppression, no matter their *class* background, they have no epistemological warrant to comment on the politics of female gender activists. They must accept, in other words, something of a 'stand with us and shut up' proposition; because there is no possibility for a man to offer any authentic critique of feminist strategy, those men who would presume to be allies can express their solidarity solely by *listening* and *amplifying* genuine feminist argument. This argument will be revisited in the final section of this chapter. For now, however, it should be noted that Gaffney had nowhere claimed that straight white men were 'the new most oppressed group'. Moreover, by imputing to him this crypto-alt-right agenda, the #CopOnComrades letter strove to erase from history a number of particular details from Gaffney's history as an activist working at the intersection of a number of different oppressive regimes; for example, Gaffney has also been a prison rights, immigrant rights and gay rights activist for many years (his mother and sister are gay). In this sense, the idea that Gaffney could be written off as simply a 'useful idiot' for the alt-right agenda appeared intellectually dishonest, to say the least. Read symptomatically, in this sense, the #CopOnComrades statement suggested a certain decadence on the part of Ireland's leading feminist voices; in the midst of shocking material inequality, their actions bespoke a contentedness to engage in a kind of 'hamster wheel' politics, conflating the policing of authentic Left ideology with progress in the Left's wider historical struggles.

Caught between the turf wars of its established political parties and the complacency of its intellectuals, then, the Irish Left may be in trouble. While the example of the Right2Water movement demonstrates concretely the significant possibilities for anti-capitalist openings in Irish common sense, the inability of the Right2Water movements to transcend their idealized hegemonic vision suggests that the prospects for a successful war of position remain weak. Equally, the failure of the Republic's Left political parties to articulate a common front is also a cause for concern. Yet the failure of the intellectuals presents at least an equally egregious failure. In an ironic and cruel twist, at precisely the moment when leftist energies had soared to the highest level since the Republic's founding, a sizeable number of intellectuals within and close to the movement embraced strategic relations of truth that sought to suspend singularity and that risked compromising thereby under the banner of political necessity what is after all supposed to be the principle payoff of the multitude's 'post-hegemonic' politics: the construction of self-confident and capable singularities of democratic, anti-capitalist self-governance.

CONCLUSION: FOR AN IRISH
SOCIALIST GOVERNMENTALITY?

In raising the case of Frankie Gaffney, the goal is not to discount the struggle for equal access to social justice of Irish women, or any of the Republic's other historically marginalized categories. Nor is it to suggest that women must wait until the proper business of a class-based revolution is carried out. Rather, it is to suggest that the struggle against capitalism will be won by those groups that can refuse the *blackmail* of having to choose, as Arditi puts it, 'between hegemony and post-hegemony' (2008, 40–41). This is the right move in a moral sense because, as Hardt and Negri point out, 'no one domain or social antagonism is prior to the others' (Hardt and Negri 2009, 342). Beyond this, however, there is also a certain strategic efficacy to identity politics, insofar as its 'primary task' is to bring about new kinds of consensus – that is, 'to combat blindness and make visible the brutally real but too often hidden mechanisms and regimes' of social subordination and to express our indignation about them (2009, 329).

Yet, as Hardt and Negri warn, the language of identity is ultimately a language of property, and while it might allow us to make visible our various subordinations, we should also remember the danger that inheres in its fetishisation, as if our identity is all that we are and all that we might ever be. Drawing from Deleuze, Hardt and Negri caution that rebellion in the name of any fixed subject, be it women, homosexuals, or the proletariat, 'ceases to be a war machine and becomes a form of sovereignty' (2009, 330). In the context of struggles within and against capitalism, identity can certainly be a powerful vector, 'since identity itself is based on property and sovereignty' (2009, 326). Equally, however, we might remember that capitalism has a history of absorbing such struggles, for identity as property 'can always be accommodated within the ruling structures of the republic of property' (2009, 330). The struggle for identity is a means, in this sense, but not an end; while identity struggles can emancipate you by giving you 'the freedom to be who you really are', they will not necessarily bring about your liberation, or give you 'the freedom to determine what you can become' (2009, 331). Identity politics thus has a second task, which is to transform our indignation into rebellion.

In this sense, what Hardt and Negri are putting forward is a posthegemonic approach, which refuses to confine the ontology of struggle to that of a perpetual quest for the most perfect or pure epistemic stance. To the contrary, it is an approach that seeks to balance the necessity of democratic representation with the strategic urgency of empowering the unrepresentable emergent singularities of the multitude, which might not yet be capable of democratic self-government, but without which a democratic communism is certainly impossible. In what may strike us as a paradox, then, Hardt and Negri suggest that identity politics also has a third task to fulfill: 'its own abolition' (2009, 332). Refusing to bind the movements to counterhegemonic relations of equivalency, the path of the multitude invites them instead to recognize exodus as a goal beyond emancipation and to consider the need to make plans towards the accomplishment of this goal.

But in the face of material austerity, what precisely does it mean for the multitude to make a plan? The risk in following the posthegemony model is that we might put too much faith in the multitude's self-activity and its potential to trigger our revolutionary exodus from capitalism. Against Hardt and Negri's claim that capitalism 'can no longer discipline the powers of the multitude' (Hardt and Negri 2008, 211), the advent of austerity suggests that the longevity of capitalism cannot be attributed solely to the production of capitalist subjectivity, the desire to be a good neoliberal, capitalist, emotionally invested worker and so on. The significance of financialisation in this sense, or what Harvey terms *fictitious capital* (2009, 214), cannot be understated, insofar as it is a power that exists primarily because of our lack of democratic access to capital and that imposes material austerity upon us, coding thereby the very habitual bases of our lives. Thus, as Jodi Dean's famous T-shirt declared, 'Goldman Sachs does not care if you raise chickens' (Srnicek and Williams 2015). It doesn't have to, because resistance solely on the terrain of biopolitics and its immanent processes of signification does not necessarily disrupt the nondiscursive power of finance, or what Lazzarato refers to as its 'asignifying semiotics' (see Christiaens 2016).

Successfully implemented, socialist governmentality might provide an answer to this question. On the one hand, through a measure of vertical integration, it gives movements an asignifying force of their own, a power measured not only in terms of the capacity to generate rebel subjectivities but also in terms of a democratic management of the communicative networks and asignifying codes of capitalism, instituting new preconscious routines and divisions of labour that capitalism cannot contain. On the other hand, it affords the parties and the movements some space to think carefully about identity and to make sure that their government obeys the norm of refusing to declare any particular segments of the population to be 'class enemies'. Of course, this is not to say that capitalism itself is not an enemy, or that the declaration of this enemy should not affect the practical order of priority in our organising. Investing our energies solely in the hamster-wheel struggle of identity politics while capitalism burns the planet is an untenable proposition in any case. Worse, it confuses the means of our struggle for its ends.

Understandably, for those committed to the struggle against austerity in Ireland, the concerns noted in this chapter may seem esoteric at best. The possibility of building any kind of genuine leftist program within the structure of the Euro may seem very remote. From this perspective, a 'Left exit' (or Lexit) strategy may be tempting, because the processes of globalisation that gave rise to the EU did not themselves occur 'beyond the state' and because wielding power 'at the national level' is the therefore the best way to secure a democratic Left hegemony (Príncipe 2016). Others agree that the national level is important but insist that Lexit is a misguided pathway that will return us to a Europe of fetishized national border controls and thereby ultimately play to the advantage of the forces of the xenophobic right. Thus is highlighted a crucial distinction between the folk-political logic of Lexit and the pragmatism of socialist governmentality. Breaking with the blackmail of having to choose between a return to the nation-state or a merely reformist call for 'more Europe', socialist governmentality constitutes a third option.

This third option would seem to be precisely what Yanis Varoufakis has in mind, with his recent call for a campaign of disobedient citizenship from within Europe: a strategy of 'willful disobedience, targeting the European Union's unenforceable rules at the municipal, regional, and national levels while making no move whatsoever to leave' (Varoufakis 2016). While simultaneously refusing identification with Europe, or any of its constituent states (see Varoufakis and Berardi 2017), Varoufakis and other leading political and philosophical figures have established a Europe-wide political party, named DiEM25. Their arguments recall the first five months of the Syriza government in Athens, prior to its capitulation to EU demands, as a window where a strategy of Greek socialist governmentality might have been pursued. That is, a window where the vertical power of the state might have been embraced on a selective basis in order better to secure an equitable economic future for the population, but on specifically internationalist grounds, without succumbing to the logic of sovereignty.

DiEM25 would appear to be calling for precisely the sort of traditional Gramscian hegemony described above. Yet the vertical integration of the strategy is a partial one. It is not so much a capitulation to reformism as a recognition of hegemony as a central material condition of possibility for the development of the movements. The struggle for hegemony, in this sense, is akin to the 'double combat' called for by Hardt and Negri, where the private must first be fought for the public before the public can be fought for the common (Hardt and Negri 2012). For the Irish people, two points alert us to the utility of a selective turning towards the apparatus of the state as part of a Europe-wide project of transforming the EU. The first is that, because horizontalist movements there still suffer from a serious lack of capacity, the struggle for the power of the state, and the public goods it can make available, remains vital. The second is that Greece was alone when it made its stand against the Troika. If the present crisis should deepen again, one cannot predict in advance the difference that a Europe-wide campaign of disobedience, precisely of the sort called for by DiEM25, may make.

BIBLIOGRAPHY

Adshead, Maura. 2015. 'Irish Responses to Austerity.' Paper presented to the 22nd International-al Conference of Europeanists, Sciences Po, Paris, France, July 8–10.

Adshead, Maura. 2017. 'Who's Left in the Wake of Irish Austerity?' *Capital & Class* 1 (280): 030981681769212. doi:10.1177/0309816817692128.

Ali, Tariq. 2015. 'Diary: In Athens'. *London Review of Books*, July 30. http://www.lrb.co.uk/v37/n15/tariq-ali/diary.

Allen, Kieran, and Brian O'Boyle. 2013. *Austerity Ireland*. London: Pluto Press.

Arditi, Benjamin. 2008. 'Post-Hegemony: Politics Outside the Usual Post-Marxist Paradigm'. In *Radical Democracy and Collective Movements Today*, edited by Alexandros Kioupkiolis and Giorgos Katsambekis, 17–44. Contemporary Politics. doi:10.1080/1356977070146 7411.

Bardon, S. 2016. 'European Commission Clarifies State Would Breach Law in Abolishing Water Charges'. *Irish Times*, August 9. https://www.irishtimes.com/news/politics/european-commission-clarifies-state-would-breach-law-in-abolishing-water-charges-1.2750793.

Boylan, L. 2016. 'Water Charges, the EU & the Establishment'. *Lynn Boylan MEP*, March 15. https://lynnboylanmep.com/2016/03/15/water-charges-the-eu-the-establishment/.

Bratsis, Peter. 2015. 'The Materiality of Power and the Physics of Change: Lessons from Henri Lefebvre, Nicos Poulantzas, and the Greek Crisis'. Presented at the Democracy Rising, Athens, July 2015. https://www.academia.edu/14259245/The_Materiality_of_Power_and_the_Physics_of_Change_Lessons_from_Henri_Lefebvre_Nicos_Poulantzas_and_the_Greek_Crisis.

Bresnihan, Patrick. 2015. 'The Bio-Financialization of Irish Water: New Advances in the Neoliberalization of Vital Services'. *Entitle Blog*, August 27. http://entitleblog.org/2015/08/27/the-neoliberalization-of-vital-services-the-bio-financialization-of-irish-water/.

Byrne, M. 2016. 'Bouncing Back: The Political Economy of Crisis and Recovery at the Inter-section of Commercial Real Estate and Global Finance'. *Irish Geography*. doi:10.2014/igj.v48i2.626.

Christiaens, T. 2016. 'Digital Subjectivation and Financial Markets: Criticizing Social Studies of Finance with Lazzarato'. *Big Data & Society* 3(2). SAGE Publications: 1–15. doi:10.1177/2053951716662897.

Clifford, M. 2014. 'People Power Is Going Down the Drain'. *Irish Examiner*, November 21. http://www.irishexaminer.com/viewpoints/columnists/michael-clifford/people-power-is-going-down-the-drain-299043.html.

Collins, Stephen. 2015. 'Labour Party Must Now Fight for Its Survival'. *Irish Times*, February 28. http://www.irishtimes.com/opinion/stephen-collins-labour-party-must-now-fight-for-its-survival-1.2120517.

Coulter, Colin. 2015. 'Ireland under Austerity: An Introduction to the Book'. In *Ireland under Austerity*. Manchester: Manchester University Press.

Cox, Laurence. 2013. 'Why Are the Irish Not Resisting Austerity?' *openDemocracy*, October 11. www.opendemocracy.net/can-europe-make-it/laurence-cox/why-are-irish-not-resisting-austerity.

Cox, Laurence. 2017. 'The Irish Water Charges Movement: Theorising "the Social Movement in General"'. *Academia.Edu*, January 25. https://www.academia.edu/31075937/The_Irish_water_charges_movement_theorising_the_social_movement_in_general.

Cullen, Paul. 2016. 'Apollo House Protesters to Meet Owners over Occupation'. *Irish Times*, December 18. http://www.irishtimes.com/news/ireland/irish-news/apollo-house-protesters-to-meet-owners-over-occupation-1.2910660.

Day, Richard J. 2005. *Gramsci Is Dead: Anarchist Currents in the Newest Social Movements.* London: Pluto Press.

Dean, Jodi. 2012a. 'Occupy Wall Street and the Left'. *I Cite*, January 16. http://jdeanicite. typepad.com/i_cite/2012/01/occupy-wall-street-and-the-left.html.

Dean, Jodi. 2012b. *The Communist Horizon.* London: Verso Books.

DiEM25. 2017. 'New Deal for Greece'. *DiEM*, June 14. https://diem25.org/wp-content/ uploads/2017/06/170614_DiEM25_NewDealforGreece_EN.pdf.

Duggan, Lisa. 2015. 'To Grexit or Not to Grexit'. *The Nation*, July 30. http://www.thenation. com/article/to-grexit-or-not-to-grexit/.

Duncan, Pamela. 2014. 'Dublin Property Prices 24% Higher in a Year'. *Irish Times*, November 26. http://www.irishtimes.com/news/ireland/irish-news/dublin-property-prices-24-higher-in -a-year-1.2015668.

Epstein, Barbara. 1991. *Political Protest & Cultural Revolution: Nonviolent Direct Action in the 1970s and 1980s.* Berkeley: University of California Press.

Errejón, Íñigo. 2014. 'Ernesto Laclau, Theorist of Hegemony'. *Verso Books Blog*, April 30. https://www.versobooks.com/blogs/1578-ernesto-laclau-theorist-of-hegemony.

Ferriter, Diarmaid. 2013. 'A Questionable Republic'. *Sunday Business Post*, July 28.

Finn, Daniel. 2011. 'Ireland on the Turn? Political and Economic Consequences of the Crash'. *New Left Review*, no. 67.

Finn, Daniel. 2015. 'Water Wars in Ireland'. *New Left Review*, no. 95: 49–63.

Fleming, Diarmaid. 2014. 'Anger at Irish Water Charges Reaches Boiling Point'. *BBC News*, October 1. http://www.bbc.com/news/business-29426733.

Foucault, Michel. 2001. 'Truth and Power'. In *Power*, edited by James D. Faubion, 111–33. New York: The New Press.

Foucault, Michel. 2003. *Society Must Be Defended: Lectures at the Collège De France, 1975–76.* New York: Picador.

Foucault, Michel. 2008. *The Birth of Biopolitics.* Edited by Michel Senellart. New York: Palgrave Macmillan.

Gaffney, Frankie. 2017. 'Identity Politics Is Utterly Ineffective at Anything Other Than Dividing People'. *Irish Times*. May 19. http://www.irishtimes.com/opinion/identity-politics-is-utterly-ineffective-at-anything-other-than-dividing-people-1.3087639.

Galvin, Andrew. 2017. 'Men of the Left vs. Intersectionality: A Response'. *Medium*, May 26. https://medium.com/@AndrewJGalvin/men-of-the-left-vs-intersectionality-a-response-4395 df418805.

Gindin, Sam, and Leo Panitch. 2015. 'The Syriza Dilemma'. *Jacobin*, July 27. https://www. jacobinmag.com/2015/07/tsipras-debt-germany-troika-memorandum/.

Gourgouris, Stathis. 2015a. 'Stathis Gourgouris: Left Governmentality in Reality'. *Analyze-Greece*, January 20. http://www.analyzegreece.gr/topics/elections-250102015/item/65-stathis-gourgouris-left-governmentality-in-reality.

Gourgouris, Stathis. 2015b. 'The Syriza Problem: Radical Democracy and Left Governmentality in Greece'. *openDemocracy*, August 6. https://www.opendemocracy.net/can-europe-make-it/stathis-gourgouris/syriza-problem-radical-democracy-and-left-governmentality-in-g.

Graeber, David. 2009. *Direct Action: An Ethnography.* Oakland: AK Press.

Gurr, Ted Robert. 2015. *Why Men Rebel.* New York: Routledge.

Hancox, D. 2015. 'Why Ernesto Laclau Is the Intellectual Figurehead for Syriza and Podemos'. *The Guardian*, February 9. http://www.theguardian.com/commentisfree/2015/feb/09/ernesto-laclau-intellectual-figurehead-syriza-podemos.

Hardt, Michael, and Antonio Negri. 2005. *Multitude.* New York: Penguin Press.

Hardt, Michael, and Antonio Negri. 2008. *Empire.* Cambridge, MA: Harvard University Press.

Hardt, Michael, and Antonio Negri. 2009. *Commonwealth.* Cambridge, MA: Belknap Press of Harvard University Press.

Hardt, Michael, and Antonio Negri. 2012. *Declaration.* New York: Perseus Books Group.

Hardt, Michael, and Antonio Negri. 2017. *Assembly.* Oxford: Oxford University Press.

Harvey, D., Michael Hardt and Antonio Negri. 2009. 'Commonwealth: An Exchange'. *Artforum International* 48(3).

Hearne, Rory. 2014. 'Protests Are a New Type of Active Citizenship Politics Here'. *Irish Examiner*, November 19. http://www.irishexaminer.com/analysis/protests-are-a-new-type-of-active-citizenship-politics-here-298452.html.

Hearne, Rory. 2015. 'From Protest to Politics: How Can We Get a New Republic?' *Irish Left Review*, April 28. http://www.irishleftreview.org/2015/04/28/protest-politics-republic/.

Henwood, Doug. 2011. 'The Occupy Wall Street Non-Agenda'. *LBO News from Doug Henwood*, September 29. http://lbo-news.com/2011/09/29/the-occupy-wall-street-non-agenda/.

Hirst, T. 2014. 'Here's the Secret Letter That Shows the ECB Forced Ireland to Ask for a Bailout'. *Business Insider*, November 6. http://www.businessinsider.com/heres-the-secret-letter-that-shows-the-ecb-forced-ireland-to-ask-for-a-bailout-2014-11.

Holland, Kitty. 2015. 'Home Repossessions Accelerate to 60 Each Week'. *Irish Times*, August 6. http://www.irishtimes.com/news/social-affairs/home-repossessions-accelerate-to-60-each-week-1.2308040.

Howlin, Gerard. 2016. 'Elitist Far-Left Has Gained Traction but Its Fascism Is Affront to Democracy'. *Irish Examiner*, October 25. http://www.irishexaminer.com/viewpoints/columnists/gerard-howlin/elitist-far-left-has-gained-traction-but-its-fascism-is-affront-to-democracy-427474.html.

Iglesias, Pablo. 2015. 'Winning an Election Does Not Mean Winning Power'. *Jacobin*, January 24. https://www.jacobinmag.com/2015/01/pablo-iglesias-speech-syriza/.

Katsiaficas, George N. 2006. *The Subversion of Politics*. Oakland: A K Press. http://books.google.com/books?id=jdyCpdUnQdoC&dq=katsiaficas&hl=&cd=2&source=gbs_api.

Kelly, Fiach. 2015. 'Anti-Austerity Alliance Out of Left-Wing Transfer Pact'. *Irish Times*, October 30. http://www.irishtimes.com/news/politics/anti-austerity-alliance-out-of-left-wing-transfer-pact-1.2412037.

Kelly, Fiach. 2016. 'The Full Document: Fine Gael-Fianna Fáil Deal for Government'. *Irish Times*, March 3. http://www.irishtimes.com/news/politics/the-full-document-fine-gael-fianna-f%C3%A1il-deal-for-government-1.2633572.

Kerrigan, Gene. 2015. 'Irish Water's Credibility Has Truly Dried Up'. Retrieved May 2, 2018, from https://www.independent.ie/opinion/columnists/gene-kerrigan/irish-waters-credibility-has-truly-dried-up-31421104.html.

Kiersey, Nicholas. 2014. 'Occupy Dame Street as Slow-Motion General Strike? Justifying Optimism in the Wake of Ireland's Failed Multitudinal Moment'. *Global Discourse* 4(2): 1–18. doi:10.1080/23269995.2014.898530.

Kiersey, Nicholas, and Wanda Vrasti. 2016. 'A Convergent Genealogy? Space, Time and the Promise of Horizontal Politics Today'. *Capital & Class*, January 1–20. doi:10.1177/0309816815627733.

Laclau, Ernesto, and Chantal Mouffe. 2001. *Hegemony and Socialist Strategy*, 2nd edition. New York: Verso.

Lapavitsas, Costas. 2016. 'One Year on, Syriza Has Sold Its Soul for Power'. *The Guardian*, January 25. http://www.theguardian.com/commentisfree/2016/jan/25/one-year-on-syriza-radicalism-power-euro-alexis-tsipras.

Lazzarato, Maurizio. 2014. *Signs and Machines*. Los Angeles: Semiotext(e).

Lee-Murray, Michael. 2015. 'Ireland's Resurgent Left'. *Jacobin*, January.

Lewis, Michael. 2011. 'When Irish Eyes Are Crying'. *Vanity Fair*, March. http://www.vanityfair.com/business/features/2011/03/michael-lewis-ireland-201103?printable=true.

Locker, Philip. 2017. 'DSA Grows to 21,000 – Toward a New Socialist Party!' *Socialist Alternative*, July 5. https://www.socialistalternative.org/2017/07/05/dsa-grows-21000-socialist-party/.

Lordon, Frédéric. 2015. 'The Euro, or Hating Democracy'. *Verso Books Blog*, June 29. http://www.versobooks.com/blogs/2075-frederic-lordon-the-euro-or-hating-democracy.

Mair, Peter. 1992. 'Explaining the Absence of Class Politics in Ireland'. In *The Development of Industrial Society in Ireland*, edited by J. H. Goldthorpe and C. T. Whelan. Oxford: Oxford University Press.

Maleney, Ian. 2014. 'An "Unmitigated Disaster": 8 Reasons It's Kicking Off in Ireland'. *Novara Media*, November 19. http://novara.media/2ditmFn.

Mason, Paul. 2012. *Why It's Kicking Off Everywhere: The New Global Revolutions*. London: Verso.

McAleavey, Richard. 2015. 'The Hard Left, Redux'. *Medium*, February 28. https://medium.com/@hiredknave/the-hard-left-redux-33c59de7202c.

McAleavey, Richard. 2017. 'My Straight White Male Life'. *Cunning Hired Knaves*, May 26. https://hiredknaves.wordpress.com/2017/05/26/my-straight-white-male-life/.

Mercille, Julian. 2013. 'Why Don't the Irish Protest Against Austerity?' *Thejournal.Ie*, November 26. http://www.thejournal.ie/readme/why-dont-we-protest-in-ireland-1177504-Nov 2013/.

Molloy, Thomas. 2012. 'Irish Meltdown Was World's Worst Since 1930s – IMF Report'. *Irish Independent*, June 28. http://www.independent.ie/business/irish/irish-meltdown-was-worlds-worst-since-1930s-imf-report-26869930.html.

Münchau, Wolfgang. 2013. 'Ireland Shows the Way with Its Debt Deal'. *FT.com*, February 10. http://www.ft.com/intl/cms/s/0/a4564eae-713a-11e2-9d5c-00144feab49a.html#axzz2KXK nfWTD.

Nagle, Angela. 2015. 'Ireland and the New Economy'. In *Ireland under Austerity*. Manchester: Manchester University Press.

O'Brien, Carl. 2015. 'Ireland at Risk of Reaching US Levels of Income Inequality, Says Study'. *Irish Times*, February 6. http://www.irishtimes.com/news/social-affairs/ireland-at-risk-of-reaching-us-levels-of-income-inequality-says-study-1.2105125.

O'Byrne, Mick. 2016. 'How Finance Is Shaping Dublin's Ongoing Housing Crisis'. *Dublin Inquirer*, February 17. http://www.dublininquirer.com/2016/02/17/mick-how-finance-shaping-dublin-housing-crisis/.

O'Connell, Hugh. 2015. 'The Story of "NO" . . . 15 Moments That Have Defined the Irish Water Protest Movement'. *Thejournal.Ie*, August 29. http://www.thejournal.ie/irish-water-protests-timeline-1963363-Aug2015/.

O'Connor, Francis. 2017. 'The Presence and Absence of Protest in Austerity Ireland'. In *Late Neoliberalism and Its Discontents in the Economic Crisis Comparing Social Movements in the European Periphery*, 32: 65–98. Cham: Springer International Publishing. doi:10.1007/978-3-319-35080-6_3.

O'Connor, Nat, and Cormac Staunton. 2015. *Cherishing All Equally: Economic Inequality in Ireland*. Dublin: Think-Tank for Action on Social Change (TASC).

O'Malley, Eoin. 2016. 'The Centre Still Holds – So FF Should Make Hay'. *Irish Independent*, March 13. http://www.independent.ie/opinion/comment/the-centre-still-holds-so-ff-should-make-hay-34534981.html.

O'Toole, Fintan. 2015. 'Radical Change the Only Way to Achieve Stability'. *Irish Times*, December 15. http://www.irishtimes.com/opinion/fintan-o-toole-radical-change-the-only-way-to-achieve-stability-1.2466369.

Panitch, Leo. 2015. 'On the Doorstep of Power'. *Jacobin*, January 25. https://www.jacobinmag.com/2015/01/panitch-syriza-election-austerity-greece/.

Power, Séamus A., and David Nussbaum. 2014. 'The Fightin' Irish? Not When It Comes to Recession and Austerity'. *The Guardian*, July 24. http://www.theguardian.com/science/head-quarters/2014/jul/24/the-fightin-irish-not-when-it-comes-to-recession-and-austerity.

Prichard, Alex, and Owen Worth. 2016. 'Left-Wing Convergence: An Introduction'. *Capital & Class* 40(1): 3–17. doi:10.1177/0309816815624370.

Príncipe, Catarina. 2016. 'How to Understand the European Union'. *Jacobin*, October 16. http://jacobinmag.com/2016/10/eu-brexit-varoufakis-europe-lexit-troika/.

Puirséil, Niamh. 2007. *The Irish Labour Party, 1922–73*. Dublin: University College Dublin Press.

Redmond, Sinéad. 2017. 'Cop on Comrades'. *Feminist Ire*, May 25. https://feministire.com/2017/05/25/cop-on-comrades/.

Right2Change. 2015. 'Policy Principles for a Progressive Irish Government'. *Right2Change*, September 11. http://www.right2change.ie/policy-principles-progressive-irish-government.

Right2Water. 2015. 'Right2Water – Strategy, Tactics, Unity'. *Right2Water*, January 6. http://www.right2water.ie/blog/right2water-%E2%80%93-strategy-tactics-unity.

RTE. 2013. '"Historic Day" as Troika Concludes Visit'. *RTE.Ie*, November 7. https://www.rte. ie/news/2013/1107/485113-troika-final-visit/.

Seguín, Bécquer. 2015. 'Podemos's Latin American Roots'. *Jacobin*, March 27. https://www. jacobinmag.com/2015/03/podemos-spain-iglesias-morales-chavez/.

Semley, John. 2017. 'The Rise of the Internet's "Dirtbag Left"'. *Macleans*, July 5. http://www. macleans.ca/society/the-rise-of-the-internets-dirtbag-left/.

Sheridan, Kathy. 2017. '#CopOnComrades: Men & Feminism'. Presented at the Womens Podcast, Dublin, July 10.

Srnicek, Nick, and Alex Williams. 2015. *Inventing the Future*. London: Verso Books.

Steward, Abby. 2017. '"We Are Staying Here", Says Home Sweet Home Movement'. *Hotpress*, January 11. http://www.hotpress.com/We-are-staying-here-says-Home-Sweet-Home-movement/19484572.html.

Surin, Kenneth. 2014. 'Empire Reconsidered: Some Reservations, Much Gratitude'. *Scribd*, October 12. https://www.scribd.com/doc/242666114/Empire-Ten-Years-After-Kenneth-Surin.

Szolucha, Anna. 2014a. 'No Stable Ground: Living Real Democracy in Occupy'. *Interface*, January 1–21.

Szolucha, Anna. 2014b. 'Real Politics in Occupy: Transcending the Rules of the Day'. *Globalizations*, October 1–17. doi:10.1080/14747731.2014.971532.

Taft, Michael. 2015. 'A Democratic Economy, a Prosperous Society, a Risen People'. *Notes on the Front*, May 5. http://notesonthefront.typepad.com/politicaleconomy/2015/05/a-democratic-economy-a-prosperous-society-a-risen-people.html.

Tierney, Rashers. 2015. 'Read Em and Weep'. *Rabble*, October 20. http://www.rabble.ie/2015/ 10/20/read-em-and-weep/.

Trommer, Silke. 2018. 'Watering Down Austerity: Scalar Politics and Disruptive Resistance in Ireland'. *New Political Economy*, 1–17. http://doi.org/10.1080/13563467.2018.1431620.

Varoufakis, Yanis. 2016. 'Europe's Left after Brexit'. *Jacobin*, September.

Varoufakis, Yanis, and Franco Berardi. 2017. '"I Am No Longer a European Given Europe's Daily Crimes" & "Thus I Resign From DiEM25" and My Response'. *Yanisvaroufakis.Eu*, August 8. https://www.yanisvaroufakis.eu/2017/07/08/bifo-i-am-no-longer-a-european-given-europes-daily-crimes-thus-i-resign-from-diem25-and-my-response/.

Watson, Mike. 2015. '"Syriza Wins Time—and Space" by Étienne Balibar and Sandro Mezzadra'. *Verso Books Blog*, February 23. https://www.versobooks.com/blogs/1885-syriza-wins-time-and-space-by-etienne-balibar-and-sandro-mezzadra.

Worth, Owen. 2013. *Resistance in the Age of Austerity*. London: Zed Books.

Zamora, Daniel. 2016. 'Bernie Sanders and the New Class Politics: An Interview with Adolph Reed'. *Jacobin*, August 8. http://jacobinmag.com/2016/08/bernie-sanders-black-voters-adolph-reed-trump-hillary/.

Chapter Seven

Worker Recuperated Enterprises

Confronting the Return of Austerity in Argentina?

Adam Fishwick

With the crisis that spread across Argentina after 2001 came an unprecedented collapse in employment, living standards and political stability. As presidents came and went over the next two years, the 'model child' of IMF-backed structural adjustment quickly became its unruly teenager. Novel forms of labour resistance emerged in these years, most notably in the form of the worker recuperated enterprises. These are workplaces, often on the edge of bankruptcy or suffering from deliberate sabotage by owners, that have been occupied by their employees. But rather than simply press demands for higher wages or workplace rights, these workers have instead sought – and often managed – to reactivate their firms. In the most famous case, that of the ceramics factory Zanón (now known as FaSinPat – short for 'Factory without a Boss'), these struggles and the successful takeover of the firm led to it producing more and better-quality goods than before under conditions of *workers' control*. What this means is that the enterprise operates without management, but instead with workplace assemblies meeting to make day-to-day decisions and 'employees' as owners controlling profits rather than being paid fixed salaries. In line with this experience, workers across Argentina have taken on bankrupt firms and – numbering now close to four hundred – run them for themselves. Borne of a necessity to survive, therefore, their resistance has begun to create innovative new ways of living.

Although geographically outside Western Europe, the significance of this case is that the lessons learned in these workplaces have begun to return to labour struggles in Greece, Italy, and elsewhere on the continent. Under the now famous slogan 'Occupy, Produce, Resist!', these worker recuperated enterprises have shown how workers, in taking control of industrial factories,

157

waste disposal services, health centres and hotels, can sustain production and their own livelihoods. More important, these experiences have shown also how workers can democratically organise their workplaces and persist within and, to an extent, against the capitalist marketplace and the austerity that returned to Argentina after 2015.

The recuperated enterprises stand clearly apart and against the neoliberal austerity introduced under Mauricio Macri, but his electoral success and economic programme still pose a unique threat to their continuing existence. At its core, the new government is attempting to reverse many of the gains that had been pushed through by many of the new forms of labour resistance in the period from 2001 to 2003. In response to mobilisations by unemployed workers and those occupying their factories, the governments of Nestor Kirchner and Cristina Fernández significantly expanded social welfare programmes, increased wages and stimulated industrial growth (see Wylde 2016). For the recuperated enterprises, Kirchner and Fernández introduced novel legal measures that supported claims to expropriation – the occupation and reactivation of a bankrupt firm – under certain conditions. But this process has long been resisted by the Right, which is now again in power with the Macri government, meaning that the struggle faced by workers on the brink of losing their livelihoods has often been long. As Marcelo Vieta (2010) has argued, the length and intensity of this struggle has increased the likelihood that, upon gaining control of the enterprise after legal – and often physical – battles, workers have been able to create new workplaces that, with assemblies making decisions, relative degrees of equal pay, and the rotation of tasks and leadership roles, look very different from the workplace as it has developed under capitalism.

Building on an autonomist Marxist perspective from within critical political economy, which is outlined in what follows, this chapter seeks to explain how worker recuperated factories might navigate the challenges arising in the current context of worsening neoliberal austerity under Mauricio Macri.[1] As the Open Faculty (Ruggeri 2016) has explained, the measures being introduced by Macri – from public spending cuts to outright political repression – have squeezed the capacity of the worker recuperated enterprises to survive. In responding to the depth of this new, emerging crisis, however, I argue that, by understanding the recuperated enterprises as the 'concrete utopias' they are understood as by Ana Dinerstein (2014a, 130–37; 2016), we can better understand their 'possibility' both to survive and to continue to create new ways of living today.

By using this notion of concrete utopia, I will show how, through the necessity of occupying workplaces and renewing production to survive, workers have created a range of new forms of living to be able to struggle against the unique form taken by these 'hard times' in Argentina today. Dinerstein has developed the notion of concrete utopia as a means of bringing a critical 'hope' to thinking about labour resistance. From this starting point, she describes the recuperated enterprises as 'the ultimate experience of solidarity and the creation of new values . . . unique as a learning process of self-management full of uncertainties and surprises' (Dinerstein 2014a, 136). In this conceptualisation, concrete utopias are a creative form of political praxis, but one that is necessarily fragile and incomplete:

> As a praxis-oriented activity within this dehumanised dynamic, concrete uto-pia is crisscrossed by the contradictions that emerge in the process. Conceived in the currents of the River of Capital, concrete utopia is compelled to navigate its open veins, its canals and passageways, stop at its stations, fall into its vessels, swim against its current. In political terms concrete utopia entails a struggle against the state. As the political form of capital, the state permanent-ly intends to incorporate, silence, domesticate, repress, that is, *translate*, the anticipatory and prefigurative nature of utopia into the grammar of order, via policy, monetisation and the law. Concrete utopia is shaped by those relations and dynamics, oppressions and social forms that she wants to obliterate. (Di-nerstein 2016, 52–53)

Consequently, this perspective permits a direct engagement with the limits, contradictions and tensions of the recuperated enterprises as sites of survival, but without simultaneously overlooking the significance of the new creative practices that have emerged within them over the last two decades.

From this point on, I divide the chapter into three sections. First, I exam-ine the importance of these spaces for surviving in recurrent crises and assess what I call the triple ambiguity of relations with the state. Second, I elaborate upon the importance of this concept of 'concrete utopia' for foregrounding the creative labour resistance that has emerged in opposition to both capital and the state's efforts to co-opt and constrain. Third, I examine how the 'social innovations' (Vieta 2010) and new forms of 'sociability' (Sitrin 2006) in the worker recuperated enterprises could overcome the new challenges arising with the Macri regime. Finally, I conclude with a reflection on the 'possibility' – as Dinerstein understands it – of the worker recuperated enter-prises and their contribution to the broader struggle in Argentina.

SITUATING THE WORKER RECUPERATED ENTERPRISES AND THE STATE

In the following section, I will assess two elements of the relationship be-tween the worker recuperated enterprises and the state. First, I discuss 'survi-val' as a modality of resistance. Second, I outline the triple ambiguity of relations with the state. I argue that, although the coming to power of Macri has produced increasingly precarious conditions for the worker recuperated enterprises (see Ruggeri 2016, parts 3 and 4), the support offered by the state has persistently been limited and contradictory, seeking to demobilise and co-opt the creative possibilities that have emerged within and across the worker recuperated enterprises.

Surviving – and resisting – in the workplace

In framing the recent impact of the recuperated enterprises in Argentina, Itzigsohn and Rebón (2015) show how they should be understood, primarily, as a means of surviving in the context of crisis. Starting from a Polanyian interpretation of social mobilisation, they argue that through a combined desire of individual self-protection and a later process of institutionalisation, participants sought to defend themselves against an objective threat of deprivation and to protect a subjective sense of the significance of 'formal' work. Using the example of Cooperativa Vieytes, they show how this 'threat to their lifeworld' was resolved:

> When the workers realized that their demands were not going to be met they looked in new directions. The workers' original goal was not to recuperate the enterprise; this idea developed along with the conflict. As the workers tell their story of the recuperation, a relative of one of the workers was familiar with another recuperated enterprise and put the workers in contact with Luis Caro, a lawyer who had been involved in the recuperation of several enterprises. (Itzigsohn and Rebón 2015, 183)

Threatened by the impending bankruptcy and intransigence of their former employer, workers turned to the newly emerging 'contentious practice' of workplace recuperation.

Importantly, such an understanding, in the view of Ruiz (2015, 31), is helpful to avoid the 'romanticised visions' of the recuperated enterprises that overly focus on the occupation and that often misunderstand the motivations of the occupiers. In her view, it has always been the 'objective . . . to recuperate rather than to seize'. Adding to this, Itzigsohn and Rebón (2015, 193) show that these actions have contributed to expanding the 'repertoire of contention'. Occupation, in this view, is driven by a desire to protect their formal employment. Learning, but sitting apart, from the history of workplace occupation in the labour movement in Argentina (Rossi 2015, 100; Fishwick 2015), recuperation was a move away from occupation to pressure negotiations or as a political tool aimed at the state.

In the view of Itzigsohn and Rebón (2015, 190), the ostensible 'legitimacy' of this tactic, framed as defending jobs and protecting the formal employment and livelihoods of participants, protected the recuperated factories from repression. Rebón, Kasparian and Hernández (2015) demonstrate the prevailing sociocultural legitimacy that persists across Argentina in support of the 'moral economy' of worker recuperation. Using a survey of adults in the

Metropolitan Area of Buenos Aires, they find overwhelming support for worker recuperation. They show that of the 73 per cent aware of these activities, 89 per cent were in favour and only 6 per cent opposed. Of that 89 per cent, moreover, 80 per cent derived their support from the importance of preserving the workplace, with only 20 per cent supporting democratic control over production (Rebón et al. 2015, 182–84). Hence the legitimacy of the recuperated enterprises is argued to derive from their role in preserving formal work.

In addition, Itzigsohn and Rebón argue that although most occupations in the years after 2001 were driven by seemingly spontaneous attempts to reclaim workplaces from unscrupulous or bankrupt employers, in subsequent years local activists, labour unions, and social movement NGOs drove their steady expansion (Itzigsohn and Rebón 2015, 191–92). According to their research, for example, in more than 90 per cent of cases of factory recuperation, the decision to convert into a cooperative was driven from outside (ibid., 186). Consequently, the shift from the spontaneous uprisings of 2001 has seen the rise of a more institutionalised mode of survival in the recuperated enterprises emerging across the country, with the process of occupation and recuperation expanding a burgeoning network of worker cooperatives legitimised by their support for and protection of the continuity of formal employment.

Yet one of the main actors in this process who they identify as advocating vociferously for the importance of formal employment in the recuperated enterprises – Peronist activist, lawyer, and head of the Movimiento Nacional de Fábricas Recuperadas por los Trabajadores (MNFRT), Luis Caro – has been shown elsewhere to have played a key role in *demobilising* the workers involved in more radical forms of resistance. In an interview in 2004 on the seizure and occupation of the Brukman garment factory, Caro is quoted as saying:

> The first time that I went to speak to the Brukman workers it had been five months that they had been in the tent. I told them 'I came to help you enter. But for that, we have to depoliticize this conflict! . . . What do we want, to change Argentina's social structure or to enter the factory? . . . What happened with Brukman?' They did not accept the cooperative. They said 'Nooo, we want workers' control' . . . this and that. And, well, what happened? They were evicted! (Luis Caro cited in Hirtz and Giacone 2013, 95)

This apolitical position on cooperatives promoted by Caro and the MNFRT has been central, in part, to their success; they comprise the status of more than 95 per cent of all the recuperated enterprises (Ruggeri and Vieta 2014). But this formal legal status is only part of the story. To fully comprehend the recuperated enterprises, we must begin by analytically separating the self-activity of workers from the limits of the legal and institutional frameworks that underpin them. This is particularly important when considering their relationship with the state.

The triple ambiguity of the state and the recuperated enterprises

Analytically separating the activity of those workers involved in occupying and recuperating their workplaces from institutional measures offered by the state requires rethinking of the relationship between participants and the ostensibly supportive – or at least permissive – political context, particularly as the current conjuncture poses new challenges for the recuperated enterprises, directly and indirectly. As noted by the Open Faculty:

> The most evident impacts are related to the general rise in the cost of supplies, the abrupt decline in consumption, the opening to imports, the [currency] devaluation that has increased imported inputs and raised domestic costs, mainly, through enormous price rises, especially for electricity and gas, for items that are indispensable for the functioning of any enterprise. (Ruggeri 2016)

Facing these conditions, it is unlikely that the new government will offer any material support to the recuperated enterprises, but rather it appears that they will continue to confront them directly. The longstanding occupation of Hotel Bauen, for example, was granted a legal expropriation order by the Senate in November 2016 that was swiftly overturned by Macri's presidential veto merely a month later in December (*La Nación* 2016).

Again, as reported by the Open Faculty, these patterns of direct and indirect confrontation are an important and emerging theme of the Macri regime and its relationship with the worker recuperated enterprises. I will address these in the final section, but it is worth noting the six main areas where this is occurring: (1) the halting or defunding of research and support programmes, particularly the Programa Trabajo Autogestionado (PTA) in the Ministry of Labour and the Comisión Nacional de Microfinanzas (CONAMI) in the Ministry for Social Development; (2) continuing systematic use of presidential veto by Macri and gubernatorial veto in Buenos Aires province to block expropriations; (3) the halting of purchases by state bodies of goods produced by the recuperated enterprises; (4) increasing judicial intransigence against worker occupations; (5) violent repression to evict and prevent these occupations, linked directly to judicial intransigence; and (6) the authorisation of the sale of recuperated enterprises to private investors rather than to the workers (Ruggeri 2016).

These changes pose a very real challenge to the existence of the recuperated enterprises. It is my contention, however, that rather than see these as fundamentally separate from the role played by the state between 2003 and 2015 – first under Nestor Kirchner and then Cristina Fernández – we must link these challenges to what I understand as the triple ambiguity of relations between the worker recuperated enterprises and the state. These are: (1) the demobilising effect of state and social institutions; (2) the limitations of established legal frameworks; and (3) the role of local government, particularly of Macri in Buenos Aires.

The expansion of new state and social institutions after 2003 was an explicit move to depoliticise mobilisation. The various social policy programs enacted under the Kirchners, such as the PTA and CONAMI, brought a range of radical demands made by workers in these enterprises under the remit of the state, channelling them into the pursuit of various state projects (Dinerstein 2014b, 127). This reflected similar efforts that emerged after the 2001 crisis, for example, with the Mesa de Diálogo in April 2002 that, supported by the UNDP and the Catholic Church, brought together a range of new 'society-based actors' (Riggorozzi 2009, 105). In combination, these mechanisms were a form of governance aimed at pacifying and incorporating the radical changes underway and bringing them under the auspices of the state. For example, Dinerstein (2007) outlines the importance of the PTA following its creation in 2004. By offering minimal legal support against eviction and limited funding for the often-difficult immediate postoccupation period, the programme prioritised support for the continued operation of the recuperated enterprise over changes to social relations in work.

Yet, interestingly, Dinerstein (2007, 538–39) also shows how the PTA unintentionally expanded the space for autonomous self-activity in the workplace. As she argues:

> As the tomas [factory occupations] are accepted and habitualised, they are depoliticised and restricted to the purpose of recovering factories rather than making them an element of the 'struggle for liberation' anticipated by many workers . . . paradoxically, the depoliticisation of the tomas by means of their institutionalisation through technical and financial support for the factories occurs simultaneously with the institutional recognition of the workers' politically stated objectives of autonomy and self-management. (ibid., 540)

The significance of this paradox – the combined processes of the institutionalisation of the recuperated enterprises and the expansion of their creative forms of political praxis in and outside the workplace – will be considered further in the following section. At this stage, it is sufficient to note that the actions of the state, while influenced by these practices in crafting the PTA, were not explicitly intended to be directly supportive of worker self-activity.

Similarly, Sitrin (2012) has shown that the state has often taken a more aggressive approach to disarming initiatives taken from below. At the graphics company Chilavert, for example, workers noted that the state intentionally disrupted local networks and efforts to develop international networks with other worker-managed enterprises in Venezuela:

One thing is clear with FaSinPat [the only permanently expropriated work-place by 2012], and I believe in many other workplaces, from the countless conversations I have had over the years: at their core they do not believe the state is on their side, but rather on the owner's side. (Sitrin 2012, 198–200)

Consequently, we can observe how participants in these spaces have nego-tiated antagonistic legal and institutional frameworks continually throughout the preceding two decades.

This antagonism becomes even clearer when we consider the role of the local state. In Buenos Aires, the recuperated enterprises have had to contend with the local governance of Mauricio Macri, the right-wing businessman-turned-president. Using his veto in 2011 and 2013, Macri deliberately blocked 'definitive expropriation'[2] as defined by the Buenos Aires bankrupt-cy law on numerous occasions, forcing the majority to persist under 'tempo-rary expropriation' status (Ruiz 2015, 36; Ruggeri and Vieta 2014, 95). These legal mechanisms have been an important battleground for workers in occupying and recuperating their factories. By forcing them to retain only a 'temporary' status, the precarity of their existence is maintained. As we will see below, this systematic vetoing of legal, permanent expropriation contin-ues under his presidency in the city and elsewhere, which has left open the possibility of beginning to attempt to roll back many of the gains made in these years.

Yet, in what follows, I will argue that the worker recuperated factories – mobilised as a means of survival and then extended beyond and against the restrictions imposed directly and indirectly by the state and social institu-tions – have been the outcome of the independent self-activity of workers and that this has profound importance for shaping the conflicts that are still to come in the face of this new assault of austerity. In creating new means of survival, operating within and in turn transforming the repertoires of conten-tion in Argentina, and navigating the triple ambiguity of relations with the state, participants in these processes of workplace recuperation have devel-oped new ways of living that can confront the challenges they now face. Considering how the idea of concrete utopia helps us to comprehend this move beyond the 'defensive moment' is to what I now turn.

MOVING FROM THE 'DEFENSIVE MOMENT' TO CONCRETE UTOPIAS

In the following section I outline how viewing the worker recuperated enter-prises from the vantage point of 'concrete utopia' enables us to understand how the need for survival generates novel, creative praxis of importance for today. On the one hand, an understanding of this as an initial 'defensive moment' is useful for conceptualising resistance in a moment of deep crisis.

On the other hand, it is somewhat limiting for explaining the significance of the creative new ways of organising work and the workplace. I use the term *concrete utopia* here in the sense offered by Dinerstein (2016, 51) to encapsulate the radical 'possibility' contained within these spaces alongside the contradictions and necessary fragility that arise from their state of continuous confrontation.

By 'defensive moment' I refer both to the immediate aftermath of the 2001 economic and political crisis that engulfed Argentina and to the spontaneity of workplace occupation and recuperation that continues to this day.[3] For the former 'moment', following several years of protests against the neoliberal austerity imposed by Carlos Menem throughout the 1990s, the economic crisis triggered by the government default in 2001 was converted into a broader political crisis by interim president Fernando De La Rúa's imposition of a 'state of siege' and violent repression in December 2001 (Onuch 2014, 101–3). These events led to a rapid expansion of mobilisation by a range of groups, including unemployed workers' organisations, neighbourhood assemblies, and the recuperated enterprises. For the latter, we can see a clear correlation between economic decline – as a proxy for the bankruptcies, nonpayment of wages and unemployment – and the cases of workplace recuperation (see figure 7.1). Crisis and the struggle for survival that constitute these periods of acute hardship provide the material conditions into which the recuperated factories have been established over the last two decades in Argentina.

Alongside this, the proliferation of the workplace recuperations should be understood in relation to the consolidation of neoliberal austerity and conflict across Latin America. From Brazil and Uruguay to Venezuela and Bolivia, throughout the 1990s and 2000s a wave of occupations occurred in an attempt to offset the widespread crises in the region and the concomitant mass unemployment this produced (Ruiz 2015, 26). Comparable cases, for example, can be drawn from the experiences of workplace recuperation in Uruguay (Riero 2015) and the Socialist Production Units established in Venezuela (Larrabure 2013). Responding to rising unemployment, to growing precarity, and to the poverty associated with these, the proliferation of workplace occupation across the region highlights the importance of defensive mobilising to survive against the crises of neoliberalism.

Nevertheless, even once they are established to secure the survival of jobs, livelihoods and even the workers' lives, workplace recuperations in Argentina have continued to face challenges (see Vieta 2010, 303–36, for details of the various microeconomic and political challenges they have faced). But although a focus on the pressures facing the recuperated enterprises is essential to developing a holistic understanding of the fragility of these experiences, privileging these structural and institutional limitations over the continuing self-activity of workers in these spaces is problematic.

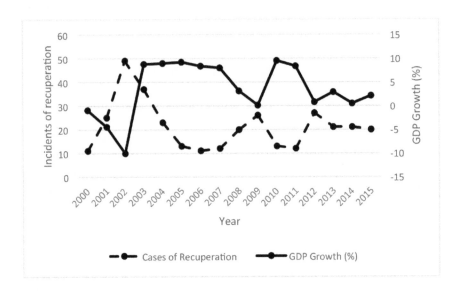

Figure 7.1.   Relationship between GDP Growth and Incidents of Workplace Recuperation in Argentina, 2000–2015. *Source*: **Adapted from Ruggeri (2016, Figure 4).**

As Dinerstein (2016, 51) argues, such narratives lead to a focus on probability, concealing a 'possibility [that] points to the existence of an excess that does *not yet* exist'. An emphasis on the probability of success against prevailing structural and institutional limitations can conceal how, in diverse and unexpected ways, these experiences can transcend constraints in the construction of 'concrete utopias' (Dinerstein 2014a; 2016).

The concept of concrete utopia offers an important way of thinking about the possibility of the recuperated enterprises even under the heightening challenges they face from the Macri regime. Not only does it enable a foregrounding of the processes of creating new ways of living, but it also does so in a way that recognises – concretely – their constraints. Rather than perceive the worker recuperated enterprises just as a necessary means of survival, or a contingent response to crisis that, without a supportive state environment, will necessarily collapse, Dinerstein understands them – as they emerged in 2001 – as 'a concrete tool to fulfil a real necessity which, in turn, facilitates the transition from fear to hope, and moves onto the unknown' (Dinerstein 2014a, 132). As concrete utopias, they are produced by the really existing context in which they emerge; they 'cannot remain intact as abstract utopias do, for they belong to the material world and are constantly reshaped by struggles' (ibid., 142).

Moving beyond the material conditions of the defensive moment, this idea of concrete utopia allows us to rethink the subjective grounds on which Itzigsohn and Rebón (2015) base their justification of mobilisation around the 'dignity' of formal work. In building a concrete utopia, Dinerstein highlights the importance of the *política afectiva* in establishing solidarity:

> *Política afectiva* is a way of transforming the world by connecting with our own emotions about what is wrong, and fight[ing] against the rationalisation of political action that distance ourselves from our humanity and dignity . . . the identities that emerged from *política afectiva* are selves of resistance involved in individual and collective acts of self-determination and hope, rather than fear and hopelessness . . . these are *not yet* subjectivities in motion, rather than descriptors of class, race, or gender. (Dinerstein 2014a, 138–39)

This idea, then, allows us to reconsider the contested meanings and subjective transformations of solidarity and sociability occurring in these spaces. For example, they can take us beyond responses to the 'dignity' of formal work, reconnecting understandings of the self within and through the creative practices and forms of social organisation that emerge.

This goes beyond any expansion of the 'repertoires of contention' to direct – but still contested – prefigurative creation (Sitrin 2016). The worker recuperated enterprises have produced new modalities of resistance, which, whether subject to defeat or opening new avenues, encompass a self-activity rooted in 'notions of territoriality, assembly activism, the demand for autonomy and the horizontalism of social relations' (Svampa 2014, 159; Dinerstein 2014a, 141). Through the struggle to build utopia:

> Today, many workers are not waiting to be faced with the closure of a company to respond; occupation of the factory when management rejects a labor contract has become a new social reality, and capitalists are aware that an occupied factory can turn into a recovered company. (Hirtz and Giacone 2013, 99)

The 'defensive movement' I identified above, consequently, is also necessarily a creative one by giving rise to new modes of solidarity, sociability and subjectivity. These concrete utopias, through their very existence, 'destabilise' as they confront and challenge the prevailing social and political order by offering something different and distinct (Brand and Sekler 2009, 63). And so, it is to how they can destabilise renewed austerity that I now turn.

WORKER RECUPERATED ENTERPRISES AGAINST MACRI: POSSIBILITY IN PRACTICE

Using this concept of concrete utopia to understand worker recuperated enterprises, the aim of this section is to assess their *possibility* in confronting the challenges of the new Macri regime. I have discussed elsewhere the importance of material, workplace, and productive changes in the recuperated enterprises as a form of 'labour-centred development' (Fishwick and Selwyn 2016). Here and elsewhere, the material practices of workers in these spaces, organising production and new ways of working, have been shown to be crucial in collectively overcoming the impact of the post-2001 crisis and for providing the basis for confronting economic 'hard times' (Vieta 2010). As Vieta argues, the wide-ranging 'social innovations' adopted at all levels within the recuperated enterprises offer '*innovative alternatives for reorganizing productive life* itself, especially during hard, crisis-riddled economic times' (Vieta 2010, 296). My point of departure in the following section is to show how, by understanding worker recuperated enterprises as concrete utopias, we can identify where and how far the 'not yet' of *material and subjective praxis* is creating new ways of organising workers' lives in the workplace in response to the challenges of the Macri regime.

To recap, these challenges are as follows: (1) indirect economic challenges of rising supply costs; (2) halting or defunding of state-sponsored support; (3) systematic use of the veto against legal expropriation; (4) halting of the purchase of goods by the state; (5) judicial penalties against worker occupation; (6) heightened violent repression; and (7) the sale of recuperated enterprises to private entrepreneurs. I will address these by focusing on the range of practices that have emerged, their material impacts, and the new sociability they have engendered that may provide the material and subjective basis for confronting these changes.

Indirect economic challenges

As explained earlier, one of the major challenges faced by the recuperated enterprises is the indirect impact of Macri's wide-ranging austerity measures. In particular, as noted by the Open Faculty report, the cost of meeting the everyday necessities for running these enterprises poses a significant new barrier to overcome (Ruggeri 2016).

Yet, as also noted in the report, recuperated enterprises have fared much better than their counterparts in the private sector, with only six firms closing since 2013 (Ruggeri 2016). One reason for this is that recuperated enterprises can rely upon a range of networks established amongst themselves, which includes direct financial support:

> Material support from other self-managed enterprises was received by 68 per
> cent of WRCs during their 'recovery' rising to 82 per cent in the longer term.
> Although only 14 percent of their clients are sister WRCs . . . given that only
> 309 such entities exist in the whole of Argentina, this demonstrates a vastly
> disproportionate preference towards doing business with them. (Ozarow and
> Croucher 2014, 997)

More important, commercial and resource relationships are complemented
by the formalisation of '"vertical integration strategies" that include the sharing of resources, markets, and expertise in order to eliminate the pressures of
competition' (ibid., 997). Vieta describes these as emergent new 'economies
of solidarity . . . prefigurative of what a noncapitalist, worker-run economy
might begin to look like'. He explains how

> competitive markets are being replaced by practices that see ERTs in similar
> or related sectors sharing orders and customers or even collaborating with or
> bartering technical expertise, the use of machinery, labour processes, raw ma-
> terials, marketing and administrative tasks, legal assistance, inventory, or other
> production inputs. (Vieta 2010, 308)

This transformation away from a competitive market environment – between existing recuperated enterprises, at least – marks a crucial development that can help them to overcome these indirect challenges posed by the
Macri regime. It can also complement the support provided by the cooperative representative organisations (Ranis 2005, 106–11) – albeit support that,
as already noted, is often imperfect – and consolidate these emergent networks.

Halting or defunding of state-sponsored support

Alongside these indirect challenges, there has been a halting or defunding of
programmes designed to support the recuperated enterprises. According to
the Open Faculty, 'studies and subsidies [provided by the PTA] . . . are
totally stopped, alongside all other activity in the programme. The government employees have no tasks'. At CONAMI, 'the budget . . . has been
reduced by a third of what was available in 2015 and in the first quarter there
have been nearly no payments' (Ruggeri 2016). Although not closing these
programmes, the deliberate slowing or altogether halting of tasks is a highly
significant development.

Yet, as has already been discussed, the earlier impact of these programmes has been ambiguous. While they have offered funding and support,
they have also played a key role in demobilising the changes underway
within the recuperated enterprises. Alternatively, the recuperated enterprises
have begun to displace the state and other social institutions. They have been

involved, for example, in delivering the bachillerato popular – a form of high school diploma based on a creative 'prefigurative pedagogy' that uses alternative educational practices linked to the everyday lives of the poor communities and the recuperated enterprises themselves (Palumbo 2017). By 2011 these covered more than ten thousand students who design and guide the curriculum on offer, with courses offered in new modes of social organisation, including 'cooperativism' (Sitrin 2012, 135).

One such programme is run at IMPA – the recuperated metalworking factory in Buenos Aires. Here, there is no attempt to conceal the purpose of the programme, highlighting its aims to construct a 'popular power' and contribute to 'the rupturing of the parameters of the hegemonic system of education' (Chervin 2016, 101). Interviewing a group of young participants, Chervin shows how, although they don't overly connect with the formal 'politics' of IMPA, there is a process of political, subjective formation occurring. To quote from one of these interviews, the student Agustina states, '[In state colleges] you don't become a person. . . . Here you learn to assert yourself. To struggle for what you want, for what you believe, and nobody puts you down' (cited in ibid., 111). As Chervin (2016, 116–17) argues, these are spaces where young students can connect their everyday experience to a contingent, political subjectivity and question and contest their own marginalisation.

This replacement and transformation of state and social institutions, therefore, has been central to extending the subjective transformations from within, but also pushing far beyond, the workplaces of the recuperated enterprises.

Systematic use of the veto

The gubernatorial and now presidential veto wielded by Macri has been an important tool aimed at restricting the consolidation of the recuperated factories. Evidence from the protracted dispute with Hotel Bauen and, as noted by the Open Faculty, the cases of the trailer factory Petinari and Hospital Vecinal de Llavallol show a clear willingness to utilise this veto (Ruggeri 2016). The challenge, therefore, is how new recuperated enterprises can overcome this legal and institutional impediment to permanent expropriation.

Yet, as we have seen over the preceding fifteen years, the willingness of Macri to use this veto against the legalisation of expropriation has not slowed the growth of worker recuperated enterprises. Not counting the spike in recuperations in the immediate aftermath of the 2001 crisis, the rate of growth has been relatively consistent and, of particular importance, so, too, has the permanence of these enterprises (Ruggeri 2010, 12–13). The use of the veto has, however, intensified the insecurity faced by recuperated enterprises. To alleviate this, particularly in the early stages of occupation, relations between communities and the recuperated enterprises have been key. At Chilavert, a recuperated graphics firm in Buenos Aires, community support was invaluable (Sitrin 2012, 136–37). Before the firm was legally recuperated, a period that lasted more than eight months, workers had to permanently occupy the plant to prevent eviction by the police. As Ruiz (2013, 480) describes, workers stationed guards at the entrances, but without the mobilisation of the surrounding community, the protracted length of the initial occupation would have been impossible. Residents and family members would physically blockade the factory, preventing police from accessing the enterprise where, inside the plant, workers continued their daily tasks and new assemblies. As one worker explains, 'When the police came . . . they couldn't do anything, we were closed in, and we were working' (cited in ibid., 480).

Significantly, the strength of these social relations, consolidated in the process of occupation, is derived from the very fact that workers themselves tend to be local residents too. In the recuperation of a waste disposal enterprise in Avellaneda, for example, the support from the community was generated by the very fact that workers in the firm – particularly those leading the struggle – were residents themselves. Most lived in the neighbourhood just four hundred metres from the site (Deux Marzi 2017, 144–45). This organic link between workplace and neighbourhood has been vital, in many instances, to sustaining these enterprises in the conflictive and insecure conditions of their formation. Recognising this invaluable contribution, workers in the enterprise stated:

> Everything that we did was because we were able to include all of the neighbourhood, all of the families of the community. That, I believe, was the added value of the struggle, because in the fight where there should have been only 90 of us, there was 1,000, because the neighbourhood was with us. (cited in ibid., 145)

This social foundation of the worker recuperated enterprises presents a means for participants to circumvent the legal impediments presented by the continuing vetoing of attempts to stabilise their situation. In line with considering these spaces as concrete utopias, and also reflecting on the challenge from the defunding of state-sponsored programmes, it is the ability to persist and extend beyond the co-opting institutional frameworks of the state that enables the consolidation of new sets of social practices to be further replicated.

Halting of the purchase of goods by the state

The return of austerity has meant public spending cuts that, besides their indirect impact on the recuperated enterprises, have also led to a cut in purchases. The Open Faculty provides examples of the sharp reduction in the purchase of uniforms by the Ministry of Security from Red Textil Cooperativa and the reduction by 80 per cent of purchases by the Ministry of Social Development from the Nueva Generación cooperative (Ruggeri 2016).

Interestingly, however, despite representing an important client for several of the recuperated enterprises, in 2010 the state constituted only 8.6 per cent of their overall sales, with other recuperated enterprises, for example, comprising 13.6 per cent alone (Ruggeri 2010, 36). Thus, although the reduction of state purchases is clearly problematic – particularly for those identified in the report that rely on the state as a client – it is a challenge that is not insurmountable. Rather, it is one that can be more fully resolved by embracing the democratising material transformations that have occurred in these workplaces.

Nonhierarchical labour processes are amongst the most well-known of the 'social innovations' introduced within the workplaces of the recuperated factories – including the preponderance of assemblies for collective decision making, job rotation and the introduction of breaks and rest times for social interaction (Atzeni and Ghigliani 2007; Vieta 2010). Alongside these, new, democratised accounting measures have been developed by the workers themselves. At Hotel Bauen, for example, these were crucial to the formation of a new 'labour-centred' emphasis on the social purpose of labour. In proposing these changes, workers at the hotel stated that 'we need organizational mechanisms that bring together Bauen's political and economic role and help everyone understand what is going on – to be socially aware and responsible' ('Roberto' cited in Bryer 2010, 52). Similar practices elsewhere have aimed at opening up the emancipatory potential of democratising accounting measures against the imperatives of profit maximisation in the competitive market and refocusing on 'an alternative form of socialisation – one that aimed to prioritise the end of society' (Bryer 2012, 38). It is precisely these changes that then present an opportunity for overcoming the impact of state disengagement from the worker recuperated enterprises, prioritising the social function of these spaces over the imperatives of profitability.

Judicial penalties against worker occupations

Moving from the relative permissiveness of the legal-institutional frameworks established after 2003, initial indications are that under Macri the judiciary will adopt a more combative position vis-à-vis the recuperated enterprises. The Open Faculty note several unprecedented examples where the legal protections that have enabled recuperation to occur have been reversed or simply ignored by the courts. For example, in the case of Frigorífico Le Lagunita, the court in Mendoza bypassed the provincial Law of Occupation to auction the bankrupt enterprise despite worker occupation, whilst in the province of Buenos Aires at Industrias RB the judge evicted workers, ostensibly protected under the Law of Expropriation, for 'trespassing' on the property of the former owner (Ruggeri 2016). Such cases point to an important shift in the legal protections that, to some extent, have guarded the recuperated enterprises from the attempts by former owners and others to close them down.

Yet legal struggle for the right to expropriation, formal occupation and legally instituted workers' control have been a consistent feature of the worker recuperated enterprises. For example, differences in the application of legal supports for the recuperated enterprises – and the long struggles involved in securing legal recognition, particularly after 2007 in Buenos Aires – have been cited as a key reason for the differential growth of these enterprises by region (Ruggeri 2010, 8–9). The structure of the legal instruments in place put severe cost constraints on workers. In the case of Brukman, for example, taking legal control under the Expropriation Law was considered improbable by the workers occupying the garment producer due to the cost of gaining ownership (Lavaca Collective 2004, 96). Moreover, the increase in complexity of the bankruptcy law after 2011 has meant that newly recuperated enterprises have faced even greater legal challenges, with the majority of those established after 2010 unable to gain a ruling in their favour – as of 2014, this figure stood at a tiny 16 per cent of all firms occupied between 2010 and 2013 (Ruggeri and Vieta 2014, 95).

Alternatively, participants in these spaces have looked to consolidate gains beyond the legal frameworks proposed by the state. To counter the growing hostility from the courts, the recuperated enterprises can intensify efforts to improve conditions at work that make these experiences sustainable. The social innovations outlined above – that include establishing equal pay arrangements, job rotation and organising managerial tasks through workplace assemblies – have been rightly described as constituting prefigurative practices in the present (Dey 2016; Larrabure 2017), with these social innovations at work marking not just a mode of survival but also one of creating anew. At Chilavert, for example, workers introduced measures that enhanced the democratisation of the workplace. Assemblies were established that met once a week to make important decisions and reflect on ongoing struggles within the enterprise. These weekly assemblies, moreover, were established in around 44 per cent of all the recuperated enterprises (Ruiz 2013, 484). Consolidating these practices may offer a bulwark against state attempts to reverse expropriations, grounding struggle against these measures in subjective connections to the enterprise in the new solidarities and sociabilities.

Violent repression against occupations

Alongside increased judicial intransigence, the state under Macri has intensified its repressive actions against worker occupations. This is not wholly new, with violent attacks from police and security personnel persisting across sites after 2003 (Lavaca Collective 2004), although this did recently decrease from 50 per cent of all occupations experiencing repression between 2001 and 2010 to 37 per cent between 2010 and 2013 (Ruggeri and Vieta 2014, 91). Under Macri, the intensity of repression against the occupying workers – as well as a range of other social movements in Argentina – is increasing. Examples of this can be seen in the violent eviction at Industrias RB, the repression of protesting workers against owners at Cresta Roja and Petinari, and increased surveillance against workers occupying the foodstuffs manufacturer Disco de Oro in Buenos Aires province (Ruggeri 2016).

A vital way to confront this renewed violence on the part of the state is to consolidate the networks and links established with local communities, as occurred in response to the 2001 crisis. These were essential to protecting and defending initial occupations. For example, at Brukman, the Cid Campeador Popular Assembly was vital to defending workers against violent eviction (Rossi 2015, 101; Lavaca Collective 2004, 64–104). These connections – between workplace and community – have only been strengthened over the past fifteen years, producing new spaces through which these enterprises can defend themselves. This process of embedding themselves more concretely in the community has meant that the targeted repression of the state against occupations becomes more difficult and less effective (Vieta 2010, 313). A waste disposal enterprise in Avellaneda, for example, enhanced relations with the community by providing employment for young people and offering health, education and sporting activities (Deux Marzi 2017, 135). As its president stated, the key objectives were 'to work with the schools, to work with the mothers . . . because in reality [environmental concerns] were a problem for all of us; we live in the neighbourhood and we have to protect its environment' (cited in ibid., 139).

This intersection of work and the community has been central to consolidating connections that earlier enabled the occupation and that may continue to allow these firms to flourish. Importantly, these barriers continue to be broken down by the very practices enacted within the enterprises themselves. As Sobering (2016) demonstrates in the case of Hotel Bauen, social innovations at work have begun to challenge gendered inequalities at work and beyond. Job flexibility, assembly decision making, equal pay across the enterprise, and the affective cultures of membership to the enterprise have, in part at least, started to 'disrupt' the gendered inequalities of the workplace. She notes, for example, how it 'makes space for family demands and major life events that are traditionally separated to the "private sphere" . . . [also]

allow[ing] some members to permanently reside in the hotel' (ibid., 140). What this demonstrates is that these new solidarities can improve not only conditions of work but also those conditions of everyday life in the gendered impacts of austerity.

Sale of recuperated firms to private entrepreneurs

A final turn that has been identified by the Open Faculty is the unprecedented move of auctioning recuperated enterprises to private investors. This combines several of the challenges already identified and helps reveal the purpose of the disengagement, intransigence and repression of the state against the recuperated enterprises – a forcing of the sale of bankrupt, occupied firms to private investors. Purchase of firms in Buenos Aires, for example, has seen either the repurposing of the expropriated enterprise or the rehiring of workers on precarious terms of employment (Ruggeri 2016). These practices mark the culmination of attempts to restrict the presence of these sites – going beyond co-option and confrontation, they are a new mechanism for closing down oppositional space.

To respond to this attempt to erase the recuperated enterprises, participants may again look to embed the practices in the workplace that generate the necessary solidarities that have ensured their continued survival and expansion to date. At work, these have included the introduction of flexible working practices, the elimination of the distinction between manual and intellectual work, slower production processes, and the 'incorporation of play and rest in the transformation of the rhythm of the working day' that prioritises 'free time' over work (Vieta 2012, 142; Kabat 2011, 376). Moreover, although the technical process of work in some of the largest plants remains relatively unchanged (Atzeni and Ghigliani 2007, 663–65), workplace hierarchies have been replaced and, although imperfectly so, recuperation has led to the democratisation of decision making via assemblies and councils deciding and resolving everyday issues on the shop floor and approving new work processes amongst flexible work teams (Vieta 2012, 143; Kabat 2011, 377–80).

Perhaps even more important, the subjective practice of autogestión – meaning 'to *self-organize and self-direct working life cooperatively*' – has been a central principle within and between the recuperated enterprises (Vieta 2010, 302–3). Consolidating this collective sociability can guard against the subversion of these occupations. New experiences of solidarity in struggle have engendered new cooperative social relations that give new meaning to work and the beginnings of more 'social production' oriented towards producing what is understood as 'social wealth' rather than profit-oriented capitalist surplus (Vieta 2012, 138; Vieta 2010, 311–12). As Sitrin argues, this is producing new relationships not only in work but also to value:

> The value of what is created and how in the autonomous communities is not
> measurable by the market or the system of value exchange . . . the value of a
> food or service exchanged is decided by those involved in the process and on
> their needs, rather than the market value placed on that particular good or
> service. (Sitrin 2012, 125)

Through this combination of material and subjective transformations – from the changes to work and the workplace and the associated changes in social relations – the recuperated enterprises will be capable of continuing to mobilise against the challenge to their very existence.

CONCLUSION

The challenge posed by Mauricio Macri since 2015 to the worker recuperated enterprises, to the popular movements, and to the people of Argentina in general, is profound. As noted by the recent report published by the Open Faculty (Ruggeri 2016), participants in the former face an unprecedented series of problems drawn directly from the measures his regime has imposed. But these sites were born of a deep structural crisis. Consequently, by understanding them as 'concrete utopias', it is possible to identify the intersection between the pressures and conflicts into which they are inserted and the novel, creative practices exercised within them to best make sense of their possible new role in a renewed struggle.

To identify the worker recuperated enterprises as a defensive mobilisation supported by the state is to underestimate the importance of the creative practices that have developed, which make *possible* the confrontation with the new 'hard times' in Argentina. Understanding how this has arisen necessitates looking beyond the triple ambiguity of relations between the state and the recuperated enterprises. In seeking to survive the vagaries of crisis, repression and impoverishment, participants in these spaces have consolidated creative new forms of workplace organisation and social relations. Overemphasising the role of the state in this process obscures the novelty of these practices and their capacity to prefigure an alternative modality of organising work and everyday life that confronts directly the worst of neoliberal austerity under the Macri regime.

Changes to the workplace, new networks that dampen capitalist competition, the opening of working space to communities, and the emergent new sociabilities that these have created are all central to transcending the new challenges the recuperated enterprises face. Importantly, understanding these spaces as concrete utopias, as Dinerstein does, allows us also to recognise and incorporate their limits into our understanding, but without shifting our gaze away from the creative, prefigurative praxis. Situating these spaces within the damaging and dangerous context of a resurgent neoliberal auster-

ity, but also against the limited institutionalisation promoted by Kirchneris-
mo, we can observe the establishment of new forms of collective sociability
that are derived from a combination of democratised working practices, collective support for new recuperations and material interaction between the
enterprises themselves, and from the opening up of these spaces to community events and alternative forms of education for some of the most marginalised populations in Argentina. All of these elements provide an invaluable
basis for resisting the challenges they now face.

Examining the ways in which the recuperated enterprises can contribute
to the wider movement against Macri also becomes clearer once we consider
their possibility as an alternative from below rather than privileging the context within which they have arisen. Reforms imposed by Macri have stimulated two processes – a resurgence of mobilisation and an increase in unemployment. Matching the extent of Macri's unemployment drive has been the
veracity of protest across all sectors of opposition. In 2016 and 2017, labour
unions, women's movements, left parties, unemployed workers' organisations and many of the social movements that emerged after 2001 have again
taken to the streets against the regime. Interestingly, it is increasingly similar
conditions that brought the recuperated enterprises into being most compre-
hensively after 2001 that now may again offer the potential for the resurgence of comparable forms of autonomous mobilisation across a range of
new sites.

The continued existence of the worker recuperated enterprises remains
precarious. But it is precisely these precarious conditions that will reshape
them as they emerge within the concrete context of their surroundings. Their
persistence should not be linked directly to the favourable conditions provided by the state. If anything, the decline of previous progressive governments offers renewed possibility for labour struggle. The so-called end of the
progressive cycle marks the end of an institutionalisation of these movements
rather than the end of these movements themselves. For the recuperated
enterprises, the question now is whether the experiences of workers' control
can be replicated and spread across the array of sectors impacted by Macri's
reforms. Crucially, the continuity of an alternative, bottom-up form of worker self-organisation provided by the recuperated enterprises presents a novel,
creative form of labour resistance and hints at a possible way out of harsh
neoliberal austerity and renewed assault on employment, welfare and work
across Argentina.

NOTES

1. This is not a comprehensive overview of the recent history of the worker recuperated
enterprises. (For a detailed account of the emergence, evolution, conflicts, and changes underway across these worker-occupied workplaces, see Vieta [2010], Ruggeri and Vieta [2014] and

Rossi [2015].) Rather, it is a reflection on the possibilities presented by the prefigurative praxis operating within these spaces as a means to overcome the challenges posed by the Macri regime both for the recuperated enterprises and for the wider popular movement.

2. This 'definitive expropriation' refers to a particular legal status, by which the occupied firms are legally – and permanently – controlled by the workers. Most of the recuperated enterprises are in a state of 'temporary expropriation' whereby they are granted legal control by the courts, but not under permanent terms.

3. According to the latest figures available from the Open Faculty, there are now 367 worker recuperated enterprises, employing 15,948 workers with more than 50 per cent of all enterprises and workers based in the Metropolitan Area of Buenos Aires (AMBA) and close to two-thirds operating in sectors of industrial manufacturing, with metalworking, foodstuffs, and textiles amongst the dominant sectors (Ruggeri 2016).

BIBLIOGRAPHY

Atzeni, Maurizio, and Pablo Ghigliani. 2007. 'Labour Process and Decision-Making in Factories under Workers' Self-Management: Empirical Evidence from Argentina'. *Work, Employment and Society* 21(4): 653–71.

Brand, Ulrich, and Nicola Sekler. 2009. 'Struggling between Autonomy and Institutional Transformations: Social Movements in Latin America and the Move toward Post-Neoliberalism'. In *Post-Neoliberalism in the Americas*, edited by Laura MacDonald and Arne Ruckert, 54–70. Basingstoke: Palgrave Macmillan.

Bryer, Alice. 2010. 'Beyond Bureaucracies? The Struggle for Social Responsibility in the Argentine Workers' Cooperatives'. *Critique of Anthropology* 30(1): 41–61.

Bryer, Alice. 2012. 'The Politics of the Social Economy: A Case Study of the *Empresas recuperadas*'. *Dialectical Anthropology* 36: 21–49.

Chervin, Mariano. 2016. 'Una aproximación a las trayectorias y representaciones políticas de las juventudes del Bachilleraro IMPA'. *Argumentos* 18: 97–119.

Deux Marzi, María Victoria. 2017. 'Competencia y comunidad: Acerca de las relaciones sociales en dos procesos de recuperación de empresas de Argentina'. *De Practícas y Discursos: Cuadernos de Ciencias Sociales* 6(8): 127–55.

Dey, Pascal. 2016. 'Destituent Entrepreneurship: Disobeying Sovereign Rule, Prefiguring Post-Capitalist Reality'. *Entrepreneurship and Regional Development: An International Journal* 28(7–8): 563–79.

Dinerstein, Ana C. 2007. 'Workers' Factory Takeovers and New State Policies in Argentina: Towards an "Institutionalisation" of Non-Governmental Public Action?' *Policy & Politics* 35(3): 529–50.

Dinerstein, Ana C. 2014a. *The Politics of Autonomy in Latin America: The Art of Organising Hope*. Basingstoke: Palgrave Macmillan.

Dinerstein, Ana C. 2014b. 'Disagreement and Hope: The Hidden Transcripts in the Grammar of Political Recovery in Postcrisis Argentina'. In *Argentina since the 2001 Crisis: Recovering the Past, Reclaiming the Future*, edited by Cara Levey, Daniel Ozarow and Christopher Wylde, 115–33. Basingstoke: Palgrave Macmillan.

Dinerstein, Ana C. 2016. 'Denaturalising Society: Concrete Utopia and the Prefigurative Critique of Political Economy'. In *Social Sciences for an Other Politics: Women Theorizing without Parachutes*, edited by Ana C. Dinerstein, 49–62. Basingstoke: Palgrave Macmillan.

Fishwick, Adam. 2015. 'Industrialisation and the Working Class: The Contested Trajectories of ISI in Chile and Argentina'. PhD Diss., University of Sussex.

Fishwick, Adam, and Benjamin Selwyn. 2016. 'Labour-Centred Development in Latin America: Two Cases of Alternative Development'. *Geoforum* 74: 233–43.

Hirtz, Natalia V., and Marta S. Giacone. 2013. 'The Recovered Companies Workers' Struggle in Argentina: Between Autonomy and New Forms of Control'. *Latin American Perspectives* 40(191): 88–100.

Itzigsohn, José, and Julián Rebón. 2015. 'The Recuperation of Enterprises: Defending Workers' Lifeworlds, Creating New Tools of Contention'. *Latin American Research Review* 50(4): 178–96.

Kabat, Marina. 2011. 'Argentinean Worker-Taken Factories: Trajectories of Workers' Control under the Economic Crisis'. In *Ours to Master and to Own: Workers' Control from the Commune to the Present*, edited by Immanuel Ness and Dario Azzellini, 365–81. Chicago: Haymarket Books.

La Nación. 2016. 'Mauricio Macri vetó la expropiación del hotel Bauen', 27 December 2016. Accessed 11 April 2017. http://www.lanacion.com.ar/1970598-mauricio-macri-veto-la-expropiacion-del-hotel-bauen.

Larrabure, Manuel. 2013. 'Human Development and Class Struggle in Venezuela's Popular Economy: The Paradox of "Twenty-First Century Socialism"'. *Historical Materialism* 21(4): 177–200.

Larrabure, Manuel. 2017. 'Post-Capitalist Struggles in Argentina: The Case of the Worker Recuperated Enterprises'. *Canadian Journal of Development Studies* 38(4): 1–16.

Lavaca Collective. 2004. *Sin Patrón: Stories from Argentina's Worker-Run Factories*. Chicago: Haymarket Books.

Onuch, Olga. 2014. '"It's the Economy, Stupid," or Is It? The Role of Political Crisis in Mass Mobilization: The Case of Argentina in 2001'. In *Argentina since the 2001 Crisis: Recovering the Past, Reclaiming the Future*, edited by Cara Levey, Daniel Ozarow and Christopher Wylde, 89–113. Basingstoke: Palgrave Macmillan.

Ozarow, Dan, and Richard Croucher. 2014. 'Workers' Self-Management, Recovered Companies and the Sociology of Work'. *Sociology* 48(5): 989–1006.

Palumbo, María Mercedes. 2017. 'Prefigurando una nueva educación: Las formas de lo pedagógico en movimientos populares en la Argentina'. *Sinéctica* 47: 1–17.

Ranis, Peter. 2005. 'Argentina's Worker-Occupied Factories and Enterprises'. *Socialism and Democracy* 19(3): 93–115.

Rebón, Julián, Denise Kasparian and Candela Hernández. 2015. 'La economía moral del trabajo: La legitimidad socialde las empresas recuperadas'. *Trabajo y Sociedad* 25: 173–94.

Riero, Anabel. 2015. 'Collective Self-Management and Social Classes: The Case of Enterprises Recovered by Their Workers in Uruguay'. In *An Alternative Labour History: Worker Control and Workplace Democracy*, edited by Dario Azzellini, 273–97. London: Zed Books.

Riggorozzi, Pía. 2009. 'After Neoliberalism in Argentina: Reasserting Nationalism in an Open Economy'. In *Governance after Neoliberalism in Latin America*, edited by Jean Grugel and Pía Riggirozzi, 89–111. Basingstoke: Palgrave Macmillan.

Rossi, Federico. 2015. 'Building Factories without Bosses: The Movement of Worker-Managed Factories in Argentina'. *Social Movement Studies* 14(1): 98–107.

Ruggeri, Andrés. 2010. 'Informe de la Tercer Revelamiento de Empresas Recuperadas por sus trabajadores: Las Empresas Recuperadas en la Argentina 2010'. Programa Facultad Abierta. Buenos Aires: Centro de Documentación de Empresas Recuperadas.

Ruggeri, Andrés. 2014. 'Informe del IV relevamiento de Empresas Recuperadas en la Argentin, 2014: Las empresas recuperadas en el período 2010–2013'. Programa Facultad Abierta. Buenos Aires: Centro de Documentación de Empresas Recuperadas.

Ruggeri, Andrés. 2016. 'Las empresas recuperadas por los trabajadores en los comienzos del gobierno de Mauricio Macri: Estado de situación a mayo de 2016'. Programa Facultad Abierta. Buenos Aires: Centro de Documentación de Empresas Recuperadas.

Ruggeri, Andrés, and Marcelo Vieta. 2014. 'Argentina's Worker-Recuperated Enterprises, 2010–2013: A Synthesis of Recent Empirical Findings'. *Journal of Entrepreneurial and Organisational Diversity* 4(1): 75–103.

Ruiz, Sandra D. 2013. 'Significaciones y prioridades en la autogestión de las ERTs argentinas: El caso de Chilavert ocho años después su recuperación'. *Cuardenos de Relaciones Laborales* 32(2): 469–90.

Ruiz, Sandra D. 2015. 'Contenidoes Políticos en la recuperación de empresas argentinas: Apuntes para una demistificación'. *Athenea Digital* 15(3): 25–46.

Sitrin, Marina. 2006. *Horizontalism: Voices of Popular Power in Argentina*. Edinburgh: AK Press.

Sitrin, Marina. 2012. *Everyday Revolutions: Horizontalism and Autonomy in Argentina*. London: Zed Books.

Sitrin, Marina. 2016. 'Rethinking Social Movements with Societies in Movement'. In *Social Sciences for an Other Politics: Women Theorizing without Parachutes*, edited by Ana C. Dinerstein, 135–49. Basingstoke: Palgrave Macmillan.

Sobering, Katherine. 2016. 'Producing and Reducing Gender Inequality in a Worker-Recovered Cooperative'. *The Sociological Quarterly* 57: 129-51.

Svampa, Maristella. 2014. 'Revisiting Argentina 2001–13: From "¡Que se vayan todos!" to the Peronist Decade'. In *Argentina since the 2001 Crisis: Recovering the Past, Reclaiming the Future*, edited by Cara Levey, Daniel Ozarow and Christopher Wylde, 155–73. Basingstoke: Palgrave Macmillan.

Vieta, Marcelo. 2010. 'The Social Innovations of *Autogestión* in Argentina's Worker-Recuperated Enterprises'. *Labor Studies Journal* 35(3): 295–321.

Vieta, Marcelo. 2012. 'From Managed Employees to Self-Managed Workers: The Transformations of Labour at Argentina's Worker-Recuperated Enterprises'. In *Alternative Work Organizations*, edited by Maurizio Atzeni, 129–56. Basingstoke: Palgrave Macmillan.

Wylde, Christopher. 2016. 'Postneoliberal Developmental Regimes in Latin America: Argentina under Cristina Fernández de Kirchner'. *New Political Economy* 21(3): 322–41.

Chapter Eight

E(a)ffective Control and Resistance in the Digitalised Workplace

Phoebe V. Moore

Digitalised methods to calculate an increasing range of activities and expression at work are evidence that management aims to control what has been called affective (Hardt 1999; Federici 2011; Dowling 2007; Gregg 2009) and emotional (Hochschild 1983/2012; Brook 2009, 2013) labour. Emotional and affective labour are, of course, neither new nor limited to digitalised work, and the long history of undervalued labour has been observed and critiqued by several feminist scholars over time. What is new about this trend is observable in the expanding use of technology to control areas of affective and emotional labour, which I have referred to as 'unseen labour' (Moore 2017), through newly digitalised workplaces with the use of location and sensory devices that threaten to capture and control our every movement, sentiment and thought, simultaneous to the blurring of the categories between work and life.

The danger in granularity where qualified and unseen work becomes quantified is the rise of barbarism, where there is no outside to the vulgarities of capitalism, where there is no culture, civility or dignity, but only brutal, corporate-driven commodification and abstraction of labour. The enlightenment held the promise of reasonable lives for all, but modern times have demonstrated several episodes where this has been significantly challenged. Adorno warned that 'to write poetry after Auschwitz is barbaric' (Adorno 1983, 34). Adorno was not warning against writing poetry but highlighted humanity's primary condition of barbarism, stressing later that the most important project after such tragic brutality must be to 'restore an unbarbaric condition' (2005, 50) where the 'sole adequate praxis after Auschwitz is to put all energies toward working our way out of barbarism' (2005, 268). The present edited collection highlights the 'hard times' we now live in. While I am not explicitly likening these 'hard times' to the Holocaust in the way Adorno notes, I argue that workplace surveillance, at its most extreme, is a form of barbarism in what are, at the very least, significantly unreasonable times. This chapter looks at workers' attempts to disrupt the new forms of the employment relationship that are being created in digitalised and potentially barbaric workplaces, where monitored and surveilled work, in giglike conditions, has rendered people's lives almost unbearable (Akhtar and Moore 2016).

The trend in workplace quantification is theorised from a post-Marxist perspective, building on recent feminist work of Dewart McEwen (2017) and Jarrett (2016), who look at the ways in which labour outside the formal employment relationship is exploited in digitalised environments, where labour is invisibilised through technologies (Crain et al. 2016; Cherry 2016). To address the latest trends in quantification and body measurement studies, this chapter contributes to the quantified self literature by identifying a substratum of these debates in body studies that I call quantified work. This critical literature focuses on the rise in the use of metrics in subordinating the body to the (supposed) mind, where calculation is inherently cognitive (Moore and Robinson 2016); surplus value is captured (Till 2014); privacy is at stake (Ajana 2017; Moore and Piwek 2018); the risks of psychosocial and physical violence are on the rise (Akhtar and Moore 2016); working time is not paid (Hayes and Moore 2016); power is deployed through metrics (Beer 2016); control is enacted within the labour process via tracking technologies (Thompson and Briken 2017; Moore and Joyce 2018); and worker quantification facilitates the social reproduction of capitalism (Jarrett 2016), invisibilises labour in digital environments (Silberman and Irani 2016) and intentionally masks 'unseen' labour (Moore 2017; also see Fuchs 2014). Self-tracking for health and well-being can be placed in the context of emerging trends in self-optimisation and the political economy of anxiety, couched in the rollback of the welfare state and rise in austerity, where, within neoliberal social relations, nothing is too precious for commodification and control. Management practices to suit such an environment are sometimes called 'gamification' if they are designed to become a pleasurable aspect of work and are part of a wellness 'syndrome' (Cederström and Spicer 2015) backed by corporate productivity and benefit packages.

This chapter looks at employee responses to being asked to use self-tracking technologies at work to improve productivity, taking note of everyday forms of resistance to this invasive level of control. New forms of work quantification in gig work on the streets and at home, automated work in factories and well-being tracking in professional environments all involve electronic tracking of labour, including, as we will see, attempts to capture affective and emotional labour, and they are capital's latest method to capture surplus value in unstable conditions of agility (Moore 2018), but the examples of workers' resistance in the empirical findings outlined here reveal weaknesses in such initiatives. So, the chapter first looks at examples of worker resistance, demonstrating that quantified, controlled work is not a *fait accompli* but is, rather, contested and contentious under conditions of neoliberal capitalism. Then, the chapter looks at the intensities of affective labour, demonstrating the unprecedented management methods being applied to ways to control new areas of previously unseen labour through new forms of quantification.

PUSHING BACK IN HARD TIMES

There are many signs of resistance to the worst effects of digitalised affective labour emerging, from everyday forms to trade union organising. Active resistance includes workers' hacking or appropriation of apps; sousveillance, where people 'watch the watcher' by using their own methods to gain access to information they do not normally have, by carrying out information and sharing jamming; using personal devices at work; situational leveraging, where, for example, people may 'steal' breaks and mask them as work; and dragging feet. Cases have also emerged in which workers use self-tracking for resistance and self-protection. In one case, a project worker without a fixed contract used self-tracking to protect himself from unpaid overtime. He tracked time spent on projects to prove he was being underpaid and to ensure his employer's compliance with the European Working Time Directive. Other forms of direct action in the context of exploitative digital labour include 'pervasive sabotage, chronic absenteeism and wildcat strikes' (Ross 2008, 7). People are beginning to resist negative working conditions in a variety of ways, including 'the use of humour, the innovation of methods to carve out slack within the work routine, dragging feet, and a strategic use of quitting' (Taylor and Bain 2003; Mulholland 2004; Woodcock 2017, cited in Moore and Joyce 2018). The current chapter views resistance as a form of organisational misbehaviour (Ackroyd and Thompson 1999) or everyday forms of resistance (De Certeau 2009), where workers' disruptive acts provide deterrents for production. Cases in the warehouse and the office discussed here show strategic break-in, a kind of analogue hacking and outright quitting seen in the case of the Quantified Workplace experiment that reflects active resistance.

Here, I outline some empirical examples of resistance to digitalised work, including gig work, warehouse wearables and office-based wellness initiatives.

Everyday forms of resistance in gig work

Mags Dewhurst is a same-day medical pushbike courier for CitySprint UK Ltd and Chair of the Independent Workers Great Britain. In an interview in 2016, I asked Ms Dewhurst about some of the changes she has witnessed over the five years she has done this work. Dewhurst told me that there is a rise in technology, such as use of handheld computers (XDA/PDA like Palm Pilots) or apps both in the courier industry and in food delivery. These technologies have digitised what used to happen on paper and are used primarily for the collection of signatures to authorise pickup and collection of parcels. The new devices and apps also allow companies to GPS track all couriers' movements live, as well as the live process of collection and delivery at every stage.

Dewhurst stated:

> Your every move and action are tracked in a digital audit trail. This is quite different from the days when couriers used to work off paper and rely solely on the use of the radio (wallow talkie) to receive jobs. Now everything is digital there is much less freedom and much higher amount of control, thus meaning we are much less 'independent', even though our contracts say we are totally free and independent.

I asked Dewhurst what, in her view, was the biggest threat to workers' rights in this context. She noted that bogus independent contractor/sub-contractor contracts are prevalent in gig economy work. She indicated that digitalisation, automation and algorithmic management have risen, stating that 'used in combination, they're toxic and are designed to strip millions of folks of basic rights'. I asked which rights were being stripped in her context of work. Dewhurst indicated, 'All of them. The only bit of legislation that protects me would be the equality act, but that would only protect certain characteristics and would be hard to win anyway. Holiday pay, NMW, sick pay, pensions, parental leave, redundancy, tax and in contributions . . . is removed via IC contracts'.

Mags and her colleagues, in response to the pressure they face in gig work,

> built a branch of the IWGB UNION. This is the mechanism we have found most effective for creating change – as it helps consolidate a fragmented community and gives people hope and strength in numbers and through collective fights. So far we have won three major pay rises of 20–30% at London's big three courier companies; City Sprint, Ecourier and Absolutely Couriers. We also won at Gophr a small app company but they recently backed out of the agreement. We are also in the process of challenging our IC status in the courts at four of the big courier companies. We've also had limited success with the Deliveroo strike in August. Although we didn't manage to stop the

new pay structure coming in, we helped the workers escalate their strike, created loads of positive publicity and helped to shine a big light on the gig economy and exposed the contradictions inherent in it – which are all present in the courier industry as well, obviously.

I asked what more could be done to organise and reform work and what was stopping people from doing it. Dewhurst indicated that the difficulty with unionising gig economy workers is that it is hard to get access to workers who are on the move constantly, where their work is scattered across large areas. Dewhurst noted that 'if we can't get legislation to force companies to let unions in from the off, which is highly likely, then unions need to try harder'. She noted that a problem is that unions often have a very negative attitude that only serves to prevent action. Dewhurst related that she often hears big unions complaining about anti–trade union legislation and lack of participation, and she blames the government for why they are not winning. In her mind,

> this is the wrong attitude and is a recipe for inaction and is defeatist. If this is the attitude, of course nothing will happen and of course you won't convince anyone to take action. What was great about the Deliveroo strike was that it was autonomous: the drivers did it by themselves, we merely assisted once it got going. It exposed the failings of government, business, and the unions!! Now slowly, the big guys are waking up and gearing up but I doubt much will happen. As ever we will rely on workers to have the courage themselves to take action and force change and that is where the real power lies.

One Warehouse Operative, Ingrid (not her real name), who has worked in one warehouse in Britain for eleven years, provided information to me about a new worn device that was rolled out in her workplace in February 2016. All warehouse work floor operatives were unexpectedly required to use the hand-worn scanner. The current researchers asked what the workers were told the devices would be used for. Ingrid indicated that management told workers that the devices would provide management with information about any mistakes made and who in the warehouse had made them, meaning that they can be provided help to not do this again.

In practice, however, Ingrid indicated that the technology has been used not only to track individual mistakes but also to track individual productivity and time spent working and on breaks. Workers were told that management would hold individual consultations on the basis of the data, but this had not happened. Instead, at a specific interval in the months that followed the devices' implementation, workers were told that people would be fired within days, and it transpired that data from devices were part of the decision-making process for whom to dismiss. Ingrid was not clear how the data was interpreted; however, as seen in her response here:

Recently they sacked 2 or 3 people, and they decided this based upon who did least work. Maybe it was in May, when things get a bit quieter at work. They sacked 3 people: one of them was lazy, so I understand why. But the other 2 were very good. A week before the sackings, the management said, 'Everyone be careful, because we are going to fire someone from the temporary staff'. So everybody speeded up.

Ingrid indicated concern that the data accumulation was in fact being rigged. In one case she and coworkers suspected that specific people were given easier tasks during a period of amplified monitoring. While Warehouse Operatives are permitted to join trade unions, Ingrid indicated that she is not part of a trade union and that she is not aware of any membership in her workplace. In any case, no consultation was held with relevant trade unions or with workers before the technology was integrated. Ingrid stated:

We're aware that the tracking might be used to put pressure on us to work faster, and it might be used to sack people. But lots of us feel that we don't care anymore. Because physically we just can't do any more.

The quantified workplace experiment and a(e)ffective resistance[1]

From 2015 to 2016, one group of professional workers in an office in the Netherlands carried out an experiment they called the 'Quantified Workplace' project (hereafter called QWP). Up to fifty employees were given the option to obtain a FitBit Charge HR Activity Tracker, and in the end around thirty-five took these devices. Some ordered different sizes, but they did not arrive or there was other confusion, leading to about twenty-five participants who were engaged at various points throughout the year that the project ran. The company contracted one data analyst, Joost Plattel, who set up individualised dashboards and RescueTime for participants. Volunteers for the project received workday lifelog emails asking them to rate their subjective productivity, well-being and stress.

Importantly, the project occurred during a period of change management as one multinational company absorbed a smaller company that had been a tight-knit group of real estate and work design consultants. The smaller company suggested and led the project. The project was part of a move towards a more agile workplace, the manager running the project informed me. The project manager indicated that his intentions were to help workers adapt to an agile working environment, where change was to be expected and red tape reduced, and to see to what extent employees' self-awareness, stress, well-being and 'well-billing' (the amount of revenue an employee generates for the company) was impacted during the period of transition (interview 10 May 2015).

In this context, workers were expected to transform affective and physical aspects of themselves by becoming healthier, happier and more productive with the use of intensely investigatory devices. The company was interested in comparing subjectively and objectively measured productivity, as linked to health and activity tracking and 'billability'. I was not given access to the data gathered by the company on whether improved activity led to higher productivity and billability. However, the project fit with the company's moves towards working anywhere, in a giglike scenario—which was encouraged at the time that the project merger was put in place—and aiming for increases in teamwork and efficiency. Furthermore, the merger was a significant *change* for all who had worked in the smaller company, and all participants in the QWP had been employed in the smaller company. So, their experience of change and affective labour were measured by the processes put into place by the QWP. Workers were expected to manage any emotional or affective impacts as the company went through a merge and acquisition process. My interviews with participants demonstrate acts of resistance that involve exit from the project because of concerns about privacy, concerns about digital devices' validity and concerns about corporate surveillance that a project of this type engenders.

Responses in the first interviews demonstrate scepticism about the validity of the FitBit's readings and a desire for more device intelligence:

> A big question for me and for a few others as well, is uh, how reliable the FitBit is. . . . this thing [FitBit] might be more intelligent than just recording my data.

One respondent in the second interviews indicated frustration:

> I don't get any answers, I just fill in my things, but I don't get an answer if it's good or not, I just want to know if I were good and just start working.

One comment in the first interviews indicated that employees originally thought there would be more 'complaints about privacy'. However, in the first interviews, three comments showed concern surrounding what types of personal data were becoming available for management perusal, increasing to twenty-one comments showing concern in the final interviews.

Responses to the question 'How/have your thoughts about the Quantified Workplace project changed?' indicate:

> I still [have] and even [have] more doubt about the project. And I don't wear the Fitbit very often. And when I will wear it, it is for myself and to see how active I am.

After monitoring my workplace behaviour over a couple of months I found out that it didn't change a lot.

It confirmed my thoughts, which I had in the beginning. It is better to change your behaviour based on your feelings rather than a device.

I learned not very much from it.

Nine interview responses indicated FitBit abandonment either for a period or altogether in the first two months. Some used the FitBit for almost the entire project, while others engaged with it for less than one month/occasionally. FitBit use decreased significantly throughout the project, reflected by the monthly total average step count recorded from all employees. There was a 30 per cent drop in average steps recorded within the first three months, and 50 per cent drop within six, with a 75 per cent drop by the end. So, results demonstrate explicit resistance to the QWP, calling into question the effectiveness of this kind of project where affective and emotional labour are managed in a period of agility (see Moore 2018).

AFFECTIVE AND EVERYDAY RESISTANCE

Affective labour is not directly 'inside' capital, nor is it a straightforward 'nonwaged reproduction of the labourer, added to labour's use value' (Clough 2007, 25). Rather, in real, affective subsumption, work happens constantly, all of the time, and is both nowhere and everywhere. Work becomes all-of-life. Indeed, 'capital produces its own outside from inside the viscera of life, accumulating at the level of the preindividual bodily capacities and putting preindividual bodily capacities to work' (ibid.). The absenting of management and individual responsibilisation in gig work is a method of controlling affective resistance by putting affect to work and reducing labour power, reducing the possibility for consciousness of labour's exploitation.

Postmodern, radical studies of the laws of value postulate that there is an 'outside' of capital that cannot be quantified, an outside that is still attainable and thus creates possibilities for emancipation (Negri 1999, 86). Federici argues that primitive accumulation continues today, and there is no longer a conceivable 'outside' of production relations whilst we live in a capitalist hegemony (2004), and the newest technologies are instrumental to its pursuits. Some new worker monitoring technologies attempt to quantify the qualitative, revealing previously unmeasured aspects of the labour process, like mood, fatigue, psychological well-being and stress. This makes workers permanently visible to management and allows the sites of everyday resistance facilitated by worker-to-worker communication to be penetrable by management, meaning it is increasingly difficult to identify any outside to capital (Moore and Robinson 2016).

Precarity is the purest form of alienation where the worker loses all personal association with the labour she performs also at the level of the affective. She is dispossessed and location-less in her working life, and all value is extracted from her in every aspect of life. Because precarious digitalised workers are constantly chasing the next 'gig', spatial and temporal consistency in life is largely out of reach. The political economy of precarity is seen in the wage share of value-added as Fordism gave way to financialised accumulation (Bengtsson and Ryner 2015); the rise in self-employment (ONS 2018); automation (Frey and Osborne 2013); the fall of the dot-com bubble; and repeated global economic crises. In the UK, statistics in 2016 and 2017 indicate that the rise in national employment figures and economic growth are dependent on self-employment such as that seen in gig economy work. More than 900,300 people worked on zero-hour contracts in 2016, which is a number that rose from 747,000 by 20 per cent in 2016 alone.

In work within the demand economy (AFL-CIO 2016) or gig economy referred to in the 'resistance' examples above, a range of new online platforms have emerged, where people buy and sell labour using computer interfaces. This involves work that happens in a 'human cloud' fuelled by such platforms as Upwork, ODesk, Guru, Amazon Mechanical Turks, Uber, Deliveroo and Handy, which are called 'online platforms' in the Digital Single Market European Commission terminology. Huws (2015) and Cherry (2011) label this type of exchange and work as 'crowdsourcing', and Huws defines it as 'paid work organised through online labour exchanges' (2015, 1). Crowdsourcing has facilitated companies' outsourcing of labour as well as introduced new platforms for freelance and self-employed work, and this trend is rising internationally likewise. The platform economy relies on self-employed contracts, and, as such, they have no access to regular employment benefits such as health care or maternity leave. Platforms are designed to reduce employer liability, and workers have very little legal protection. Gig work puts intensive strain on workers' corporeality and consciousness, often leading to emotional anxiety and panic. Gig workers, who are expected to be continuously agile (Moore 2018), must be prepared for constant change and life disruptions, happy to make personal changes, always on the move and always trackable. So, work, identity and life blur in conditions of digitalised precarity. Workers are often in a position where they cannot log out or switch off (Gregg 2010). Gig workers 'struggle to be left alone rather than to be included, a type of refusal that would have looked strange to their Fordist predecessors' (Fleming 2015, 83).

In gig work, subjectivities are required to be resilient to instability and subjects are expected to take full responsibility for personal wellness rather than associate stress and illness with poor working conditions. So gig work is conducted in a process of social reproduction of capitalist labour relation within the context of the reproduction of accelerated capitalist subjectivities of competition and flexibility (Dalla Costa and James 1971; Fortunati 1996; Jarrett 2015, 2016; Gill and Bakker 2003; Kofman 2012; Haider and Mohandesi 2015; Kofman and Raghuram 2015; Dowling 2016; Weeks 2011; Hoskyns and Rai 2007). Affective work reaches below, behind and above the corporeal. Measuring this type of labour becomes a form of control by means of the 'modulation of affect' by both recording and trying to control bodily capabilities by providing self-tracking devices, and thus 'varying the resistance of a body' (Bogard 2010).

In digitalised and gig work, the inevitability of machinic developments takes precedence, even beyond client satisfaction (though that is, of course, important). Affective gig labourers do not engage in creative production using their own affective capacities in an emancipatory sense. They are engaged in a type of negative affective repression by which the required subordinate performances corrode their own psychosomatic and bodily well-being. Attempts to regulate and modulate affect and to externalise its costs are part of this process. Affective labour is, however, by definition innumerable. However, in gig work, every moment of our labour is calculated and measured using algorithmic mechanisms with increasing intensity, not so that it can be remunerated, but because precarious workers' corporeal collapse could result in resistance and reduce companies' profits.

Lorusso (2017) refers to precarity as a form of Derridean 'hauntology' and Fisher's *Ghosts of My Life* (2014) because precarity is not 'fully part of the present' but rides on an 'anticipation shaping current behaviour', or the dream that present activities will lead to something better, a goal-oriented vacuum of constant anxious strife or the failure of the present to become what we hoped. From an autonomist viewpoint, precarity is a systemic capture of the hopeful movements of exodus of the 1960s/1970s, when resistance often took the form of 'refusal of work' by the 'slacker' or 'dropout' (Shukaitis 2006), with refusal to submit to Fordist work routines (Brophy and De Peuter 2007, 180–81). Capitalism is said to have pursued this exodus into the field of life beyond work and captured escaping flows by expanding labour into these spaces (Mitropoulos 2006; Neilson and Rossiter 2005; Federici 2008; Frassanito Network 2005) and appropriating radical ideas, introducing a wave of flexibilisation and selling it as liberation (Berardi 2009) and blurring work-life boundaries in the process. In effect, capitalism followed the fleeing workers into the autonomous spaces of the qualitative and restructured these spaces along quantitative lines to bring the workers back into capitalism. Continuous appropriation manifests capitalism's continued capability to reinvent itself when faced with resistance (Berardi 2009, 77).

From a labour process perspective, technology *itself* has not caused the conditions of precarity. Rather, the use of data from technologies in management methods such as the 'agility system' I discuss (2018) involves the invisibilisation of power relations that intensify age-old practices of scientific management and related worker control. But worker organising and resistance has begun to reveal the revived agency in labour power as a response to the latest incarnation of Ricardo's machine question. For solidarity to fully emerge amongst digitalised workers, class consciousness in the Marxist sense is necessary. Some have claimed that class has fundamentally changed vis-à-vis concepts of labour. Virno (2004) wonders whether the multitude is too centrifugal to hold a class consciousness 'of its own'. Standing (2011) has asked whether a 'multi-class' configuration that identifies the precarity matters, since it is identifiable in other ways. Work ascribes worth to our species-being (Sayer 2005), and people find dignity and self-worth within labour. Technology and social media have been a medium for social uprising and resistance (Gerbaudo 2012), and digital activism's 'firebrand waves' have been escalating since the early 1990s (Karatzogianni 2015). Fishwick argues that critical subjective connections in the labour process are crucial for resistance, where

> contestation in and around the production process is central to the formation of the working class as a political subject. Not only does it create objective conditions of shared experience, it also allows for a collective subjective interpretation of these experiences that extends beyond the workplace and permits the articulation of coherent and salient political interests as a class. (2015, 215)

Ross notes that the expectations placed upon the precariat are a 'warmed over version of Social Darwinism' (2008, 36). It is easy to see how this operates in practice, as the value of social performances is *entirely reduced* to managerial metrics.

New pursuits in labour control exceed the study of physical movements of scientific management, as concrete labour is increasingly subject to abstraction as new ways to identify and calculate previously unseen labour become apparent and more subject to commodification in the process. This employer prescription eliminates any possibility for negativity by highlighting well-being (Davies 2016; Cederström and Spicer 2015). With this realisation, and 'even if the measurement of this new productive reality is impossible, because affect is not measurable, nonetheless in this very productive context, so rich in productive subjectivity, *affect must be controlled*' (Negri 1999, 87). As we will see, work design methods have begun to reflect the conviction that 'affect must be controlled'. Quantification recognises unseen labour, such as affective labour, as productive, but not as an exchange worthy of consistent or useful reward, as pointed out by Jarrett (2015). It is a new terrain for territorialisation to locate profit for capital.

Beller predicted that the development of capital was not likely to proceed without the development of technologies for the modulation of affect (1998, 91). Affect enables or disables our power to act (through the body), and its power lies in its singularity and universality (Negri 1999, 85). These ideas prefigure and inspire the Deleuzian distinction between active and reactive forms of affect or force. Affective labour is the internal work that takes place before emotions are expressed and is linked to the biological aspects of work, whereby 'labour works directly on the affects; it produces subjectivity, it produces society, it produces life. Affective labour, in this sense, is ontological – it reveals living labour constituting a form of life' (Hardt 1999, 99).

One control method is seen in healthcare worker training that is explicitly designed to modulate and regulate affect (Ducey 2007). Gregg (2010) outlines the blockages to any affective communication induced by email and pseudo office intimacy garnered by such activities as Secret Santas and other games that prevent affective relationships. Cognitive behavioural therapy and related psychology highlight emotion and affect regulation for stress management at work, and one group has provided the tools titled Affect Regulation (Psychology Tools 2017).

Firth defines affect as a 'necessary part of social and ecological assemblages, which passes through the unconscious field' (2016, 131). Negri (1999) expands on the unseen aspects of affect and posits that the use value of such labour cannot be quantified in contemporary conditions in the same way that work was controlled during previous eras because such labour exists in a 'nonplace', the immaterial. But affective labour becomes a 'moral' obligation imposed by corporate power.

Lordon's *Willing Slaves of Capital* looks to the work of Spinoza and Marx to ask why people continue to serve capital and have not overcome it, given its abuses. Affect and its power to act can be triggered by the positive and the negative (which is often overlooked in the literature on affect). A 'last straw' can trigger the multitude, whence institutional power, in the Spinozan sense of 'pouvoir', can no longer contain people's 'sadness', and our interaffections and enlisted conatus will drive us to revolt. Lordon shares Spinoza's point of 'indignation', where political affect is brought to bear. Joy, desire and passion (and unseen labour, as I argue) are classically appropriated by capital. Lordon asks whether the social reproduction of capitalism could be appropriated to reproduce subjectivities of resistance, where 'collective human life reproduces itself', he says, and 'the passions that work to keep individuals subordinate to institutional relations can also, at times, reconfigure themselves to work against those same relations' (Lordon 2014, 138–39).

Attentive stress and disposability are intensified by unrealistic expectations fostered by a quantified, machine-like image of human productivity, further intensified by permanent indebtedness leading to a sense of permanent inadequacy (Gill 1995). Tracking and monitoring technologies appear to provide objective data on human capabilities, but this claim elides their social context. They measure only users, creating an illusion that the precarian worker – constructed by the affective and social field of which these technologies are a part – is identical with humanity, the defining point of human bodily capabilities, and the point from which we should start – an outer limit of 'human nature' that restricts political and social possibility. While to some degree measuring emotion, feeling and bodily responses, dividing and distributing work with new technologies at a granular level involves the capture of affect *stricto sensu* – the social and psycho-structural underpinnings of affective responses. Such technologies only measure variance within the range defined by precarian affect, providing an illusory, pseudo-objective view of what might be possible outside this range.

Worse still, the ideology of quantification of all of life and work perpetuates the image that the mind controls the body, and thus, from a Spinozian perspective, serves to contain the body's power within a mental frame largely constituted by neoliberal ideology and subjectivity (the managerial self, quantified productive performance, magical voluntarism). Butler's work on *Precarious Life* looks at the body as containing mortality, vulnerability and agency (2004, 26). While this text is not about resistance as such, her recognition of the shared 'vulnerability of life' (Lorey 2010) and her call to leftist politics to orient our 'normative obligations of equality and universal rights' around our corporeality and vulnerability (ibid.). Perhaps now is the time for the precariat to identify itself (ourselves) and identify a real alternative, an alternative that does not prey on insecurity but builds solidarity, a constituting of the political without the requirement for a single leader, a rhizomatic formation of activation, without requiring a class identity in the orthodox sense.

Precarity is now used in academic and public discourse to mean the abandoned worker, the vulnerable, the person whose life is tied up with ongoing risk and stress. At the international level, discussions on a new labour convention about violence against women and men in the world are current. At the 'From Precarious Work to Decent Work' ILO 2011 Workers' Symposium on Policies and Regulations to Combat Precarious Employment, trade unionists, ITUC, the Global Union Federations, workers' groups and trade unionists met to discuss the symptoms of rising precarity noted by the Occupy Together movement, escalating unemployment and underemployment and the crisis of democracy and collapsing economies in the West. The documents produced from these meetings outline the problem and highlight strategies for viable responses, including how to organise or, better put, enable informal workers' organisation. The Labour arm of the ILO, AC-TRAV, composed the *Symposium on Precarious Work* in 2012 to look for ways to mitigate the fact that 'people everywhere, it seems, are suffering from precarity as a result of economic and financial crisis, and weak Government policy responses to these' (ACTRAV 2012, 1). What these actions didn't predict was the dramatic rise in gig work that has pervaded many areas of industries, on the streets as well as in offices.

In the early 2000s I talked to a range of precarious digital workers on their experiences of work at the Fab Lab centre in Manchester. The emerging picture is a picture of overwork and stress that contradicts dominant images of the freedoms of creative and digital labour:

> I have dealt with unreasonable expectations and impossible management cultures in full time work. . . . I would like less stress and more freedom to work on what I want, as this is where the real 'innovation' happens.

> I deal with constant overwork and funding problems.

> The main problems are the economic recession, people losing control over their lives.

> Play? At the moment it's all work.

> Near deadlines stress is a real problem, and whatever the ergonomics, sitting for 12-plus hours a day is bad for your health and posture.

> We need realistic expectations. You can work eighty hours a week for a while, but you must remember that it won't do you good in the long term.

These quotes from IT and creative industries gig workers reveal a set of persistent recurring problems, including unreasonable performance expectations and pressure (through incentives and self-conception of capability and necessity). There is a growing acceptance that jobs require flexibility, volunteering and the extraction of surplus value; this means that an emerging form of self-perception keeps precarious gig workers in a 'condition of animated suspension' (Berlant 2011, 256).

CONCLUSION

Digitalised work unites the body and mind under the sign of mind, as techniques of managerial (mental) control, what Rose (2001) terms the 'politics of life itself'. The difficulty, however, is that this politics does *not* speak to 'life itself', any more than Fordism or medievalism. What it speaks to is a particular *quantitative, spatial representation* of life. Emphasising empowerment, Negri and Hardt (1999) illustrate affect and immaterial labour in the post-Fordist climate as providing possibilities for resistance and formation of communities. The emphasis on affect in management strategies can be seen

to be tied up with a legacy of labour control and social reproduction discussed by Hartmann in 1979 (Hartmann 1979a, 1979b). As a tool of resistance, affect functions in this system as a structure that enables or disables
our power to act (through the body). One can contrast an instrumental relationship, where the body is 'used' by the mind to pursue rational goals, with
an expressive relationship, in which bodily or affective forces express themselves in the world, through the mind. Work in the digitalised contexts
occurs in an intensely instrumentalised relationship between workers, clients
and often invisible forms of management.

I conclude by assessing the possibilities for a(e)ffective resistance in digitalised work. Affect is the 'power to act that is singular and at the same time
universal' (Negri 1999, 85). This prefigures and inspires the Deleuzian distinction between active and reactive forms of affect or force. Affective labour
is the internal work that takes place before emotions are expressed and involves the possibility for subconscious labour power that could lead to resistance but also subconscious affective self-repression. It is linked to the biological aspects of work, whereby 'labour works directly on the affects; it
produces subjectivity, it produces society, it produces life. Affective labour,
in this sense, is ontological – it reveals living labour constituting a form of
life' (Hardt 1999, 99).

For Spinoza, affect was an intensely embodied concept that refers to the
active ways in which bodies affect one another and coproduce social life (not
always in conscious ways). The full, positive realisation of affect means that
the 'power to act' is enacted and solidarity is immaterial, becoming also
conscious and corporeal. So, affect transcends what is immediately conscious. For this reason, affective resistance is a serious threat to systems of
workplace operation such as interface management in the gig work context.
Simply put, affective solidarity would lead to the most difficult form of
resistance to stop since, akin to invasive management techniques of technological control to infiltrate all aspects of life, affect already infiltrates all-of-
life (as does digitalised labour in the way I have theorised it). When workers
become conscious of affect, or their power to act, they also become conscious of their ability to impact one another and to challenge abuses at work
(Moore 2015).

Simondon (1958/1980) discusses transindividuality as a link to emancipation through describing technical objects as having an infinite number of
possible uses when they are individualised but notes that their convergence is
the point at which they are useful and become a system. He looks at the case
of a 'made to measure' car, indicating that only nonessential parts are contingent and work 'against the essence of technical being, like a dead weight
imposed from without' (18). Simondon defends the human as the organiser
of the technical, stating that automation is never perfect nor complete and
always contains a 'certain margin of indetermination' (4). He states that 'far

from being the supervisor of a squad of slaves, man is the permanent organiser of technical objects which need him as much as musicians in an orchestra need a conductor' (4). In a similar way, people can recognise their individual existence without becoming atomised or hostile, and instead realise that our interrelations are what strengthen us and prevent us from abdicating and delegating our humanity to a robot (2). Marx observed during his lifetime the ways in which early industrialisation turned 'living labour into a mere living accessory of this machinery, as the means of its action, [which] also posits the absorption of the labour process in its material character as a mere moment of the realisation process of capital' (Marx 1858/1993, 693). These augural comments continue with '[machinic] knowledge appears as alien' and 'external' to the worker where the worker is 'superfluous' (brackets added) (1858/1993, 605). In this text, Marx identifies the machine in the labour process and describes its capacity for quantification and division and of abstracting labour, commenting that 'the worker's activity, reduced to a mere abstraction of activity, is determined and regulated on all sides by the movements of the machinery, and not the opposite' (1858/1993, 693). In this way, Marx identifies agency, and even authority, to the machinery, where 'objectified labour confronts living labour within the labour process itself as the power which rules it; a power which, as the appropriation of living labour, is the form of capital' (ibid.). The means of labour, Marx wrote, is transformed, controlled and absorbed by machinery. It is very likely that workers are beginning to resist both traditional forms of management and machinery itself (see Moore 2017).

Digitalised work, in the contemporary context of agility and precarity, ultimately demonstrates that machines are now more than ever before the symbols for 'the ordering of life itself' (Merchant 1990, 227): accelerating the labour process to the cliff edge of what is possible to endure, dragging workers with them. Workers' responses to the digitalised aspects of gig work as well as workers' explicit disengagement with the quantified workplace company-led project outlined here, demonstrate awareness of the tensions surrounding new control mechanisms; ongoing struggles in the contemporary labour process where agile is a key meme; and the urgency of review of all-of-life management strategies. This chapter explores where and how resistance emerges to a brave new world of all-of-life work, where monitoring and tracking of unseen labour may become ubiquitous. Future research must look at the risks this poses for workers and at forms of resistance that emerge against modulation and control methods in the quantified workplace.

NOTE

1. Lukasz Piwek aided with data analysis for this project.

BIBLIOGRAPHY

Ackroyd, Stephen, and Paul Thompson. 1999. *Organisational Misbehaviour*. London: Sage.

ACTRAV. 2012. '"From Precarious Work to Decent Work" Outcome Document to the Workers' Symposium on Policies and Regulations to Combat Precarious Employment International Labour Organisation, Bureau for Workers' Activities'. Switzerland: International Labour Organisation. Accessed 18 May 2017. www.ilo.org/wcmsp5/groups/public/---ed_dialogue/---.../wcms_179787.pdf.

Adorno, Theodor W. 1983. 'Cultural Criticism and Society'. In *Prisms*, 17–34. Cambridge, MA: MIT Press.

Adorno, Theodor W. 2005. *Minima Moralia. Reflections on a Damaged Life*. London and New York: Verso.

AFL-CIO. 2016. *Our Principles on the On-Demand Economy*. Accessed 18 May 2017. http://www.aflcio.org/Issues/Jobs-and-Economy/Our-Principles-on-the-On-Demand-Economy.

Ajana, Btihaj. 2017. 'Digital Health and the Biopolitics of the Quantified Self'. *Digital Health* 3: 1–18.

Akhtar, Pav, and Phoebe Moore. 2016. 'The Psycho-Social Impacts of Technological Change in Contemporary Workplaces and Trade Union Responses'. *International Journal of Labour Research* 8(1–2): 102–31.

Beer, David. 2016. *Metric Power*. Basingstoke: Palgrave Macmillan.

Beller, Jonathan. 1998. '"Capital/Cinema" Deleuze and Guattari'. In *New Mappings in Politics, Philosophy and Culture*, edited by Eleanor Kaufman and Jon Heller, 76–95. Minneapolis: University of Minnesota Press.

Bengtsson, Erik, and Magnus Ryner. 2015. 'The (International) Political Economy of Falling Wage Shares: Situating Working-Class Agency'. *New Political Economy* (20)3: 406–30.

Berardi, Franco. 2009. *Precarious Rhapsody*. New York: Minor Composition.

Berlant, Lauren. 2011. *Cruel Optimism*. Durham: Duke University.

Blackman, Lisa, and Couze Venn. 2010. 'Affect'. *Body & Society* 16(1).

Bogard, William. 2010. 'Digital Resisto(e)rs'. *Essays in Critical Digital Studies*: cds012. Accessed 18 May 2017. http://ctheory.net/ctheory_wp/digital-resistoers/.

Brook, Paul. 2009. 'The Alienated Heart: Hochschild's Emotional Labour Thesis and the Anti-Capitalist Politics of Alienation'. *Capital and Class* 33(2): 7–31.

Brook, Paul. 2013. 'Emotional Labour and the Living Personality at Work: Labour Power, Materialist Subjectivity and the Dialogical Self'. *Culture and Organization* 19(4): 332–52.

Brophy, Enda, and Greig De Peuter. 2007. 'Immaterial Labor, Precarity and Recomposition'. In *Knowledge Workers in the Information Society*, edited by Catherine McKercher and Vincent Mosco. Lanham, MD: Lexington.

Butler, Judith. 2004. *Precarious Life: The Powers of Mourning and Violence*. London: Verso.

Cederström, Carl, and Andre Spicer. 2015. *The Wellness Syndrome*. Cambridge: Polity.

Cherry, Miriam A. 2011. 'A Taxonomy of Virtual Work'. *Georgia Law Review* 45: 951–1013.

Cherry, Miriam A. 2016. 'People Analytics and Invisible Labor'. *Saint Louis University Law Journal* 61(1): 1–16.

Clough, Patricia T. 2007. 'Introduction'. In *The Affective Turn: Theorising the Social*, edited by Patricia Clough and Jean Halley, 1–33. Durham and London: Duke University Press.

Crain, Marion, Winifred Poster and Miriam Cherry. 2016. *Invisible Labour: Hidden Work in the Contemporary World*. Oakland: University of California Press.

Dalla Costa, Mariarosa, and Selma James. 1971. *The Power of Women and the Subversion of Community*. Brooklyn, NY: Petroleuse Press.

Davies, Will. 2016. *The Happiness Industry: How the Government and Big Business Sold Us Well-Being*. London: Verso Books.

De Certeau, Michel. 2009. 'The Practice of Everyday Life'. In *Cultural Theory and Popular Culture: An Anthology*, edited by John Storey, 546–77. Harlow: Pearson.

Dewart McEwen, Karen. 2017. 'Self-Tracking Practices and Digital (Re)productive Labour'. *Philosophy and Technology*. Ahead of Print DOI: https://doi.org/10.1007/s13347-017-0282-2.

Dowling, Emma. 2007. 'Producing the Dining Experience: Measure Subjectivity and the Affective Worker'. *Ephemera* 7(1): 117–32.

Dowling, Emma. 2016. 'Valorised but Not Valued: Affective Remuneration Social Reproduction and Feminist Politics beyond the Crisis'. *British Politics* 11(4): 452–68.

Ducey, Ariel. 2007. 'More Than a Job: Meaning, Affect, and Training Health Care Workers'. In *The Affective Turn: Theorising the Social*, edited by Patricia Clough and Jean Halley, 187–208. Durham and London: Duke University Press.

Federici, Silvia. 2004. *Caliban and the Witch: Women, the Body and Primitive Accumulation*. New York: Autonomedia.

Federici, Silvia. 2008. 'Precarious Labour: A Feminist Viewpoint'. *In the Middle of a Whirlwind*, WordPress Online. https://inthemiddleofthewhirlwind.wordpress.com/precarious-labor-a-feminist-viewpoint/.

Federici, Silvia. 2011. 'On Affective Labour'. In *Cognitive Capitalism: Education and Digital Labour*, edited by Michael Peters and Ergin Bulut, 57–73. New York: Peter Lang.

Firth, Rhiannon. 2016. 'Somatic Pedagogies: Critiquing and Resisting the Affective Discourse of the Neoliberal State from an Embodied Anarchist Perspective'. *Ephemera* 16(4): 121–42.

Fisher, Mark. 2014. *Ghosts of My Life: Writings on Depression, Hauntology and Lost Futures*. London: Verso.

Fishwick, Adam. 2015. 'Paternalism, Taylorism, Socialism: The Battle for Production in the Chilean Textile Industry, 1930–1970'. In *Handbook of the International Political Economy of Production*, edited by Kees van der Pijl, 211–28. London: Edward Elgar.

Fleming, Peter. 2015. *Resisting Work: The Corporatization of Life and Its Discontents*. Philadelphia: Temple University Press.

Fortunati, Leopoldina. 1996. *The Arcane of Reproduction: Housework Prostitution Labour and Capital*. New York: Autonomedia.

Frassanito Network. 2005. 'Precarious, Precarization, Precariat?' Accessed 18 May 2017. http://www.metamute.org/editorial/articles/precarious-precarisation-precariat.

Frey, Carl Benedikt, and Michael A. Osborne. 2013. *The Future of Employment: How Susceptible Are Jobs to Computerisation?* Oxford Martin School, University of Oxford. https://www.oxfordmartin.ox.ac.uk/downloads/.../The_Future_of_Employment.pdf.

Fuchs, Christian. 2014. *Digital Labour and Karl Marx*. London: Routledge.

Gerbaudo, Paolo. 2012. *Tweets and the Streets: Social Media and Contemporary Activism*. London: Pluto.

Gill, Stephen. 1995. 'The Global Panopticon? The Neo-Liberal State, Economic Life and Democratic Surveillance'. *Alternatives: Global, Local, Political* 20(1): 1–49.

Gill, Stephen, and Isabel Bakker, eds. 2003. *Power Production and Social Reproduction*. Basingstoke: Palgrave Macmillan.

Gregg, Melissa. 2009. 'Learning to (Love) Labour: Production Cultures and the Affective Turn'. *Communication and Critical/Cultural Studies* 6(2): 209–14.

Gregg, Melissa. 2010. 'On Friday Night Drinks: Workplace Affects in the Age of the Cubicle'. In *The Affect Theory Reader*, edited by Melissa Gregg and Gregory Seigworth, 250–68. Durham and London: Duke University Press.

Haider, Asad, and Salah Mohandesi, eds. 2015. 'Social Reproduction'. *Viewpoint Magazine* 5.

Hardt, Michael. 1999. 'Affective Labour'. *Boundary 2* 26(2): 89–100.

Hartmann, Heidi. 1979a. 'Capitalism Patriarchy and Job Segregation by Sex'. *Signs* 1(3): 137–69.

Hartmann, Heidi. 1979b. 'The Unhappy Marriage of Marxism and Feminism: Towards a More Progressive Union'. *Capital & Class* 3(2): 1–33.

Hayes, L. J. B., and Sian Moore. 2016. 'Care in a Time of Austerity: The Electronic Monitoring of Homecare Workers' Time'. *Gender, Work and Organisation*. Ahead of print. DOI: 10.1111/gwao.12164.

Hochschild, Arlie Russell. 1983/2012. *The Managed Heart: Commercialisation of Human Feeling*. Oakland: University of California Press.

Hoskyns, Catherine, and Shirin Rai. 2007. 'Recasting the Global Political Economy: Counting Women's Unpaid Work'. *New Political Economy* 12(3): 297–317.

Huws, Ursula. 2015. 'A Review on the Future of Work: Online Labour Exchanges, or "Crowd-sourcing" – Implications for Occupational Safety and Health'. Discussion Paper (Bilbao, European Agency for Safety and Health at Work). https://osha.europa.eu/en/tools-and-publications/publications/future-work-crowdsourcing/view.

Jarrett, Kylie. 2015. 'Devaluing Binaries: Marxist Feminism and the Values of Consumer Labour'. In *Reconsidering Value and Labour in the Digital Age*, edited by Christian Fuchs and Eran Fisher, 207–23. New York: Palgrave Macmillan.

Jarrett, Kylie. 2016. *Feminism, Labour and Digital Media: The Digital Housewife*. London: Routledge.

Karatzogianni, Athina. 2015. *Firebrand Waves of Digital Activism 1994–2014: The Rise and Spread of Hacktivism and Cyberconflict*. Basingstoke: Palgrave Macmillan.

Kofman, Eleonore. 2012. 'Rethinking Care through Social Reproduction: Articulating Circuits of Migration'. *Social Politics* 19(1): 142–62.

Kofman, Eleonore, and Parvati Raghuram. 2015. *Gendered Migrations and Global Social Reproduction*. Basingstoke: Palgrave.

Lordon, Frédéric. 2014. *Willing Slaves of Capital: Spinoza and Marx on Desire*. London and New York: Verso.

Lorey, Isabel. 2010. 'Becoming Common: Precarization as Political Constituting'. Accessed 18 May 2017. http://www.e-flux.com/journal/17/67385/becoming-common-precarization-as-political-constituting/.

Lorusso, Silvio A. 2017. 'A Hauntology of Precarity'. Institute of Network Cultures, Enteprecariat, 21 February 2017, accessed 18 May 2017. http://networkcultures.org/entreprecariat/a-hauntology-of-precarity/.

Marx, Karl. 1858/1993. 'Fragment on Machines'. In *Grundrisse: Foundations of the Critique of Political Economy*, translated and with a foreword by Martin Nicolau. London: Penguin Books.

Massumi, Brian. 2002. *Parables for the Virtual: Movement Affect, Sensation*. Durham: Duke University Press.

Merchant, Carolyn. 1990. *The Death of Nature: Women, Ecology and the Scientific Revolution*. New York: HarperCollins.

Mitropoulos, Angela. 2006. 'Precari-Us?' *Mute* 29: 88–92. Accessed 18 May 2017. http://www.metamute.org/editorial/articles/precari-us.

Moore, Phoebe. 2015. 'Tracking Bodies, the Quantified Self and the Corporeal Turn'. In *Handbook of the International Political Economy of Production*, edited by Kees van der Pijl, 394–408. London: Edward Elgar.

Moore, Phoebe. 2017. *The Quantified Self at Work, in Precarity: Work, Technology and What Counts*. London: Routledge.

Moore, Phoebe, and Simon Joyce. 2018. 'Black Box or Hidden Abode? Control and Resistance in Digitalised Management Methods'. Paper presented for Lausanne University workshop digitalization and labor governance (24–25 November 2017), unpublished.

Moore, Phoebe, and Lukasz Piwek. 2018. 'Tracking Affective Labour for Agility in the Quantified Workplace'. *Body & Society*.

Moore, Phoebe, and Andrew Robinson. 2016. 'The Quantified Self: What Counts in the Neoliberal Workplace'. *New Media & Society* 18(1): 2774–92.

Mulholland, Kate. 2004. 'Workplace Resistance in an Irish Call Centre: Slammin', Scammin' Smokin' an' Leavin''. *Work, Employment and Society* 18(4): 709–24.

Negri, Antonio. 1999. 'Value and Affect'. Translated by Michael Hardt. *Boundary 2* 26(2): 77–88.

Neilson, Brett, and Ned Rossiter. 2005. 'From Precarity to Precariousness and Back Again: Labour, Life and Unstable Networks'. *The Fibreculture Journal FCJ-022* 5. Accessed 18 May 2017. http://five.fibreculturejournal.org/fcj-022-from-precarity-to-precariousness-and-back-again-labour-life-and-unstable-networks/.

ONS (Office of National Statistics). 2018. 'Trends in Self-Employment in the UK: Analysing the Characteristics, Income and Wealth of the Self-Employed'. Available https://www.ons.gov.uk/employmentandlabourmarket/peopleinwork/employmentandemployeetypes/articles/trendsinselfemploymentintheuk/2018-02-07.

Parker, Sharon K. 2014. 'Beyond Motivation: Job and Work Design for Development, Health, Ambidexterity, and More'. *Annual Review of Psychology* 65: 661–91.

Psychology Tools. 2017. 'Affect Regulation/Emotion Regulation'. Accessed 18 May 2017. https://psychologytools.com/technique-affect-regulation.html.

Read, Jason. 2003. *The Micro-Politics of Capital: Marx and the Prehistory of the Present*. New York: SUNY Press.

Rico, David F. 2010. 'Lean and Agile Project Management: For Large Programs and Projects'. In *Lean Enterprise Software and Systems*, Lecture Notes in Business Information Processing, edited by Pekka Abrahamsson and Nilay Oza, 37–43. Heidelberg: Springer.

Rose, Nikolas. 2001. 'The Politics of Life Itself'. *Theory, Culture and Society* 18(6): 1–30.

Ross, Andrew. 2008. 'The New Geography of Work. Power to the Precarious?' *Theory, Culture & Society* 25(7–8): 31–49.

Sanchez, Luis, and Rakesh Nagi. 2010. 'A Review of Agile Manufacturing Systems'. *International Journal of Production Research* 39(16): 3561–60.

Sayer, Andrew. 2005. 'Class, Moral Worth and Recognition'. *Sociology* 29(5): 957–63.

Shukaitis, Stevphven. 2006. 'Whose Precarity Is It Anyway?' *Fifth Estate* 41(3). Accessed 18 May 2017. https://www.fifthestate.org/archive/374-winter-2007/whose-precarity-is-it-anyway/.

Silberman, M. Six, and Lilly Irani. 2016. 'Operating an Employer Reputation System: Lessons from Turkopticon, 2008–2015'. *Comparative Labour Law and Policy Journal* 37(3): 505–41.

Simondon, Gilbert. 1958/1980. *On the Mode of Existence of Technical Objects*. Translated by Ninian Mellamphy. Ontario: University of Western Ontario.

Smith, Gavin J. D. 2016. 'Surveillance Data and Embodiment: On the Work of Being Watched'. *Body & Society* 22(2): 108–39.

Standing, Guy. 2011. *The Precariat: The New Dangerous Class*. London: Bloomsbury.

Taylor, Phil, and Peter M. Bain. 2003. 'Call Centre Organizing in Adversity: From Excell to Vertex'. In *Union Organising: Campaigning for Union Recognition*, edited by Gregor Gall, 153–72. London: Routledge.

Thompson, Paul, and Kendra Briken. 2017. 'Actually Existing Capitalism: Some Digital Delusion'. In *The New Digital Workplace: How New Technologies Revolutionise Work*, edited by Kendra Briken, Shiona Chillas, Martin Krzywdzinski and Abigail Marks, 241–63. London: Palgrave.

Till, Chris. 2014. 'Exercise as Labour: Quantified Self and the Transformation of Exercise into Labour'. *Societies* 4(3): 446–62.

Virno, Paolo. 2004. *The Grammar of the Multitude*. New York: Semiotext(e). Accessed 18 May 2017. http://www.generation-online.org/c/fcmultitude3.htm.

Weeks, Kathi. 2011. *The Problem with Work: Feminism Marxism Antiwork Politics and Postwork Imaginaries*. Durham: Duke University Press.

Conclusion

Connecting the Diversity of Working-Class Survival, Disruption and Creation

Adam Fishwick and Heather Connolly

Our project began with the ambitious task of connecting the complexities of working-class resistance across a diversity of spaces – from social movements and digital labour to workplace organising and trade union renovation – through a variety of disciplinary lenses. In bringing together scholars engaged in solidarity with the subjects of our studies, our collective aim was not only to showcase marginalised experiences of struggle but also to learn from the diversity of experiences, practices and challenges to further aid our understanding of these activities in our own contexts. By bringing this diversity into dialogue, the volume has shone new light on how actors mobilising within and against the vagaries of austerity or 'hard times' are making a difference in reshaping the worlds in which they live.

The three core questions posed in the introduction to our volume – and elaborated in a variety of ways by our contributions – ask: (1) How are people *surviving* in the context of increasing hardship? (2) In what ways are actors *disrupting* the institutions and structures that reproduce the political economic order? (3) To what extent can we observe resistance(s) that are *creating* something new within and against this? In addressing these, the contributions in this volume reflect on the different ways in which actors have survived, disrupted, and created in their specific contexts of hard times. This concluding chapter will seek to tie these together with a short series of reflections on some of the main themes that have been brought into conversation through contributions to the volume and discussions we have held in the development of this project. Reflecting the organic process through which this has developed, the aim is to open up some potential new avenues for thinking around three areas. The first looks to our understanding of working-class resistance and the impact of the varied practices of surviving, disrupting and creating. It asks how we can understand the experiences we have analysed as meaningful in a time when the ostensible direction is to an intensification of hard times – a consolidation of what we might call instead a new 'barbaric times'. Second, we address the importance of 'being unreasonable', drawing again on the cases we have identified, but also in response to the concerns of our participants in how to contest the worst impacts of hard times today. The struggle to survive, the need to disrupt, and the imperative of creating new ways of being has been shown to require going beyond institutional, organisational and societal limits. Finally, we address what can be learned from looking across the diverse spaces of resistance highlighted in our chapters and from the distinct disciplinary lenses mobilised by our contributors in their chapters. To address this problem, the section brings the chapters explicitly into dialogue and looks to the strength of this diversity for working-class resistance against the hard times we face before closing with some suggested pathways ahead.

FROM EFFECTIVE TO MEANINGFUL RESISTANCE

One of the central themes raised in our volume relates to the development of effective working-class resistance. What are the techniques and tactics adopted for surviving the worsening conditions of today? And how far do they enable us to improve the situation in which we live? How can disruptive practices – those aimed at undermining the functioning of the state or capital accumulation – produce a tangible impact on policy or the strategic decision making of firms? Can resisting actors create new ways of living that not only disrupt but also prefigure the possibility of a better future? And what might that future look like? These are questions at the very core of this volume, addressed in different ways across our chapters, reflecting the diverse, inter-disciplinary lenses applied by our contributors and the shared commitment to collective solidarity that is at the heart of each of our contributions.

In his chapter on Ireland, Nicholas Kiersey addresses these questions via the issues of temporality. He examines the intersection of vertical strategies interacting with the state and other institutions and horizontal strategies aimed at constructing new 'socialist governmentalities'. It is, he argues, the space and time generated through the vertical engagement – the building of electoral coalitions and the pressure for social democratic reform – that can allow for the 'slow exodus' of horizontally organised movements. David Bailey and Saori Shibata demonstrate a more immediate sense of effective resistance in their comparison of disruptive protest in Japan and the United

Kingdom. Drawing on several examples, they show how an understanding of the spatially grounded practices of contestation can highlight the modalities of resistance that are most likely to affect change in the current conjuncture. For example, in distinguishing these two cases of what they term *low-resistance* economies, they show how 'militant refusal' is most effective in the United Kingdom, where organised political interests are weaker, but that in Japan more conventional, organised practices have delayed and minimised the implementation of austerity measures.

This issue of effectiveness is also a central theme of the two chapters addressing the role of immigrant workers in trade unions. Rossana Cillo and Lucia Pradella highlight how logistics workers in Italy are amongst the most effective organised workers in the country, mobilising against significant constraints as they are imposed by both traditional trade unions and the heightening precarity of their working lives in the outsourced cooperatives for whom they often work. Building on Beverly Silver's (2003) seminal understanding of associational and structural power, however, they show that it is the structural location of logistics workers – a condition generated directly by the deepening of global, neoliberal capitalism – that enables them to develop a new, alternative modality of resistance. For Heather Connolly and Sylvie Contrepois, influence comes from the effective incorporation of immigrant workers – the *sans papiers* – into the French trade unions and the organisational changes that they have affected.

However, underpinning each of these contributions is a sense – either implicit or explicit – of the challenges to working-class resistance. Amongst the lived experiences documented in the volume are a range of narratives that bring hope as to the possibility of enacting social change through conflict and contestation emerging at work, in everyday life or in changing subjectivity and sociability. But at the same time there is recognition of defeat. As noted in the introduction to this volume, our intention is not to fetishise that which remains marginal – and which is rendered even more difficult in the conjuncture of hard times. Each of our contributors acknowledge failure as framing often ephemeral moments of effective resistance. The Focus E15 protests garnered international attention but were dissipated with the swift relocation of belligerents by an ostensibly favourable local authority (see Mckenzie in this volume); the heightening levels of precarious and stressful monitoring of work in the digital economy, despite the various acts of refusal operating at the micro level (see Moore in this volume); the direct and indirect pressures imposed under Macri that are challenging the very survival of the worker-recuperated enterprises in Argentina (see Fishwick in this volume); and the continuing forms of discrimination and exploitation faced by immigrant workers in France (see Connolly and Contrepois in this volume).

Our focus, consequently, turns to thinking about this question of effectiveness by what makes these experiences of working-class resistance *mean-

ingful. Here we frame this contribution in two ways linked to the redrawing of conflict lines and the meaningful epistemological claims that can be made from our volume (Cox and Nilsen 2014) and to that which is left behind in the aftermath of protest and resistance (Dinerstein 2014). In thinking about the meaning of resistance and social conflict more generally, Laurence Cox and Alf Nilsen (2014) seek to explain social structure as the outcome of competing agencies – namely, the struggles of those seeking to sustain and deepen the prevailing socioeconomic order and those looking to change it. In these terms, structure is not immovable or immutable, but rather the 'sediment of movement struggles' from above and from below (Cox and Nilsen 2014, 57). And, consequently, the outcome – or defeat – of emerging new practices of working-class resistance serves to redraw new lines of social conflict, highlighting the agency necessary to sustain the prevailing order and pinpointing new practices and strategies to be developed in response.

Alongside this, Cox and Nilsen also draw out important epistemological claims that can make sense of this question of meaningfulness as it relates to those cases discussed in our volume. They posit theory and knowledge production not as a primarily academic process, but rather

> the building blocks of theory are ordinary people's efforts to make sense of and change their social experience; theory is produced wherever this happens. The producers of theory are – potentially – everyone who reflects on their experiences so as to develop new and improved ways of handling problematic aspects of that experience. (ibid., 8)

It is in this sense, therefore, that, as is noted above, our authors have openly privileged the praxis of those actors and organisations upon which they focus. Hence, we can reflect on this as a starting point for making sense of the meaningfulness of resistance, identifying here a series of understandings that are produced through practice, 'collectively produced rather than individual possessions; dialogical and contested rather than monolithic; and practice-oriented rather than narrowly cognitive or propositional' (Cox and Nilsen 2014, 12–13).

Reflecting this sense, moreover, we also understand this meaningfulness through that which is left behind as much as that which is directly produced by resistance. Ana Dinerstein (2014) helps us to understand this in terms of the 'excess' left over from attempts to disrupt and build through resistance. Synthesising various radical autonomist perspectives on this question, Dinerstein explains how this has been viewed as the construction of subjects that are not wholly subsumed by capital or, in the terms of John Holloway, the 'overflowing that emerges out of the mismatch between doing (our power to do) and abstract labour' (Dinerstein 2014, 48). In translating this into the 'key of hope', she points us toward 'the not yet mode that speaks of an unrealised or an existing-oppressed reality' to escape the repetition of 'rebellion and integration' (ibid., 71). This provides an invaluable lens for perceiving what we frame here as the meaningfulness of resistance inasmuch as we have refocused on new, changing practices and perceive what is left behind from struggles that arose (see Price in this volume). These have provided directions for situating new modalities of disruption, raising new prospects for strategies of survival and, perhaps most important, mapping open blueprints for the way ahead, engendering new ways of being and addressing comparable epistemological concerns of knowledge produced within and through struggle.

So in moving from the question of effectiveness to meaningfulness our contributions and discussion have considered not only the tangible, material impacts of working-class resistance – be they significant policy change, the re-composition of institutions or organisations, gains in workplace and citizenship rights or improved standards of living – but also what, if anything, is left behind. This ranges from the diffusion of new strategies and tactics adopted in the course of protests and acts of resistance, including those that were 'effective' and those that were not, the consolidation of new subjectivities that incorporate emerging solidarities within and across diffuse networks that characterise these marginal sites and spaces, the development of new knowledges, or ways of thinking and interpreting the world grounded in the very practice of seeking to change it, and, finally, the emergence of new lines and sites of struggle that coalesce around the absorption or suppression of our resisting subjects. It is, then, to the constitution of these tactics and strategies, these emergent subjectivities, the new knowledges, and new sites of conflict that we now turn in the following section.

THE IMPORTANCE OF BEING UNREASONABLE

At the very core of our approach in this volume is the idea that protesting and resisting requires an active denial of the way things are – as John Holloway states:

> In the beginning is the scream. We scream. When we write or when we read, it is easy to forget that the beginning is not the word, but the scream. Faced with the mutilation of human lives by capitalism, a scream of sadness, a scream of horror, a scream of anger, a scream of refusal: NO. (Holloway 2010, 1)

And so, it is precisely from the open rejection of austerity and hard times – or what we may now begin to think of as barbaric times, reflecting this continued 'mutilation of human lives' – that our contributors begin their claim as to the imperative of being unreasonable. Being unreasonable means not just the recognition of what is wrong or the opening of discussion to resolve or to negotiate away the crises that surround us. Our contributions have shown that being unreasonable means demanding new resources – be they material, institutional or subjective – for survival, preventing the implementation of new policy measures, new workplace 'innovations' and the restructuring of means to reproduce ourselves through disruption, or seeking to exit the prevailing order and build beyond it.

Being unreasonable, however, manifests differently across spaces. As is shown in our volume, the capacity to be unreasonable is conditioned by the material and subjective resources available to belligerent actors (a term we use here in a positive, not pejorative way) by the historically and geographically conditioned context of what, for example, social movement theorists term *repertoires of contention*, although this is a conceptual framing that is perhaps belied by the imperative of unreasonableness underpinning our volume, and by the presence (or not) of democratic channels for pursuing social change by other means. In our contributions, the notion of unreasonableness is framed in various ways, conditioned in part by these factors and in part by the disciplinary lenses through which we observe these practices. Yet it is at the fore throughout. For Saori Shibata and David Bailey, it is in the acts of 'militant refusal' or the variegated spectrum of disruptive practice that shape policy trajectories. For Nicholas Kiersey, it is in the establishment of a space for the construction of a new subjective mode of organising – a productive or creative 'socialist governmentality'. For Lisa Mckenzie, it is in the mobilisation of some of the most marginalised actors in society fighting back simply to remain in their homes and in their communities.

The imperative to be unreasonable, however, is complicated further in the workplace. Here the challenge, and the risk, is heightened by a sphere in which capitalist control and the capacity to enforce the precarious and exploitative conditions of hard times are pervasive. Nonetheless, it is being unreasonable in the workplace that has been shown to produce meaningful resistance in this volume. For Heather Connolly and Sylvie Contrepois, it is the refusal to accept the precarious conditions of work and life granted to immigrant workers in France that is at the core of the successes of the *sans papiers* movement. Facing the intransigence of the state and firms and challenging the limits of the traditional trade unions, these workers mobilise their precarious situations through networks and in collective solidarities to create a new space within the prevailing socioeconomic order. For Rossana Cillo and Lucia Pradella, the mobilisation of this precarious condition of immigrant workers targets the circulation of capital itself by explicitly disrupting the logistics industry in Italy for the furtherance of the goals of these workers to build a better life at work and beyond. For Phoebe Moore, the challenge to be unreasonable in the face of heightening surveillance and exploitation through new technologies at work is even greater. Efforts to exert control not only over the material but also the affective modes of life are increasingly central to the modern workplace, but, as she shows, they perhaps also offer a basis for resistance. Incidences of refusal and subversion in digitalised labour are documented in diverse workplaces, with important implications for new modalities of unreasonable resistance. For Adam Fishwick, it is the ability to subvert the workplace itself and to deny the subsumption of work to labour in the occupation and recuperation of enterprises in Argentina.

Each of these distinctive modalities of resistance offer ways forward for unreasonably confronting hard times today (and, again, we mean this in a positive rather than pejorative sense). Here we can frame these claims around a further two understandings that speak to our contributions and to the reflections we have developed so far, in terms of the successes of 'impractical movements' (Engler and Engler 2016) and in the need to prevent the appropriation, co-option, or 'translation' of meaningful protest and resistance (Dinerstein 2014). First, then, reflecting on their recent book, *This Is an Uprising*, Mark Engler and Paul Engler (2016) write in praise of what they term *impractical movements*. They argue that 'outbreaks of hope and determined impracticality provide an important rebuttal to the politics of accommodation, to the idea that the minor tweaking of the status quo is the best we can expect in our lifetimes'. They show the importance of 'mass defiance' to social change by drawing on several historical and contemporary cases in the United States from the civil rights movement in the 1960s to the actions of DREAM Act students – the children of undocumented migrants – today. As with the cases of our chapters, it is by confronting powerful institutions and challenging the precariousness of their existence that individuals in different times and places collectively overcome elements of the worsening conditions they face. By being impractical – or acting unreasonably – meaningful change becomes possible.

However, it is the incompleteness of this change that also needs to be accounted for – and again this touches upon an important theme of our volume – namely, that working-class resistance faces often insurmountable barriers. As well as being disarmed and suppressed by the repressive apparatus of the state or other institutions, resisting actors oftentimes find their mobilisation co-opted, appropriated, or 'translated' into the prevailing socioeconomic and political order. Importantly, and returning to our discussion of refocusing on that which is left behind – on the excess – we consider how to confront this. As Ana Dinerstein (2014), argues, this is an invaluable avenue that opens new questions:

> The new question facilitates a movement from translation to untranslatability. That is, what are the signs, ideas, horizons, practices, dreams, i.e., elements, that cannot be recuperated and integrated into the logic of the state, the law or capital? The new question indicates a new moment in radical social enquiry as it opens a new space for the exploration of excess. (Dinerstein 2014, 22)

Surpassing this asks us to foreground those acts and practices of unreasonable protest and resistance. Within these, then, we can begin to identify the moments of 'excess', the acts and actions that are 'untranslatable' and that move us beyond these hard times.

In framing the acts of working-class resistance we explore in this volume as unreasonable, we clarify further what we can identify as meaningful. Our interdisciplinary analytical lenses on these practices as they manifest in spaces of the workplace, the trade unions, digital labour and social movements can begin to provide us with a sense of the shared grounding of these activities. While diverse and context dependent in concrete terms, and necessarily so, it is in the impractical, the unexpected, the untranslatable or the confrontational moments that we can draw together seemingly disparate and diverse acts of survival, disruption and creation. Bringing these together, drawing out the concrete meanings and combining the diversity of these actions can enable us to open new scholarly and strategic thinking on not only how actors are confronting these hard times but also how they may begin to overcome them. It is to this question of how we learn from these varied understandings and to the final question informing our volume ('where to next?') that we now turn in this concluding section.

WHERE TO NEXT? LEARNING ACROSS DISPARATE SITES AND SPACES OF RESISTANCE

So far in this volume we have emphasised the diversity of experiences of working-class resistance, drawing on examples in social movements, digitalised labour, trade unions and the workplace. Bringing forth the richness of experience across diverse sites and spaces and understanding them from the perspective of employment relations, international political economy, politics, media studies and sociology is an important contribution of this book. Highlighting practices that are often marginalised in both the social and the scholarly realms and foregrounding how we can conceive of these as meaningful in a real sense derives from our engagement in solidarity with these subjects. Understanding the imperative to be unreasonable in these contexts, moreover, demonstrates both the urgency and the immense difficulties faced by these actors and organisations in moving from the localised sites of their activity into a wider field beyond their immediate surroundings. Communicating more widely what we understand here as 'meaningful unreasonableness' is a vital challenge. Therefore, in addressing the question of building a broader challenge to the consolidation of hard – or even barbaric – times, we turn in this final section to start to identify how we can draw together these distinctive practices as they materialise within and across different sites and spaces.

For Saori Shibata and David Bailey, it is the centrality of disruptive practice that is the key lesson for understanding working-class resistance. In its myriad forms, the impact of such practice is vital to understand how different modes of governance are developed and implemented across national contexts. In this sense, we learn that even in 'low resistance' models, such as the United Kingdom and Japan, where the tradition of radical social conflict is constrained, the most militant acts of refusal and disruption or the persistence of struggle against austerity continue. These are not just bubbling along beneath the surface but illustrate the real potential of radical mobilisation to transform the lives of those who engage in it. Although the seemingly inexorable march of austerity continues apace in these two cases, the intervention of contestation by diverse actors can challenge – or even reverse – its trajectory.

For Nicholas Kiersey, the challenge is to overcome the limits of horizontal 'folk politics' as experienced in Ireland. Here, then, the act of disruption requires a concomitant effort to engage vertically in the development of a socialist governmentality within and against prevailing political institutions. To overcome the devastating effects of hard times, to develop the material and subjective resources to build anew, what is required is time. By creating resources for survival through mediation with the state, time is allowed for new subjectivities to develop and for material connections to be built between resisting subjects. In the process, radical mobilisation can be turned not only to the shifting trajectory of policy measures that embed these hard times but also to our 'exodus' from the material conditions that reproduce them.

For Lisa Mckenzie, disruption is a necessity that derives from the search for survival. And it is an act that meets continually with its own, often more forceful and more violent, resistance from above. It warns against accommodation with actors embedded in political institutions, whose incentives and imperatives derive from a distinct and distant material basis than that from which our resisting actors typically mobilise. In demanding access to the means to survive – in this case, the right to housing and to remain in their community – alliances with ostensibly sympathetic political organisations may lead to the appropriation of resistance. In pacifying it, moreover, the demands so central to the initial disruptive moment can be repackaged and removed from the process, leading to demobilisation, defeat and worse. This provides us with an important warning sign about how to obtain time and space to develop the material and subjective dimensions for extending resistance.

As Heather Connolly and Sylvie Contrepois show in an alternative setting, however, this direct engagement with powerful institutions – in this case the French union federation, the CGT – can be vital to consolidating survival in the most precarious conditions. They demonstrate how efforts to repurpose organisational resources to pursue alternate ends can present invaluable grounds for consolidating relations of solidarity and securing real material gains. Immigrant workers in France have utilised the institutional structures of the CGT to gain time – time away from the struggle to survive under precarious conditions of work and citizenship, and time to build concerted resistance to the day-to-day exploitation they face. Hence this renovation of a new, potentially radical, trade unionism offers an important avenue for thinking about the question of appropriation of struggle as a contested dynamic, and how engagement can bring benefits if grassroots mobilisation remains strong.

Rossana Cillo and Lucia Pradella offer important insights from the case of immigrant workers in Italy for understanding the foundations of this grassroots mobilisation – the importance of structural power. The structural location – geographically, economically, or politically – of resisting actors can amplify their power to disrupt the normal functioning of the prevailing socioeconomic order. Many of our contributors focus on marginalised actors, but here we see how some of the most precarious workers – again, precarious both at work and in terms of residency – can strengthen the impact of their mobilisation. Support from sympathetic institutional actors – this time, again, the trade unions – can assist organisational capacity, but it is mobilisation on the ground, the capacity to contest the fundamental exercise of power in these hard times, that we see as generative of meaningful resistance.

For Phoebe Moore, this derives from the new material conditions of the modern workplace. Technology plays an increasingly prominent role in heightening exploitation and the precarity of work and everyday life – surveillance and other forms of monitoring and tracking represent a new, intensive mode of exercising capitalist control. But as noted in the very beginning of our volume, innovation at work and elsewhere is also the starting point for innovations in resistance. There is a clear and growing rejection or subversion of the various techniques utilised at the most fundamental – what Moore terms the affective – level to diminish our capacity to resist and to heighten the anxiety and fear that characterise these hard times. Identifying these new and emerging micro-level practices for survival and disruption thus becomes an imperative for scholars seeking to understand where to next.

The question of 'where to next?' is perhaps at the heart, most concretely, of Adam Fishwick and Stuart Price's contributions to this volume, addressing this to thinking about the creative practices of resistance prominent in the worker recuperated enterprises of Argentina and to the bases of a left libertarian political project in Catalonia today. The idea that precarity and the intensification of repression can be the basis for deriving new modes of solidarity – or in fact that precarity and the threat of worsening material and subjective conditions of work and life have *always* been the basis for radical modes of solidarity and sociability – allows us to tie together the various contributions and identify the connection between them.

As hard times intensify, so, too, does the potential for new energies for working-class resistance to emerge. To reiterate a point made in the introduction, what our volume shows is that where individuals feel aggrieved and grievance is felt as an injustice, there is always the possibility for individual and collective resistance to develop. As observed in each of the chapters, the brutal inventiveness and innovations of capitalism present new imperatives to fight back – these are not necessarily sites of progressive social change but comprise overcoming the heightening difficulties of reproducing ourselves under the brutality of capital accumulation and disrupting the worst impacts of efforts to embed these realities. Nonetheless, within these practices we can often identify the mobilisation of tangible change. The capacity to protest and resist is often generated in sites and spaces where control, exploitation, dispossession and repression are at the worst, so it is to uncover the potentials and possibilities in this unceasing confrontation to which we must all now turn.

Our volume opens potential new avenues for considering how we make sense of this confrontation and how the theoretical lens of survival, disruption and creation might present us with new avenues for research and political practice. First, across different settings and in diverse sites and spaces of resistance, our contributors have demonstrated the interconnectedness of these three moments of radical political praxis. They have shown how the very act of seeking to survive can provide the possibility of disrupting the workings of capital accumulation and devastation. The solidarity generated by disruption can present those who exist on the margins with the potential to construct new ways of organising their daily lives that may extend beyond the meeting of immediate needs into creating new modes of political organisation or new forms of production and social reproduction. At the same time, this creation provides new ways of surviving as such experiences are co-opted or pushed further into the margins, in turn generating new modalities of disruption. Hence, we can observe how Dinerstein's (2014) conceptualisation of autonomy via notions of 'excess' and 'translation' discussed above becomes invaluable for tracing this movement of practice across the porous spatial and temporal boundaries that constitute these different moments of resistance.

In furthering this discussion, one crucial move will be to extend the range of cases beyond the broadly Western European focus of the volume. How does the postulated intersection between survival, disruption and creation hold in contexts where social and political contexts of hard times – combining austerity, precarious everyday lives, authoritarianism and more – are exponentially more destructive to everyday life? Moreover, some of the most significant experiences of radical social change and working-class resistance emerge from cities and countries across the Global South (see, for example, Ness 2015; Ngwane et al. 2017). Understanding how these experiences can shed new light on how resistance can be meaningful and extend across these three moments in working-class resistance is a key avenue for extending this project. The intention of this volume is to continue to learn from working-class practices of resistance themselves. By placing the agency of the working class at the fore of our understanding, each of these chapter contributions, in different ways, situates this in the epistemological claims of Cox and Nilsen (2014), rendering these experiences 'the building blocks' of the volume's theoretical contribution. Expanding the framework that has been developed in this volume will, therefore, require incorporating a wider range of disparate and geographically dispersed experiences, making connections between these sites and how they navigate and survive the unique constellations of hard times. This volume, we hope, can act as a starting point, not only for better understanding of how resistance can be meaningful but also, and more important, for seeing how this meaningfulness can be translated into wider, interlinked forms of disruptive and creative confrontation in a worsening world.

BIBLIOGRAPHY

Cox, Laurence and Alf Gunvald Nilsen. 2014. *We Make Our Own History: Marxism and Social Movements in the Twilight of Neoliberalism*. London: Pluto Press.

Dinerstein, Ana. 2014. *The Politics of Autonomy in Latin America: The Art of Organising Hope*. Basingstoke: Palgrave Macmillan.

Engler, Mark and Paul Engler. 2016. 'In Praise of Impractical Movements'. *Dissent Magazine*, 9 March 2016. Accessed 28 April 2017. https://www.dissentmagazine.org/online_articles/civil-rights-marriage-equality-bernie-sanders-impractical-movements.

Holloway, John. 2010. *Changing the World without Taking Power: The Meaning of Revolution Today*. London: Pluto Press.

Ness, Immanuel. 2015. *Southern Insurgency: The Coming of the Global Working Class*. London: Pluto Press.

Ngwane, Trevor, Luke Sinwell and Immanuel Ness. 2017. *Urban Revolt: State Power and the Rise of People's Movements in the Global South*. Chicago: Haymarket Books.

Silver, Beverly. 2003. *Forces of Labor: Workers' Movements and Globalization since 1870*. Cambridge: Cambridge University Press.

Index

About the Contributors

David Bailey is Senior Lecturer in Politics at the University of Birmingham. His research and teaching are on left parties, protest movements, political economy and how these tend to interact, especially in the European context. He has recently published articles in *Socio-Economic Review*, *British Journal of Political Science*, *Comparative European Politics* and *New Political Economy*. He has a recently published book, *Beyond Defeat and Austerity: Disrupting (the Critical Political Economy of) Neoliberal Europe*, coauthored with Mònica Clua-Losda, Nikolai Huke and Olataz Ribera-Almandoz, which considers the disruptive effect of workers' resistance in the UK, Spain, and on the process of European integration.

Rossana Cillo is a PhD student in Sociology at the Université Libre de Bruxelles and a research fellow at Ca' Foscari University of Venice. Her research interests include racial discrimination at work, immigrant workers and trade unions, labour exploitation in agriculture, posted workers and precarious work of youth. Among her recent publications: *Nuove frontiere della precarietà del lavoro: Stage, tirocini e lavoro degli studenti universitari*, Edizioni Ca' Foscari (edited collection), and 'Immigrant Labour in Europe in Times of Crisis and Austerity', *Competition and Change* 19(2), 2015.

Heather Connolly is Associate Professor in Employment Relations at the University of Leicester. Her in-depth qualitative research in France, the Netherlands, Spain and the UK explores how trade union activists respond to contemporary challenges, and particularly the innovative role that unions might play in the social inclusion of migrant workers. She has articles published in *Work, Employment and Society* and the *European Journal of Indus-*

trial Relations and was a British Academy Mid-Career Fellow from 2017 to 2018.

Sylvie Contrepois is a sociologist and a member of the Centre de Recherches Sociologiques et Politiques de Paris – Equipe Cultures et Sociétés Urbaines (CRESPPA-CSU). She has core expertise in industrial relations and has led several EU DG employment-funded research projects. She recently developed research on industrial relations in multilingual environments at work. She coauthored, with Professor Dominique Andolfatto, the book *Syndicats et dialogue social, les modèles occidentaux à l'épreuve* (2016).

Adam Fishwick is Senior Lecturer in Urban Studies and Public Policy at De Montfort University. His research explores the political economy of development in Latin America, with a focus on its relationship with workplace resistance and the labour movement. He is also interested in alternative development models in the region and beyond and has published recently in *Development and Change*, *Labor History* and *Geoforum*.

Nicholas Kiersey is Associate Professor in Politics at Ohio University.

Lisa Mckenzie is Sociology Research Fellow at the London School of Economics and author of *Getting By: Estates, Class and Culture in Austerity Britain* and coeditor of *Building Better Societies*. Her research focuses on class inequality and British working-class culture. She has published recently in *Competition and Change* and *British Journal of Sociology* and appears regularly in the media, including *The Guardian* and Radio 4.

Phoebe V. Moore is an internationally recognised expert on technology, work and global governance and is primarily interested in workers' rights and social justice. She is based at Leicester University as an Associate Professor of Technology and Politics. Her publication record includes three monographs and several edited books, journal articles and chapters. Dr Moore regularly appears in the media, including most recently *Financial Times* and Radio 4.

Lucia Pradella is Lecturer in International Political Economy at King's College London. Her research focuses on imperialism, the working poor in Europe and alternatives to neoliberalism and the global economic crisis. She is the author of several journal articles and two monographs: *Globalisation and the Critique of Political Economy: New Insights from Marx's Writings* (2014) and *L'Attualità del Capitale: Accumulazione e impoverimento nel capitalismo globale* (2010). She coedited *Polarizing Development: Alternatives to Neoliberalism and the Crisis* (2014).

Stuart Price is Chair of the Media Discourse Group, De Montfort University, as well as the author and editor (respectively) of the forthcoming books *Corbyn and the Media* (2018) and *Investigative Journalism: Global Perspectives* (2018). He is, with Ruth Sanz Sabido, the editor of *Sites of Protest* (2016) and *Contemporary Protest and the Legacy of Dissent* (2015) and is also the author of *Worst-Case Scenario?* (2011), *Brute Reality* (2010), *Discourse Power Address* (2007) and a number of books on media and communication, including *Communication Studies* (1996). Current research is devoted to the 'Catalan crisis' and state power.

Saori Shibata is Lecturer in Political Economy at Leiden University. Her research focuses on the political economy of Japan, including changing patterns of contestation, industrial relations, models of growth and new forms of social movement unionism. She has articles published in the *British Journal of Industrial Relations*, *British Journal of Political Science*, *Capital and Class* and *Japan Forum*.